Elementary Teacher's
Arts and Crafts Ideas
for Every Month of the Year

Elementary Teacher's
for Every

Parker Publishing Company, Inc.

Arts and Crafts Ideas
Month of the Year

Ireene Robbins

West Nyack, New York

Elementary Teacher's Arts and Crafts Ideas
for Every Month of the Year
by Ireene Robbins

© 1970, BY
PARKER PUBLISHING COMPANY, INC.
WEST NYACK, NEW YORK

LIBRARY OF CONGRESS
CATALOG CARD NUMBER: 79–111076

PRINTED IN THE UNITED STATES OF AMERICA
ISBN–0–13–260687–9
B & P

DEDICATION

To my greatest motivators . . . Lillian and Robbie

A WORD FROM THE AUTHOR

This collection of effective art ideas will help the teacher satisfy the need for imaginative variations in the art program, within the limits of time and material at her disposal.

For a period of years, I was involved in Teacher Training Art Workshops. Teachers would request over and over that we offer them ideas which could be used in the classroom, and ideas for *holiday* art.

The format of this book is built around *seasonal* art and the ideas are listed monthly. I selected seasons as a basis for the many ideas listed because as an art educator, I know that it is a great source of stimulation for children's art work. Notice, also, that the summer months have not been omitted. These chapters will contain craft ideas which can be used by the teacher throughout the entire year, or can form the basis of a summer camp craft program.

Each chapter contains a number of lessons for a particular month, in simple understandable language. Using this practical guide can set into motion an interesting and exciting sequential program which will offer a challenge to both teacher and the pupil. The material is the result of twenty years of art experience with children, and has been planned to aid the classroom teacher with simple, succinct guidelines to more effective art lessons.

At the conclusion of each chapter, I have listed a number of subjects that can be used as drawing projects. Children need lots of drawing, but drawing with a specific goal. They relish art, but structured art. Use the lessons, but let the children be as creative as they wish.

At the close of these lessons let the child show his completed work to the other boys and girls. Let him discuss it. Ask questions, and encourage them to do likewise. What could have been added or deleted from your picture? How could you have made your work more interesting? These lessons can become an integral part of the art program for elementary teachers, with over 200 tangible art ideas that can be used in the classroom by the *classroom teacher*.

Art teaching can be a rewarding and exciting happening to you and to the children. *You can do it!*

Ireene Robbins

Contents

CONTENTS

CONTENTS

12. August 239

September

This month announces the presence of autumn. School reopens and this can be a happy or sad time for boys and girls. It is a time for making new friends and renewing old school acquaintances. It is a harrowing experience for children who are attending school for the first time. Will they know how to get home? Will they take the correct school bus? How will they ever remember the number of their house? The leaves are beginning to turn. There is a new kind of color on the horizon. The children are eager for new experiences. Let's consider some art ideas for this time of the year.

How Did You Feel the First Day of School?

Water Paint Cartoon

Are all the faces smiling when school reopens? What are the children really thinking and feeling? Make this a spontaneous lesson—once a decision is made, let it become a reality, so let's use paint.

Basic Materials: 18 by 24 inch easel paper, water paint, brushes, container of water, newspaper.

Procedure:

- Ready the painting materials so the children can work as soon as you make the statement, "How did you feel on the first day of school?"

Figure 1–1

- Have the children make a large oval on their paper. Discuss how you make a smile or how you make a frown. Tell them this is like a newspaper cartoon so the lines on the picture can be simple.
- Ask them to draw the way they felt, and then have them complete the picture to make it themselves.
- Let them look in a mirror if they forgot the color of their hair or eyes.
- When the children have finished their likeness suggest that they paint a thought bubble from their head in the picture to a spot somewhere at the top of the paper. (See Figure 1–1)
- Next have them paint a small picture in the thought bubble of why especially they are happy or sad to be back at school.

Why not display these cartoon-like pictures on a large bulletin board for your first P.T.A. meeting? Won't the parents be surprised to see their child's reaction to school reopening?

Back to School—Happy or Sad

Collage of Cut Out Magazine Pictures and Paper

Did you as a teacher ever wonder how the children really felt about returning to school? This project will prove how really candid and uninhibited the children are. They will tell you precisely how they feel about school opening. The lesson involves the use of a collage which is a simple and effective way to produce an abstract composition employing various materials, but using one main idea. Suggest that the children make a *Back to School—Happy or Sad Collage*. This can be done by drawing individual pictures or cutting pictures out of magazines. An interesting treatment is obtained by a combination of the two.

Basic Materials: old magazines, crayons, manila paper, scissors, paste, 12 by 18 inch colored construction paper.

Procedure:

- Draw pictures on the manila paper with crayon of why you are happy or sad school has opened. Clip these out.
- Next, thumb through the magazines and clip out any pictures which would express feelings of sadness or happiness over the September opening of school. For instance, pictures of people swimming, playing, bicycling, or fishing might be reasons for being sad that school has opened. Pictures of classrooms, children at group games, children reading or studying might be reasons why some children would be glad that school had reopened.

- Choose the pictures from both groups that you would like to incorporate in the design. The original drawings or the magazine pictures used alone will be fine, too.
- The collage is made by cutting the pictures into various sizes and shapes and arranging the pieces on a sheet of large paper until the composition is pleasing to the student.
- Next the pieces are picked up and one by one pasted and returned to the original spot. (See Figure 1–2)

Figure 1–2

When the collages are completed put them side by side to fill an entire bulletin board. Cut out large black letters saying, *Back to School—Happy or Sad* and pin or staple them over the huge collage mural. What an impressive display!

My House

Three Dimensional Paper Bag House

Young children often come to school in the fall, tense and forgetful. Here is a way to break the tension, and also find out pertinent information like addresses for your class records.

Basic Materials: a paper bag with a rectangular bottom, crayons, paint, glue, scissors, assorted colored construction paper, a piece of 9 by 12 inch cardboard.

Bonus Materials: pebbles, sponge bits, fabric scraps, sand.

Procedure:

- Puff out the bag so the rectangular bottom will stand up when it is placed on a flat surface.
- If the bag seems too high for the house, cut the top of the bag until the size is satisfactory. (See Figure 1–3A)
- Next carefully refold the bag to its flat shape and with crayons or paint draw the windows, doors, the siding material on the house, porch, flower boxes, or any other pertinent thing which will identify it with the child's real home.
- Do both the front and the back of the house.
- If you spread the side of the bag carefully, even that portion can be colored.
- Reopen the bag and paste the rectangular bottom to the cardboard base. The bag can be stuffed with a crumpled sheet of newspaper to give it stability. (See Figure 1–3B)

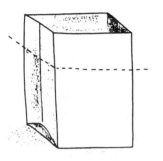

Figure 1-3A

Figure 1-3B

- Take a 4 by 6 inch piece of construction paper and fold this in half the short way. Carefully place it on top of the opened bag. This is the roof. (See Figure 1–3C) If it seems too large, trim it with scissors wherever necessary.
- Now tack the paper roof to the bag with a bit of glue or tape to make it secure.
- Add the chimney with cut paper.
- Print the address on the front door, or make a rural delivery mailbox and place the address on it.
- Suggest that the children add three-dimensional touches by using sponges dipped in green paint for shrubs and bushes; bits of colored paper cut into flowers, trees or a fence; cut cloth glued to a section of the windows for curtains; pebbles and sand glued to the base for a walk or path. (See Figure 1–3D)

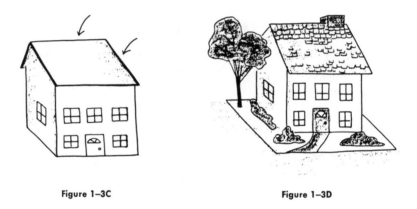

Figure 1-3C   Figure 1-3D

The children will be so enthusiastic that they will not want to stop with one building. Let them continue with other bag constructions until an entire city is completed—Classville, U.S.A. Why not display it in the school corridor? Start the month of September with your own custom made community.

Cellophane Leaf Hangings

Transparent Cut Paper

Here is a lesson which is different and will make your classroom gay and fall-like in appearance. It is also a wonderful way to make individual collections of leaves that everyone will enjoy.

Basic Materials: colored cellophane about 12 by 18 inches, a metal hanger, manila paper, assorted colored construction paper, glue, scissors.

Procedure:

- Draw various leaf shapes on a piece of manila paper.
- Cut them out for your leaf patterns.
- Trace the leaf patterns that you have made on different colored pieces of construction paper.
- Cut these out also.
- Next using the 12 by 18 inch cellophane paper as a background, arrange the colored leaves in a pleasing composition.
- Pick up each paper leaf, place glue on it and replace it to its original position on the cellophane.
- Add bits of paper cut into acorns or seed shapes and glue these scattered among the leaves for added interest.
- Fold the top edge of the cellophane paper over the straight bottom edge of the hanger about one half inch.
- Glue this firmly. (See Figure 1–4A)
- Next cut two strips of black paper about 1 by 12 inches, and paste one at the top and one at the bottom of the hanging. (See Figure 1–4B)

Figure 1–4A

Figure 1–4B

The leaf transparency is ready for show. It already has a hook, so suggest that the children find a spot that might be used for displaying their September project. One of the nicest places for display would be to hang them from the light fixtures. In this way they can be observed from back and front at the same time. How wonderful they look when the sun shines through.

Stand-up School Bus

Three Dimensional Paper Tent Fold

School buses could almost be called synonymous with school opening. This is an art lesson which is three dimensional and a bit different in technique. The children will enjoy making this project.

Basic Materials: 12 by 18 inch manila paper, crayons, scissors.

Procedure:

- Take the 12 by 18 inch paper and fold it the short way. This becomes a *Tent Fold,* and will stand if you prod the paper just a bit.
- Draw a picture of a bus in the rectangular block areas of one side of the folded paper. The open ends are the bottom of your picture, the fold is the top of the vehicle. (See Figure 1–5A)
- Cut away portions of the paper to make the bus appear more realistic. Do

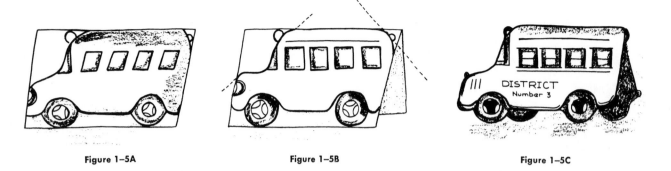

Figure 1–5A   Figure 1–5B   Figure 1–5C

not cut too much of the fold, or the project will not stand. (See Figure 1–5B)
- Sketch in lightly the windows, doors, fenders, bumpers of the bus.
- Next paint or crayon heavily all parts of the bus.
- When one side of the bus is completed turn the paper over, and do the other side. (See Figure 1–5C)
- Suggest that the children put friends in each window of the bus, or perhaps they could draw their favorite bus driver at the wheel. Ask them to number their bus.

The class might enjoy standing their buses in a line for a September Bus Parade. What an exciting sight that would be!

This project can be utilized in many ways. All types of vehicles can be made in the identical way outlined. Changing the size and color of the paper will make all the difference. You might suggest in another lesson that the children design a sleek car, truck or train out of a sheet of colored construction paper.

Tower Your Initials

Cardboard Construction

It doesn't matter who it is, everyone loves to have personal objects about him. Here is a project with a personal aspect, and one most desirable for children to work with—especially since it is the beginning of the new year at school. It is a wonderful way to utilize a name or initials in a new and different manner.

Basic Materials: 4 by 6 inch corrugated cardboard, a piece of shirt cardboard, scissors, glue.

Bonus Materials: silver foil, paint, crayons, magic markers, colored pencils.

Procedure:

- Have the children sketch on scrap paper their initials or the letters in their first name, if it is a short name.
- Suggest that they experiment with different letter forms until they find the letter type that suits them.

- Redraw the letters to a size 3 or 4 inches high.
- Cut out the trial letters, trace them on shirt cardboard, and next cut out the cardboard letters. The cardboard construction is interesting just as it is. However, you can now enhance them with bonus materials.
- Decorate them on both sides in any fashion desired. Crayons, paint, silver foil, magic markers, colored pencils or a combination of two or more of the media mentioned will be exciting. Suggest that this project is extremely personal, and that students create their own designs and be as innovative as possible.
- When the letters have been completed, notch them in two different places. (Notch means cutting a slit in the letter with a pair of scissors.) (See Figure 1–6A)
- Start connecting the letters by fitting them in the notches of the other letters. Build the letters up in a tower shape. This is not difficult if you are sure to insert the notch of one letter into the notch of another. The process automatically locks the letters together. (See Figure 1–6B)
- Next incise a slit in the corrugated cardboard base just large enough for a portion of your bottom letter to fit into, and glue them firmly together. (See Figure 1–6C)
- The base may stay in its original form, or it also can be decorated.

The students will enjoy playing a game with this project. Line the *Towering Initials* on the window sills of your classroom. After a day or two see how many names and initials the children can associate with the members of their class. Offer a small reward for the person who identifies the most names from the Towering Initial display.

Carry Home Portfolio

Crayon Techniques

Youngsters, especially the younger ones, love to take projects home to show their parents. This endeavor is a good one for them because it is functional, and it also can be an excellent way to renew or teach some basic crayon fundamentals. Here is the easiest way I know of to make a wonderful paper portfolio.

Basic Materials: 12 by 18 inch manila paper, crayons, scissors, scrap construction paper, paste.

Procedure:

- If the children have not used crayon in your class before, it is a good idea to demonstrate the following crayon techniques. These are funda-

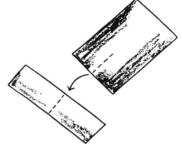

Figure 1–6A

Figure 1–6B

Figure 1–6C

mentals that all children should be introduced at an early age. The crayon is a tool that is easily acessible, and has many possibilities.

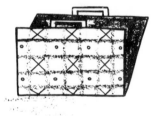

· Round flat back.

·Tip of crayon.

· Side of crayon.

Figure 1–7A

- There are three basic ways to use the crayon as a tool. (1) The tip is used for drawing or defining lines. (2) The side (broken, unwrapped pieces) is used for broad bands of color. When pressing with the side of a crayon put pressure on one end of the side of the crayon and shading will be obtained. (3) The round flat end can be placed on paper and pressed and twisted to make small round repeated shapes. (See Figure 1–7A)
- The teacher will find it most profitable to demonstrate these techniques on a sheet of paper taped to the blackboard. After the demonstration, allow ample experimentation by the children on pieces of scrap paper.
- Manila paper is then given to the students, and they create an all over design on the paper using the various crayon techniques.
- Next the paper is folded in half in booklet form.
- Handles are made by cutting two pieces of construction paper in a bridge form ⊓.
- Fasten these one each to the middle of the open ends of the booklet. Like magic a personal carryall has been produced. (See Figure 1–7B)

Figure 1–7B

Suggest to the children who finish before the others that they can draw pictures inside their folder of all the possible things they could carry in it. It is interesting to discover what the child thinks he can carry home in his paper portfolio. Watch the proud expressions on the faces of the children when they carry their handiwork home with the papers of the day in it.

Getting to Know You!

Montage of Photographed Pictures

This is an excellent project for September. It not only introduces a new art term—*Montage,* but it is an excellent opportunity for the boys and girls to work in a group. Here is an interesting way to produce a picture with photographed pictures.

Basic Materials: old magazines, newspapers, sheets of construction paper at least 18 by 24 inches, scissors, paste.

Procedure:

- Suggest that the children work in groups of 5 or 6 people. The group can decide whether they would like the people they want in their montage to have happy, sad, funny, or scary faces.
- When the decision is made, all students will thumb through the magazines and newspapers and cut out the pictures that they find. Cut the faces so that uninteresting areas around the faces are taken away.

- Next take turns pasting the faces to the background paper in any manner suitable.
- The faces can be tilted, placed upside down, sideways, any way you choose.
- Use lots of faces, big ones, little ones—all sizes.
- Overlap the faces in some areas, allow space around some of the pictures in other areas.
- Continue with this procedure until the arrangement of faces form an exciting new picture. (See Figure 1–8)

Figure 1–8

Suggest that the boys and girls find an area in the room where they think their montage would look best. Let them be the decorators. Some of the montages can be labeled with cut out letters or magic markers and used for posters announcing a school or local event. The montage is eye-catching and can be used again and again in various other ways. Make a car, alphabet, clothes, or house montage. They are all fun!

Your Dream School

Chalk on Wet Paper

Wouldn't it be wonderful if school reopened in September and we as teachers and students could work or study in the school of our choice? Today for an art lesson let us suggest that the children draw precisely what they think their dream school should be like. The results should be very revealing.

Basic Materials: 18 by 24 inch manila paper, chalk in various colors, a container of water, sponges.

Procedure:

- Wet the manila paper by quickly rubbing the wet sponge all over the paper.
- While the paper is still wet, quickly make a large sketch of the school on the paper with chalk.
- Continue to work on the paper until all the areas have been filled in.
- By this time the children will find that the paper has dried somewhat, but the paper is not to be remoistened.
- Continue to work filling in the details.
- Go back to main portions of the picture and make them stand out by pressing heavier with the chalk. (See Figure 1–9)

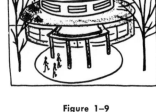

Figure 1–9

When the picture has been completed, spray it with fixitive, or if this is not available, hair spray can be used. Mount the dried pictures on a piece of gray or black paper for display. Invite another class to come in and vote on the school they think would be their *Dream School*.

September Placemats

Magic Markers and Paper

Snack time is a usual school procedure. Why not make it a gala affair by making a monthly placemat? Let us start with one for September.

Basic Materials: a sheet of 12 by 18 inch oaktag or an old window shade cut into 12 by 18 inch pieces, assorted colored magic markers.

Procedure:

Figure 1–10

- Think of a simple motif that could be adapted easily to a placemat design and make an experimental sketch on scrap paper with pencil.
- A September placemat could possibly be an apple (for the teacher), school bells, school items like pencils, pens, books; or it might be a simple leaf pattern.
- When the sketch is satisfying, transfer the idea to the placemat lightly with pencil, then go over it with the colored magic markers.
- The design could be an all over design, a center design, or a design placed in each corner. (See Figure 1–10)
- The placemat can be shellacked or sprayed with hair spray for added wear.

Wouldn't it be fun to have a few extras on hand so that you could invite the Principal in to have a snack with the class? He or she would be delighted with the hospitable gesture.

Pencil Case for September

Paint

At the beginning of the year everyone comes to school with bright and shiny pens and pencils. A personal pencil case would be a wonderful art project in which to house this new paraphernalia.

Basic Materials: a paper towel tube, scissors, brushes, tempera paint, scrap pieces of shirt cardboard, pieces of yarn, a paper punch.

Procedure:

- Cut about two inches off the top of a paper tube.
- Make the caps for closing the top and bottom of the tube in this manner.
- Cut a strip of lightweight cardboard about 2 inches wide by 6 inches long.

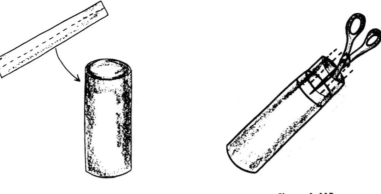

Figure 1–11A

Figure 1–11B

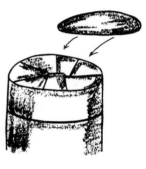

Figure 1–11C

- Fold this strip in half the long way.
- Open it, and wrap it around the top of the tube so that the crease in the cardboard is at the top edge of the tube. (See Figure 1–11A)
- Paste the cardboard strip to itself, and slide it carefully off the tube.
- Next cut the cardboard circle from the top down to the crease in about 6 or 7 places all around the circle. (See Figure 1–11B)
- Fold these strips in toward the center of the circle. As they are folded in to the middle, the strips will form the top.
- Cut out a small circle the size of the tube top from a scrap of cardboard.
- Paste this on the turned in strips for a completed top. (See Figure 1–11C)
- Repeat this process for the bottom cap, and glue the completed cap to the bottom of the tube, so you have only the top which will have a removable cap.
- Next decorate the tube with paint in any way desired. Use bold splotchy color and patterns if you want a pencil case that can be found easily.
- When the case is dried, punch a hole on each side of the tube, and attach a piece of yarn for a handle. (See Figure 1–11D)

The children will love their pencil cases, but don't stop with this project. A case like this would make Mom a wonderful holder for kitchen utensils, and Dad will be delighted with one for holding fireplace matches or pipe cleaning equipment.

Figure 1–11D

What's in a Name?

Crayon

This project is another September Getting-to-Know-You Better lesson. It might be suggested for use during the early part of the school year when teachers are still not familiar with the names of people in their class.

Basic Materials: crayons, 12 by 18 inch manila paper.

Procedure:

- Fold the manila paper in half the long way.
- Open the paper, and on the inside along the upper half of the fold have

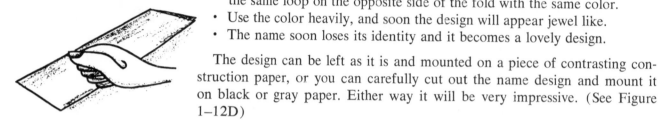

Figure 1–12A

the children write their name heavily with black crayon. (See Figure 1–12A)

- Refold the paper with the name inside.
- Next with the side of a pencil, book or box, rub over the area of the paper where you have just written your name. (See Figure 1–12B)
- Check by opening the fold to see whether the impression of the black crayon has rubbed off on the lower half of the folded paper.
- When the light impression appears, go over the name to make it as dark as the first writing. You now have a double image of the name. (See Figure 1–12C)
- Hold the paper the long way, and start to fill in portions of the name.
- If you fill a loop on one side of the paper with a color, remember to fill in the same loop on the opposite side of the fold with the same color.
- Use the color heavily, and soon the design will appear jewel like.
- The name soon loses its identity and it becomes a lovely design.

Figure 1–12B

The design can be left as it is and mounted on a piece of contrasting construction paper, or you can carefully cut out the name design and mount it on black or gray paper. Either way it will be very impressive. (See Figure 1–12D)

Display the names by tacking them to a huge bulletin board. Hang a sign entitled *What's in a Name?* across the top of the display.

Figure 1–12C

Figure 1–12D

Personal Bookmarks

Ball Point Pen and Paper

Back to school means back to studying. The children will enjoy making this project because they will have their own personal way of keeping track of pages in their texts.

Basic Materials: old envelopes, ball point pens, scissors.

Procedure:

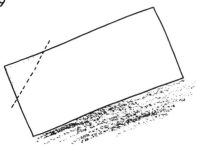

Figure 1-13A

- Cut the corners from any old envelope.
- This becomes your bookmark. (See Figure 1–13A)
- With the ball point pen, print your initials on the bookmark.
- Decorate the initials by filling in areas heavily with ink, and by adding designs around the printed letters. (See Figure 1–13B)

If a bookmark is uninteresting, it can be discarded, and others can be made. Suggest that the children make several bookmarks, not only for themselves, but as a surprise gift for someone in the family. It would be a nice treat for Mom to receive when you return home after school, wouldn't it?

Figure 1-13B

September Nature Assemblage

Project with Natural Materials

There is such varied foliage in September. Why not take advantage of this idea while the materials are asking to be used?

Take your class on a nature adventure tour and collect items for the project. Outline the reason for the tour, and if possible correlate the project with a science lesson.

The children should carry a bag or container with them on their tour. Along the way, point out interesting colors and nature items. The children will begin to find beautiful colored leaves, stones, bits of moss, bark and any number of miscellaneous types of foliage for their assemblage.

Basic Materials: a collection of natural items from nature, a piece of 12 by 18 inch oaktag, glue, scissors, scotch tape.

Procedure:

- Following the nature walk have the children spread out the goodies they found while on their trip.
- Have them choose the various items they particularly want to use in their project, and have them discard the rest.
- Next arrange the chosen items on the cardboard in an interesting fashion.
- The items can be arranged to form a picture, or they can be arranged in rows for display. Either way, stress that the arrangement should be pleasing to look at. (See Figure 1–14)

Figure 1-14

I mentioned previously that perhaps the art lesson could be correlated with a science lesson. Why not enhance the assemblage by labeling the various items collected with the correct scientific name? This could be done with the use of the magic marker, and it will add much to the project.

In the science corner of your room the Nature Assemblages could be displayed on tables or tacked to a bulletin board with a huge sign saying, *Fruits of our September Nature Adventure.*

Mock Ancient Leaf Designs

Ball Point Pen Project

The Orientals have a very unusual way of drying leaves, pounding portions of the leaf matter away, and making the veins appear as an interesting leaf design.

Your class can assimilate this by using the following method. It is time consuming, but the reward obtained from the project is well worth the time.

Basic Materials: a leaf, a piece of 9 by 12 inch paper (white or manila), and a ball point pen.

Procedure:

Figure 1-15A

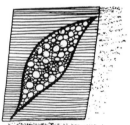

Figure 1-15B

- Trace the leaf shape on the chosen paper with the ball point pen. When the leaf has been traced, the interior of the leaf is filled in with small round circles.
- Each circle is touching the other but not overlapping. (See Figure 1-15A)
- The circles can be varied in size. Draw in a very large one occasionally, but basically the shapes should be approximately the same size.
- When the leaf has been filled in entirely with circles, the children can make any type of interesting background. However, here are a few suggestions.
- Draw straight lines to cover the entire area of the background. Do not draw the lines over the leaf. (See Figure 1-15B)
- Draw repeated larger circles in a different color pen all around the leaf and extending to the edge of the paper. (See Figure 1-15C)
- Follow the leaf design with lines of your own making. Repeat these intermittently until the background is completely filled in. (See Figure 1-15D)

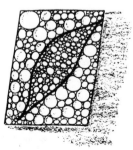

Figure 1-15C

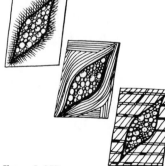

Figure 1-15D

When the leaf designs are completed, mount them on a piece of black paper. They make a wonderful border above the chalkboards. (This project is one that parents will choose to frame when they are brought home by the children. They are very impressive.)

Map Your Route

Pencil and Crayon

The first month of school is a wonderful time for children to make a map of their route to school. This is not an easy task, but the children will enjoy doing it once they try the project.

Basic Materials: a shirt cardboard, pencil, crayons, 12 by 18 inch white paper.

Procedure:

- Just before school lets out, give each child a shirt cardboard and suggest that they draw a trial map of their route home. They do not have to go into exacting detail, but suggest that they start with school and include main streets, buildings or other landmarks which will aid them when they redraw the map on another piece of paper.
- School was the beginning of the map, and their house should be the destination.
- Suggest that they recheck the route on the map they made when they return to school the following day.
- During the art lesson give each child a piece of white paper and ask them to redraw their school route map using the basic cardboard map as a reference.
- The final map can include additional landmarks and directional points.
- The map can remain drawn with pencil; however, it can be made more attractive and meaningful if the key points are crayoned in heavily. (See Figure 1–16)

An interesting booklet of pupils' maps can be made by compiling the maps together in book form. One of the students who enjoys making book covers can design a cover for the booklet. The children can take turns using a classmate's map to find a route to their friend's house.

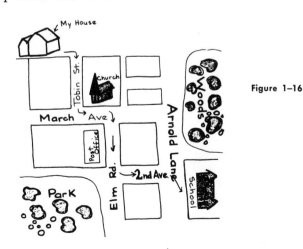

Figure 1–16

Where Did You Go Last Summer?

Mixed Media

The children have interesting experiences during the summer months. Using some of these experiences in an art project can be a very worthwhile adventure. Why not make your room a temporary travel agency? Great! Let's decorate the room with travel posters.

Basic Materials: 18 by 24 inch colored construction paper, paint, brushes, magic markers, miscellaneous bits of colored paper, colored pencils.

Procedure:

Figure 1–17

- Suggest that the children make a poster of what they did during the summer. Stimulate interest and conversation with the aid of commercial posters. (If a child did not travel, ask him to sell his home town to other travelers.)
- When the enthusiasm is high, give each child a piece of scrap paper, and have him sketch in pencil an idea which he thinks will sell his travel experience to someone else. Suggest that the poster be made so exciting that everyone will want to journey to the place depicted.
- Stress that one idea for a picture, and words kept at a minimum, will make the poster more desirable.
- When the pencil sketch is satisfactory, have the pupils redraw the idea on the large paper.
- The fun of making a poster is to decide what materials you would like to use to make them really impressive.
- Allow the children to choose from the assortment you have laid out for them to use.
- Many types of media can be used, or a child may want to partake of only one. Let them decide! (See Figure 1–17)

Hang the posters on the walls of your room. Your Travel Agency is decorated. Invite another class to visit your agency. Ask your children to be ready as agents to sell their trip to people who inquire about their poster. The introverts as well as the extroverts will shine with this approach. Try it!

Hidden Treasures

Crayon

Surprise the children with the question, "What's in your desk?" Ask them to take out an assortment of items, and you now have the beginning of a wonderful fun lesson. Do the lesson in September and try it again in June. It will be interesting to see how the items change.

Basic Materials: crayons, 12 by 18 inch manila paper, and an assortment of items taken from each pupil's desk.

Procedure:

- When the children have taken various paraphernalia from their desks, ask them to trace the various items on the paper in a hodgepodge manner. There should be objects like scissors, a book, pencils, pens, erasers, a pad, a purse, just anything found in a school desk.
- Overlap portions of the various objects to cover the entire paper. (See Figure 1–18A)
- When the paper has been covered with tracings in an interesting composition, next suggest that the children fill in various areas with color until the entire piece of manila paper has been covered with crayon.
- Use the crayon heavily so the picture appears as an interesting color design.
- Next with a black crayon outline the shapes that were first traced.

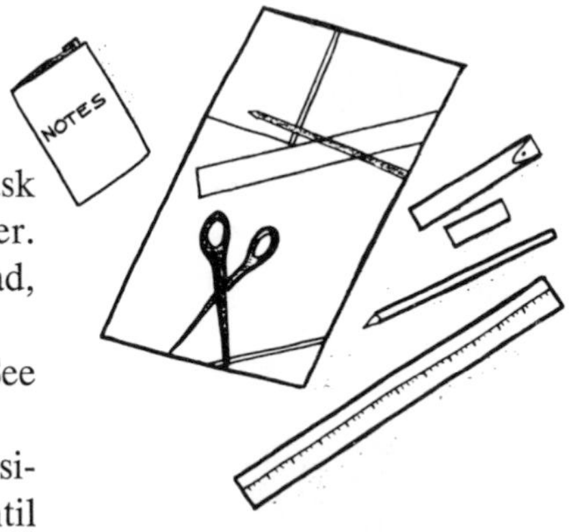

Figure 1–18A

The picture becomes a bold crayon abstract. Why not use these colorful pictures as a cover for one of the many booklets that are made in class? If it is folded in half, the short way, it is just the correct size. Perhaps the children could cut letters from black paper and paste them to the cover. What an exciting English, History, or Penmanship booklet cover this abstract drawing will make. (See Figure 1–18B)

Figure 1–18B

Tape a Magic School

Masking Tape and Water Color Paint

Why not tape a school? It isn't really difficult, and how different a lesson it would be. September is a wonderful time to try this project. School is still holding the "limelight."

Basic Materials: masking tape wrapped on toothpicks, so each child can have his own portion to use, water color paints, a container of water, brushes, manila paper about 12 by 18 inches, scissors.

Procedure:

- Ask the children to make a picture of the school on the manila paper, but instead of drawing it with a tool, ask them to construct it with bits of masking tape.

Figure 1–19A

- Illustrate how this is done with a piece of paper tacked to the bulletin board. On the illustration, construct a square with 4 pieces of tape forming the box or rectangular shape which eventually becomes the beginning of a building. (See Figure 1–19A)
- Suggest that the children attempt the construction of a school on their paper using a basic rectangle or square for the beginning of their school.
- It isn't long before the children will begin to create other constructions with their tape which will eventually become their school and its background.
- Suggest that the children cut the tape narrow in some areas for subjects like a flag pole or playground equipment.
- The children will decide when they have added enough tape to make the picture their school.
- The next step is to paint the entire picture with water color. This can be done by using one color all over the picture, or using strips or splotchy color all over the paper, tape and all.
- When the paint has dried, have the children carefully remove the tape from the picture. What occurs is almost magic. The areas covered with tape remain unpainted, while the other areas of the picture are covered with the water color paint. (See Figure 1–19B)

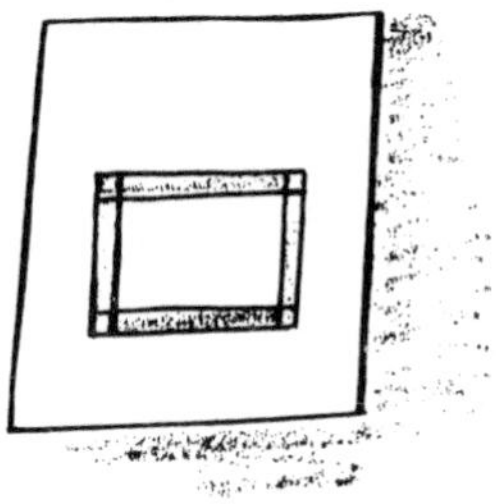

Figure 1–19B

The children will enjoy showing their work to their classmates. As they complete their pictures, have them come up and display their project for peer perusal. Explanations and comments are welcome! Show and Tell with creative work will never lose popularity.

Jane's Puzzle

Paint

There aren't many days during September that the children are forced to remain indoors during lunch period. However, this month is an excellent time to prepare for long periods of indoor weather. Here is an easy art project which will give countless hours of joy to the children. Not only in the making of the project but in its future use. Try this delightful idea for personal puzzles.

Basic Materials: a sheet of sturdy cardboard, compass, tempera paint, brushes, scissors, a plastic bag.

Procedure:

- Trace the largest circle possible on the cardboard with the compass.

Figure 1–20

- When this is completed, have the children print their name in the circle from its top to its bottom. (See Figure 1–20)
- Use the entire circle.
- If your name is not long enough to print in the circle, add letters of your last name to it.
- Next paint the broken areas and spaces of your name with the tempera paint. Two or three colors can be used, or if you choose, use as many colors as you think are necessary.
- Soon the name will become just a design, and the circle picture will be colorful and exciting.
- Allow the painting to dry thoroughly, then cut the circle into all shapes and sizes.
- Do not make the pieces too small. You now have a wonderful round picture puzzle.

Each child should be sure to enclose all of the pieces of his puzzle in the plastic bag which has been labeled with his name.

Have all the puzzles put into a large box. Entitle the box *Fun Puzzle Box,* or some such title. Then during inclement weather the children have a definite place to go to find a worthwhile pastime. Everyone will soon know who has made the most interesting puzzle. It will be the first one to be sought by all.

FUN THINGS TO DRAW DURING SEPTEMBER

1. How did you come to school on the first day it opened?
2. Draw a picture of your new teacher.
3. Draw what you did on Labor Day.
4. Draw a picture of your principal.
5. Draw what you miss most during the summer.
6. How does mother look in the morning?
7. What do you see out one of your class windows?
8. Draw a picture of your class in portrait form.
9. What does your school look like inside?
10. Draw a picture of what you would like to be doing right now.

2

Octuber

The trials and tribulations of school opening are over. The teacher and students have settled down for the new school year.

October begins the autumn season which is one of the most colorful times of the year. The trees are shedding leaves, the countryside is ablaze with magnificent color.

This month marks the time for U.N. and Fire Prevention Week, Child Health and Poetry Day. It is also the time to celebrate Columbus' birthdate, and one of the most colorful children's fun days—Hallowe'en.

In this chapter we have varied suggestions and techniques for all the special days mentioned plus special sections on Columbus Day and Hallowe'en.

Autumn Mobile

Colored Paper and Natural Material

Autumn is one of the loveliest times of the year. Artists have tried to capture on canvas for many years the profusion of color that exists when the leaves change color. This project is a different way to record this season. Here is a suggestion for a wonderful October mobile.

Basic Materials: thread, assorted colored paper, scissors, a small branch (a wire coat hanger if the branch is unavailable).

Procedure:

Figure 2–1

- Cut out a number of autumn leaves from a variety of colored paper. Use colors which remind you of the changing leaves.
- Next put a small hole in each leaf, reinforce the hole with a piece of transparent tape.
- Cut the thread in different lengths, and attach one end to the leaf, and the other to the branch.
- Do not put all the leaves in one area or in an even line on the branch. Irregular placement is much more exciting.
- From time to time look at the branch mobile. If you have added too many pieces, take some off, or if the mobile has too many empty spots, add some pieces. (See Fig. 2–1)

When the mobile is the way you want it, find an interesting place to hang it. One suggestion would be to hang it from the light fixtures. Invite the class next door to visit your colorful overhead autumn spectacle.

Sad Scarecrow

Charcoal

Everyone has feelings. Sometimes we feel happy or sad, sometimes we feel grouchy or indifferent. No matter how we feel we seem to portray it in our facial expression. Let us try to capture the feelings of a sad scarecrow in this October project.

Basic Materials: 12 by 18 inch manila paper, charcoal.

Procedure:

Figure 2–2

- What are some of the scarecrow's characteristics? Try to make a mental picture of how you think he might appear. Start your picture with a sketch of his face. Make it huge! Fill the paper with face.
- Now add his features and as much clothing as you have room available on your paper. Have you drawn the face sad? How about a scarf?
- Don't forget to add wisps of straw coming from areas that may have popped open. Make the straw look like straw. Draw the lines straight and crisp.
- When the sketch is completed, go back to certain areas of the picture. Use the charcoal in as many ways as you can. Press hard for dark areas, lighter for middle shading, and very light for pale shading.
- Show texture in his clothing by using stripes, plaids, polka dots, or create new textures. (See Figure 2–2)

- Other background scenery can be added—trees, farmhouse, cornstalks, fences, crows.

An interesting way to display these sad scarecrows would be to line them up on the bulletin board, and entitle the exhibit *October's Sad Scarecrow Brigade*.

Autumn Trees

Crayon and Tissue Paper

October is a wonderful time to utilize the tree silhouette. Children of all ages will benefit by a lesson which will encourage them to look and actually see the beauty nature offers us.

Basic Materials: 12 by 18 inch manila paper, crayons, paste, assorted colored tissue paper.

Procedure:

- Take the class for a walk on the playground or park where you can point out the growth and formation of various types of trees. Discuss the way the trunk is formed, the V shape that appears when a branch forms, how a branch sprouts to form other branches.
- When you return from the trip, give each child a sheet of paper and ask him to draw with black or brown crayon one of the trees he saw on the excursion. Be sure that the tree is large, and fills the paper. (See Figure 2–3A)
- Next make available an assortment of colored tissue paper, preferably red, yellow, orange, green and brown.
- Now have the children tear the tissue into pieces of various size and paste them to the crayoned branches. Overlap some pieces, allow others to remain apart from other color. (See Figure 2–3B)
- When enough color has been added, have the children cut out their tree.

One way to display the trees would be to mount them on a sheet of black paper and cover a bulletin board with them. Another way would be to attach them to the school windows with scotch tape. The children will have their own personal forest in the classroom.

Figure 2–3A   Figure 2–3B

Fire Prevention Posters

Mixed Media

Fire Prevention Week occurs during the month of October. Here is a project which will make children cognizant of fire prevention at all times.

Basic Materials: 18 by 24 inch construction paper, crayons, magic markers, assorted scraps of colored paper, scissors, paste.

Procedure:

Figure 2-4

- Have a discussion period prior to the art lesson about the hazards of fire. How can we help to show people how important it is that they practice fire prevention ideas? The children will come forth with all kinds of interesting ideas. Stress that they try to think of an idea that is not used by another classmate. When enthusiasm for the subject is high suggest that they start making posters.
- Give each child a sheet of large paper, and let him choose crayon, cut paper or magic marker to work with. He may combine the use of all media if he desires.
- Suggest that the poster be kept simple, and the ideas and lettering remain as large as possible. Stress the fact that posters are to be seen from a distance. (See Figure 2-4)

When the posters are completed, have the children take turns showing their project.

Perhaps the posters can be improved if the peer group suggests brighter color, or an addition of some point on a poster.

When everyone is satisfied with their poster, a wonderful place to exhibit them might be in the school or town library. The librarian will be delighted to display Fire Prevention Week posters.

Print of Columbus Ship

Cardboard Graphic

Did you ever do a graphic with your class? It sounds like something difficult, doesn't it? Really it is not. Making a graphic means making a piece of art work that can be duplicated again and again by making a print of it. There are many ways to produce a graphic. This graphic will be produced with a cardboard plate. Since it is October, and there is much talk at this time about Columbus and his exploits, let us make a graphic about a subject pertaining to him. How about a print depicting one of his ships?

Basic Materials: light weight cardboard, 6 by 8 inch rectangle of corrugated paper, glue, scissors, water base printing ink or thick tempera paint, brush, a spoon, newsprint.

Procedure:

- Cut out pieces of the lightweight cardboard to form a ship and the sails of a Columbus era ship.
- Place them on the corrugated rectangle which will be the plate for your printing.
- Add pieces of cardboard until the assembled ship is satisfactory.
- Next remove each piece of your proposed ship and replace it after glue has been applied. (See Figure 2–5A)
- When the picture plate is completed cover the entire surface by painting it with water base printing ink or thick tempera paint.
- Quickly lay newsprint paper on the wet plate, and rub the entire area carefully with the bowl of a spoon.
- Carefully lift the paper away from the plate. You now have a duplicate of the ship you cut from the cardboard. Repeat the process for as many prints as you desire. (See Figure 2–5B)

Figure 2–5A

Perhaps your school is having a Columbus Day Program. Wouldn't the prints make wonderful invitations? Remember this project for other programs or some form of holiday cards. A rabbit print for Easter cards, an evergreen for Christmas, heart prints for Valentine's Day.

Commemorative Columbus Plates

Crayon

Commemorative plates have been a collector's item for many years. Do you know someone who has such a collection? Making a commemorative plate for notable people would be an interesting project, wouldn't it? Why don't we try making one for Christopher Columbus?

Figure 2–5B

Basic Materials: compass, 12 by 18 inch manila paper, crayons, scissors.

Procedure:

- If you have one, show the children the china plate entitled Blue Willow. (Substitute other picture plates to illustrate a commemorative plate.) Tell the children the story of the picture.
- Suggest that they make a picture plate for Columbus' birthdate.
- Using the compass, draw a circle on the manila paper the plate size desired.

Figure 2-6

- Draw another circle within the first circle for the border of the plate. Cut out the paper plate.
- Next draw a few trial sketches on scrap paper of an idea dealing with Columbus' life.
- When you like your sketch, decide whether you want to use it as a repetitive design around the plate or just a scene of his exploits in the center of the plate.
- Now redraw the sketch on the plate and color it heavily with crayon. (See Figure 2–6)

Mount the completed plates on black paper and display them in rows or in clusters around the room. They will be an excellent way to celebrate the memory of the great voyager, Christopher Columbus. In the following months why not draw commemorative plates for other famous people? The children would certainly have a wonderful collection with which to remember your class.

What Columbus Feared Most

Crayon and Chalk

October cannot pass without some recognition of Christopher Columbus. Why not try a new art approach with this familiar subject?

Basic Materials: crayon, colored chalk, 18 by 24 inch manila paper.

Procedure:

- During a Social Studies discussion you may touch upon reasons why Columbus and his crew feared a trip to the new world. It surprises most girls and boys when they discover that unknown monsters were in the main responsible for the frightened crew. The monsters were actually sea creatures unfamiliar to men at that time, and were manifested in early sketches as dreadful man eating monsters.
- Ask your students to imagine that they are members of Columbus' crew.
- Have them draw huge scary sea monsters and crayon them vibrantly.
- Highlights can be added with colored chalk. (See Figure 2–7)

One good way to display the pictures would be to place them in a school corridor, and label the pictures, *What Columbus Feared Most—Do You?*

Figure 2-7

Columbus' Ship in Silhouette

Paint

Children love to paint. Why not let them attempt to paint a ship—Columbus vintage.

Basic Materials: 12 by 18 inch white paper, paint brush, container of black paint.

Procedure:

- Suggest that the children sketch with pencil their interpretation of a Columbus ship. They have seen so many pictures of the Nina, Pínta and Santa Maria that this should be an easy task.
- When the sketch is completed, paint the entire ship with black paint.
- Fill in all the solid areas so the sketch becomes a silhouette.
- Allow portions of the white paper to show through in the form of port holes, foam on waves, ladders, the anchor. (See Figure 2–8)

Mount the pictures on black paper and cover a large bulletin board with them. A good title for the display might be *Sailing Along with Columbus.* Can your class think of another title?

Figure 2–8

Picture Book of the Life of Columbus

Crayon and Magic Marker

Group projects are an effective way to produce really worthwhile art work. Here is an idea which you will find most rewarding. A joint project in picture form of Columbus' life.

Basic Materials: 12 by 18 inch manila paper, crayons, magic markers.

Procedure:

Columbus Sets Sail!

Figure 2–9

- Prior to the lesson discuss fully the following topics:
  1. Columbus as a boy.
  2. Columbus the Inquirer.
  3. Columbus the Explorer.
  4. Columbus the Adventurer in the New World.
  5. Columbus and his despair.
- Next divide the class into five groups with each group choosing one of the listed topics.
- Have the children illustrate their topic and print a short statement of the picture beneath it with magic marker. (See Figure 2–9)
- When the pictures are completed, compile them in topic order. Choose one of the students to illustrate a cover for the booklet.
- Fasten the booklet together by punching two holes at the side of each picture at the binding point. Insert a piece of rug yarn or ribbon in the holes and fasten the entire booklet together.

Suggest that the students in your class take turns in visiting other classes to read their picture booklet to them. The youngsters will love to show off their picture story book of Columbus.

Illustrate a Haiku

Crayon

Have you had difficulty in developing poetry appreciation in your class? Perhaps a new type of poetry can be introduced which may stimulate a fresh and different interest. The Haiku is a new approach. It is an unrhymed Japanese poem of three lines containing five, seven, and five syllables respectively and referring in some way to one of the seasons of the year. (If you have difficulty with poems of this sort, a librarian will advise you.)

Since we celebrate Poetry Day during October, let's try this lesson.

Basic Materials: 12 by 18 inch manila paper, crayons.

Procedure:

- Have the paper and crayons available for use by the class.
- Choose a book of your choice and recite a Haiku to the class. Show them the illustrations pictured.

- Ask the children to close their eyes and, as you read another Haiku, have them make a mental picture of parts of the poem. Discuss the pictures visualized by the class.
- Next read several new Haikus, and ask the class to choose one that they would be interested in illustrating. The enthusiasm will be high, so let the children create. (See Figure 2–10)

When the pictures are completed, let the children present their work to the class. Have the children try to guess the Haiku that was illustrated.

The lesson will lead to the possible writing of newly created Haikus during an English class. Perhaps a Haiku booklet could be made by each pupil along with original illustrations for the booklet. A Haiku library shelf with original manuscripts could be a focal point in a corner of the classroom.

As I stand outside.... And the wind blows against me. I hear winter come.

Figure 2–10

Special Section on Hallowe'en

Hallowe'en Via the Daily Newspaper

Newspaper and Paint

It is always fun during an art period to use a material which is unique for a project. What could be more apropos than using newspaper to paint a Hallowe'en picture?

Basic Materials: newspaper want ads, orange and black paint, brushes.

Procedure:

- Give each child a sheet of newspaper, a paint brush, and a container of orange and black paint.
- If the children work in pairs the paint can be placed between them.
- Suggest that they think of various things that could be painted for a Hallowe'en picture. Witches, bats, owls, ghosts, goblins, pumpkins, cats are all good subjects. (See Figure 2–11)

When the pictures are completed, mount them on gray or black paper. They are such handsome pictures, why not display them in the school cafeteria for all to enjoy? Won't people be surprised to see paintings on newspaper ads?

Figure 2–11

Zany Katz

Crayon

The cat is a great Hallowe'en favorite, but why not try a new approach in developing an art project involving him?

Basic Materials: 12 by 18 inch manila paper, crayons, scissors, paste, 12 by 18 inch black paper.

Procedure:

- Ask the children to sketch a picture of a cat in any position they desire.
- When it is completed, suggest that they redesign their sketch so the cat's personality is completely changed. The head could be designed as striped, the legs polka dotted, the body in plaid or floral pattern, the tail could be patchworked. All sorts of new patterns and designs could be created.
- Next crayon the animal (newly created) with vibrant color.
- The cat appears as a new and unusual animal. Cut him out and mount him on black construction paper. (See Figure 2–12)

Use the Zany Katz as a border around the classroom. Perhaps it can be labeled, *Zany Katz on Parade.*

Figure 2–12

The Magic of Hallowe'en

Household Bleach

Here is a great painting medium—household bleach. Your class will enjoy the mysterious way a picture can be painted with this common liquid.

Basic Materials: a plastic cup of bleach, Q tips, a sheet of orange paper.

Procedure:

- Give each child a sheet of paper, several Q tips and the cup of bleach. (*Caution*—do not use brushes, and warn the children that bleach is injurious to clothing.)
- Next ask the children to paint a picture using the bleach as their paint. They will soon discover that areas that are bleached begin to lose color. The orange paper becomes white where the bleach has been applied. (See Figure 2–13)
- What a scary Hallowe'en picture evolves. Let the children make several pictures using various colored background paper.

Figure 2–13

- Perhaps one of the pictures can have added touches of crayon when the bleach has dried. Experiment, it's fun!

Why not have the class vote on the magic picture they think is most Hallowe'en in flavor? The winner could be the recipient of a black or orange lollipop.

Pumpkin Mobile

Crayon and Paper Construction

Children will enjoy creating these delightful pumpkin mobiles. Suggest that they attempt to make their pumpkin face have a feeling: jolly, sad, frightened, remorseful. It will be interesting to see what the response will be.

Basic Materials: 12 by 18 inch orange paper, crayons, scissors, thread.

Procedure:

- Cut out a huge pumpkin from the orange paper, and decorate it with crayon. Have you expressed feeling in the face of the pumpkin?
- Next cut away portions of the pumpkin face and replace parts of them by tying the pieces back in place with thread.
- Make sure that the returned pieces have been cut sufficiently, so they will move freely in their new position.
- When the front of the mobile is completed, carefully turn it over and complete the other side identical with the front. (See Figure 2–14)

Figure 2–14

Display the pumpkin mobiles by hanging them on the light fixtures of the classroom. They will be an announcement to all that Hallowe'en is near.

Trick or Treat Bag

Crayon and Magic Marker

What boy or girl wouldn't be delighted to create his very own trick or treat carryall? Just your suggestion about it will bring accolades from each pupil.

Basic Materials: a sturdy rectangular bottomed paper bag, crayons, magic markers, 24 inches of yarn.

Procedure:

- Fold the top of the bag down so it makes a 2 or 3 inch cuff inside the bag.

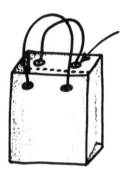

Figure 2–15A

- Decide where you want the holes made for the yarn handles. At these points place a piece of masking tape for reinforcement and punch holes there.
- Cut the yarn in two equal pieces and attach them in the reinforced holes for the handles. (See Figure 2–15A)
- Next design the bag back and front with all sorts of Hallowe'en motifs. It is very effective if only yellow, orange, green and black crayons are used in the decorations.
- Use the crayon heavily, and accentuate areas with magic marker. (See Figure 2–15B)

Why not offer a treat to the child who creates the best trick or treat bag? The school nurse might be a good judge, ask her.

Figure 2–15B

Merry Skeletons

Painted Window Ornaments

Here is an excellent idea for a Hallowe'en project. The materials are at a minimum and the final results very dramatic.

Basic Materials: 18 by 24 inch black paper, white tempera paint, easel brushes, scissors.

Procedure:

Figure 2–16

- Discuss the bone structure of a skeleton with your class. The skull, ribs, how the arms and legs are joined, what hands and feet look like in bone structure.
- At the blackboard demonstrate how dots and dashes of chalk become a skeleton.
- Suggest that the children attempt to make a picture of a skeleton with pencil on a piece of scrap paper.
- Next give each child black paper, a plastic cup of white paint and an easel brush.
- Now they can paint a skeleton on the paper, but suggest that they make the skeleton in motion—perhaps dancing. (See Figure 2–16) It will only take a few strokes to obtain a very impressive dancing skeleton. Why not make more than one?
- When the paintings are dry, cut out the skeletons, allowing the black paper to remain as the foundation.

Tape the skeletons hodgepodge on the classroom windows with the painted side out. What a handsome and different window decoration these dancing skeletons make.

The Family Pumpkin

Crayon and Cut Paper

Let's make a Pumpkin Family for Hallowe'en. The idea is a simple one, but very effective!

Basic Materials: 9 by 12 inch orange paper, 12 by 18 inch manila paper, scissors, paste, crayons.

Procedure:

- Have the children cut out as many pumpkin shapes as they would like to have in their Pumpkin Family. Don't forget baby pumpkin or Grandma or Grandpa Pumpkin.
- Next paste the pumpkin heads on the background paper.
- Draw the faces for each pumpkin, and proceed with a body, clothing, hair, jewelry—all kinds of added decoration.
- Decide where and what the family is doing and draw a suitable background. (See Figure 2–17)

When the pictures are completed, display them side by side on the bulletin board. A good title might be: *The Daily Lives of the Family Pumpkin.*

Figure 2–17

What Is in the Haunted House?

Mixed Media

Have you ever been in a haunted house? I have, and it was a scary adventure. I am sure I saw things that really never existed. The imagination is a funny thing! Why not suggest that the children draw a haunted house for Hallowe'en?

Basic Materials: 18 by 24 inch manila paper, crayons, paint, scissors, paste, assorted construction paper, netting, cellophane, tissue.

Procedure:

Figure 2–18

- Sketch a picture of the eeriest old house you can create.
- Color areas of it with crayons or paint. (Both mediums used is great fun!)
- Cut out the house and carefully cut out the windows and doors on three sides so they become little shutters.
- Next paste the house to a sheet of background paper; however, be sure that the shuttered windows and doors remain open.
- One at a time open the shutters and draw something frightening in each one. (See Figure 2–18)
- Add other materials to the house. Perhaps cellophane or tissue over some windows, or pieces of netting cut into ghost-like shapes in others. Don't add too much or you may cover things which are interesting.

A good idea to utilize after the art lesson would be to have the class write a story about the haunted house. These would be a unique touch when mounted together and displayed in the school corridor for all to read and use.

Pumpkin Heads

Crayons

Here is a great fun lesson. Try it! The basic idea of the lesson is to see how many varieties of faces can be created on pumpkin shapes.

Basic Materials: 12 by 18 inch orange paper, scissors, paste, crayons, 12 by 18 inch gray or black paper.

Procedure:

- Cut out as many pumpkin heads as possible from the orange paper. Cut the heads in a variety of sizes, none smaller than the size of a lemon.
- Next paste the heads on the gray or black paper, scattering them so the paper is filled with pumpkin shapes.
- Now decorate each head differently with crayon. The faces can be of people, animals, fish, birds, flowers—see how creative you can be! (See Figure 2–19)

Figure 2–19

Display the pictures on a huge bulletin board with a possible title: *Pumpkins with a Thousand Faces*. Another possibility would be to take the completed picture and staple it into a large cylinder. A handle of yarn could be attached at the top and it would become a wonderful Hallowe'en ornament.

Mock Scratchboard Masks

Crayon

October—Hallowe'en! How about making a mask—a different kind of mask? You can make yourself into anything at all. A mask lets you pretend that you are something that you might for a moment like to be. If you want, you can make your mask sad, scary, old, young or funny. This mask everyone will enjoy making. It can be worn or you may just like to use it as an interesting wall decoration.

Basic Materials: 12 by 18 inch manila paper, crayons, scissors.

Procedure:

- Sketch a large oval shape on the manila paper.
- Very lightly pencil in the facial features on the mask, but accentuate each one. The nose can be huge, pointed, pugged; the eyes can be bulging, slanted, squinting; the mouth might be thin, thick, round, long, short. Think of many different ways that you can make the features original and grotesque.
- Now crayon heavily all portions of the mask. Use only bright colors in a variety of shades. (See Figure 2–20A)
- Next take your black crayon and completely crayon over your entire mask. Make sure none of the color you first put on your mask shows through.
- When you have reached this point, cover your working area with newspaper.
- Open your scissors and hold them open in your hands so the point of one side becomes a scratching tool. (A nail file, inkless pen, orange stick, or any sharp tool can be used in place of the scissors.)
- Now carefully start to scratch away the black area of crayon from your mask. Scratch lines going in one direction if you can, but be careful that your scratching tool does not dig a hole in your paper. (See Figure 2–20B)
- When the black areas are removed decide what you would like to do with your mask. You may cut it out and mount it on construction paper for display, or you may want to paste it to a piece of cardboard, cut it out and wear it. You decide.

Figure 2–20A

Figure 2–20B

A fun game to play with the class would be to have each person guess how the mask makes its owner feel. Try it!

Spatter a Ghost

Spray Gun and Paint

Sometimes we overlook some excellent art possibilities in the use of common household tools. A spray gun can become one of the most exciting tools that can be found. Fill it with diluted tempera paint or ink and it is ready to be utilized in an art lesson. Here is a wonderful way to use the spray gun in an October project.

Basic Materials: a spray gun, dark construction paper, white ink or white paint diluted with water to ink consistency, newspaper, paper tissues, glue, weeds, yarn.

Procedure:

- Cover your work area with plenty of newspaper.
- Carefully arrange your weeds on the dark paper background, and spray the white liquid over the entire arrangement, however, do not cover the dark paper with it. When you have a white silhouette shape of the weeds, stop spraying. (See Figure 2–21A)
- Allow the paint to dry and carefully remove the weeds and put them aside for later use. Your paper now has an eery looking silhouette on it.
- Next take two tissues. Roll one into a ball, and put this into the center of the other tissue. Twist the tissue around the balled tissue. You now have a little ghost.
- Put paste on the head and lower portion of the little ghost and place him somewhere on the weed silhouette. More than one ghost can be added. (See Figure 2–21B)

Figure 2–21A

Figure 2–21B

- Now with crayon just add a bit of color here and there on the picture. Perhaps a wisp of green, brown or yellow among the white weed silhouette will be sufficient. You may want to add a gnarled tree or haunted house. Don't add too much or it will take away from the exciting effect obtained from the spray gun.

Mount the picture on a sheet of gray paper, and hang them around the room. What an eery atmosphere the pictures give the class.

Remember the weeds we set aside after we made our silhouette? Now is the time to make use of them. Pick over the weeds and choose only the ones you like. Now add another color to the spray gun and respray portions of the weeds with the new color.

Allow the weeds to dry thoroughly, and then tie them together with a piece of colorful yarn. The weeds have now become a wonderful dried bouquet to take home to mother. Your unique present will certainly be admired by her.

Oh, You Ugly Witch

Crayon Batik

Witches, concoctors of brews and magic potions—dreaded people with special powers. I guess I have never seen one, but in my mind I picture them as unusual creatures with long thin crooked noses, straggly hair and weird unkempt clothing. How do you think they look? Why not have everyone in the class create a witch, and they can be compared for appearance. I hope these creative interpretations aren't too frightening.

Basic Materials: assorted sizes of manila paper, crayons, easel brushes, diluted orange and black paint.

Procedure:

- Have the children choose the size manila paper they desire. A tall thin witch might be best drawn on a 12 by 24 inch paper. A short witch might need a 12 by 12 inch paper. Wouldn't it be fun to make a giant witch 7 feet tall on wrapping paper?
- First sketch the witch lightly on the paper chosen. Develop the witch the way you think she looks.
- Next crayon heavily all areas of the witch and any background you may have added.
- When the crayoning is completed, take the picture to a paint station. This is an area which has been prepared for painting. Newspapers cover the floor in the area, and the paint and brushes are in a position for easy manipulation.

- The paint that is to be applied to the crayoned witch must be diluted about two parts paint to two parts water. Test the solution on a piece of crayoned scrap paper to make sure the consistency is correct. If the paint is bright and transparent and will roll off the crayoned areas it is fine. If it is too thick and covers the crayon, add more water to it.
- Choose the black or the orange paint to work with. Now start at the top of the paper and with a large easel brush paint directly over the entire picture. The paint does not adhere to the crayon because it is made of wax. When the paint is diluted with water it will not cover the crayon. (See Figure 2–22)

Figure 2–22

- One caution, never repaint the picture—this would spoil the wonderful transparency that we get from the first painting. In fact the picture will become more interesting if portions of it are not painted. Let the paper show through the way it does in a water color painting.

When the pictures are mounted and displayed, why not have a contest? Perhaps the children from your grade section could take a vote on the Ugliest Witch displayed.

Pumpkin Centerpiece

Paper Construction

Need a centerpiece for Hallowe'en? Here is a good idea which is simple and most effective!

Basic Materials: six pieces of 9 by 12 inch orange paper, paste, scissors, assorted scraps of colored paper.

Procedure:

- Cut six large circles from the orange paper. You decide the size of the circle.
- Fold the circles in half.
- Paste the half of one circle to the half of another until you have only one circle left.
- Paste this entirely to the two halves of the circles already together.
- The pasted circles form a large stand-up pumpkin. (See Figure 2–23)
- Next cut features for the pumpkin construction, and a stem for the top from the assorted colored paper.
- Now paste him on a piece of colored paper for a little stability.

What a wonderful addition to your Hallowe'en party.

Figure 2–23

Napkin Baskets

Origami Fold

Want an inexpensive basket for your Hallowe'en party, and one that is easy enough for your class to make? Once you have utilized this fold you will probably use the basket idea for every holiday party.

Basic Materials: paper napkins, an empty glass.

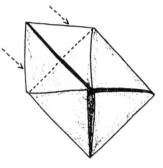

Figure 2–24A

Procedure:

- Open the napkin.
- Fold each corner into the middle.
- Again fold the corners into the middle. (You now have folded the corners in toward the center two times.) (See Figure 2–24A)
- Carefully turn the folded napkin over.
- One more time fold the corners into the center of the napkin. (This makes the third time in all that you have done this.)
- Place the empty glass in front of you bottom up. It will make the base for the basket you are going to produce. Pick up the napkin fold and place it with the side you have just folded down on top of the glass. (See Figure 2–24B)
- Use the palm of your hand to press the napkin shape firmly on the glass. Now carefully start to peel back the folded corners starting with the four large outside corners. Carefully turn the glass as you peel the corners.
- When these are turned down on the glass, peel back the next four corners.
- Press the peeled back corners against the side of the glass all the way around so the napkin takes the shape of the inverted glass. (See Figure 2–24C)

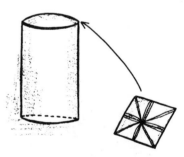

Figure 2–24B

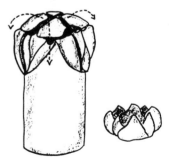

Figure 2–24C

- Now carefully take the basket shape off the glass base. You now have a very adequate paper basket. It is nice the way it is, but you can add cut paper decorations or a pipe cleaner handle to it.

Let the children who finish first make a basket for the nurse, Principal, school secretary.

The paper basket can be utilized in another way. If one basket is placed within another, the shape becomes a flowerette which would make a wonderful springtime bulletin board display.

Fright Environments

Shoe Box Sculpture

Have you visited a museum or gallery lately that was featuring Environments? They are man made areas which you enter and experience from within and without. All sorts of mechanical devices, lights, and materials are used to give you sensations. It might be a little difficult to develop an actual environment in a school, although there are some schools where environments have been constructed.

Why not have your class build a scaled down environment out of a shoe box? Since Hallowe'en is a holiday noted for unusual happenings, let's suggest that we create Fright Environments.

Basic Materials: shoe box, all sorts of paper, scissors, string, glue, paint, brushes, bits of miscellaneous material like—screen, glass, mirror, plastic, fur, lace, styrofoam, yarn, tissue—just any junk available.

Procedure:

Figure 2–25

- Discuss an Environment.
- Suggest that the students build one in the shoe box, and make it have the sensation of fright. (There will be many manifestations—some students may build one with a cemetery in it. Others may place all kinds of goblins, ghosts or monsters in them. Others may build one in the shape of a coffin. I hesitate to mention more because the children will develop such creative works.) (See Figure 2–25)
- The materials should be readily available and the children should feel free to get additional materials when needed.

When the Environments are completed, allow the children a Show and Tell period in which to exhibit their creations to their classmates. Then the Environments could be tacked on the bulletin board, one on top of the other. You might entitle the display—*A Skyscraper of Fright Environments.*

Hallowe'en Happening

Rubber Cement Resist

Occasionally it is exciting to do an art project that it is difficult to anticipate beforehand. The materials used act in an unpredictable way—so the project is really a happening. Try this version of Rubber Cement resist with your class.

Basic Materials: rubber cement, 9 by 12 inch orange paper, India ink, brush.

Procedure:

Figure 2–26A

- Lift a mass of rubber cement from its container with the applicator brush.
- Carefully dribble the cement around the paper, and let the glue fall freely, but do not let it drop in one spot. (See Figure 2–26A)
- When the cement has thoroughly dried, paint a coat of India ink directly over the entire sheet of orange paper.
- Allow the ink to dry, then with your finger carefully rub away the cement to expose the pattern made by the resistance of the cement. (See Figure 2–26B)
- If some lines are not interesting in the pattern, ink them out, or add ink to areas of the orange paper that you would like to change.

Very interesting shapes emerge. Perhaps by turning the picture in a variety of ways, some surprise pictures will evolve. Ask your class to explain their expressionistic interpretation to others in the class.

Figure 2–26B

Hallowe'en Spelled Out

Colored Pencil

Let a holiday word be the basis for an interesting art lesson.

Basic Materials: colored pencils, 9 by 12 inch manila paper, ruler.

Procedure:

- Hold the manila paper the short way on the desk.
- Draw lines at one inch intervals down the paper.
- Start in the top space and write the word Hallowe'en with a colored pencil.
- As soon as the word is written begin to write it again. Continue to re-

write the word until the entire paper is filled with Hallowe'en. (See Figure 2–27)

· Now go back to the first time you wrote Hallowe'en, and design it with colored pencils.

· As you work make sure once you have designed a letter like the L, that the next L must be identical in decoration.

· When the entire word Hallowe'en is designed continue to decorate the other words exactly in the same manner as the first word Hallowe'en. The results will be a nicely designed page of color with the word Hallowe'en completely losing its identity.

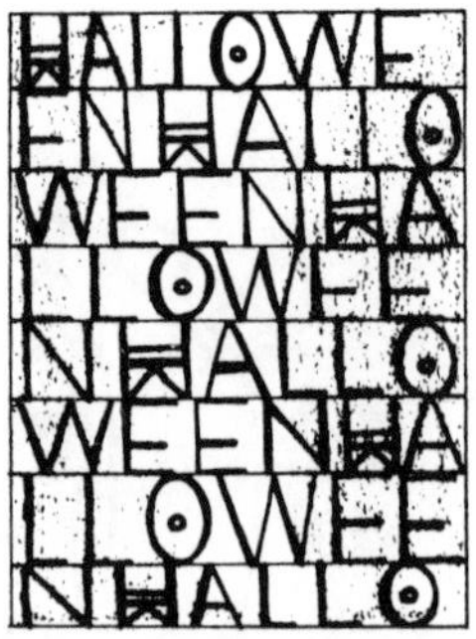

Figure 2–27

A good way to display these would be around flower containers or jars. They will help to keep the room bright and cheery for some time.

INTERESTING THINGS WE CAN ALL DRAW

1. Draw a picture for U.N. Week.
2. Draw a Hallowe'en costume parade.
3. Draw "You" in your Hallowe'en costume.
4. How does a tree look in summer, winter, spring, fall?
5. Draw a game you like to play.
6. Draw a ghost party.
7. Draw a funny, sad, happy, scary mask.
8. Draw a monster.
9. Draw one of the school administrators.
10. Draw the foods that are best for you to eat for Child Health Day.

November

3

November commemorates some very special days. American Education Week, Election Day, Veterans Day, Children's Book Week and Thanksgiving. Each one of these days is an important time, but we can make them more impressive by utilizing some creative art ideas for the specified days.

Tools of the Trade

Pastels

A nice way to celebrate American Education Week would be to use in an art period some of the books that are handled in an every school day. How can this be accomplished? Try this suggestion.

Basic Materials: 12 by 18 inch manila paper, crayons, assorted books from a desk.

Procedure:

- Ask the children to take as many books as possible from their desks that can be traced. These might include pads, notebooks, and textbooks.
- Next trace the objects on the manila paper with pencil.
- Overlap portions of each one so you have a conglomeration of books

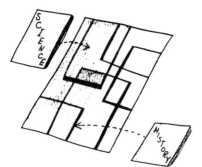

Figure 3–1A

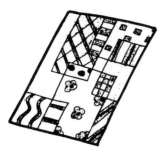

Figure 3–1B

which flow in shape into other book shapes. Trace an object more than once if necessary to produce interest. (See Figure 3–1A)

· When all the tracing has been accomplished, start to fill in areas of the book picture with design and color.

· Use the pastels heavily, and make as many designs as you can think of in the broken areas of space. Some suggestions might be plaids, polka dots, checkered, flowered, stripes.

· The areas in between the tracings can either be colored in with black chalk or paint, so the entire piece of manila paper is covered with color. (See Figure 3–1B)

When the picture is completed, bend it into a cylinder shape and staple it. Use the cylinder shapes for colorful standing decorations around the room for the month of November.

Vote—Bumper Stickers

Mixed Media

Children often hear about Election Day as a part of a discussion at the dinner table or the appearance on T.V. of a notable political candidate. Why not use the art period as a time to dramatize the importance of Election Day?

Basic Materials: 9 by 24 inch manila strips, crayons, red, white and blue paper, scissors, rubber cement.

Procedure:

· Discuss beforehand with the class why this important part of our Democracy—Election Day—must not be overlooked. Suggest that you use an art lesson to publicize voting. Here is one way. Make a bumper sticker.

· Cut out large letters—V, O, T, E from the red, white or blue paper.

· Cement them on the manila paper strips in an interesting manner.

· Use the Statue of Liberty, the Liberty Bell, the Eagle, Washington's or Lincoln's Monuments as symbols of our country to add to the strips with crayon or cut paper.

· Keep the strip simple so it can be seen and read easily. (See Figure 3–2)

Figure 3–2

Bumper stickers are for car bumpers usually. Perhaps Mom or Dad will put them on the family car. Another suggestion would be to tape them on your bicycle or school door. Either way we are announcing that people—Vote!

Veteran's Day Patriotic Plaques

Etching on Metallic Foil

A plaque is something we see quite often. It is a marker that is put on a building or placed in an important place to remind people of an important incident. They are usually made of a strong metal, most often bronze which has been cast from a mold.

Boys and girls would have difficulty in the elementary grades with casting metal, but we can have fun working with another material which will look like metal when it is finished, even if we know it is not as strong.

Basic Materials: 5 by 8 inch cardboard, aluminum foil, paper cement, scissors, a dull tool like an orange stick, lollipop stick, the back of a paint brush.

Procedure:

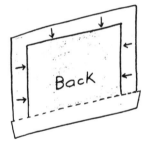

Figure 3–3A

- Cut the cardboard the size you would like. Do not make it too large. If you wish, it can be cut into an interesting shape like a triangle or a diamond. You decide.
- Next carefully tear off a piece of aluminum foil a little larger than the cardboard shape that you cut out.
- Wrap it around the cardboard and fasten the edges with glue; you now have a comparatively strong metallic paper shape. (See Figure 3–3A)
- On a piece of scrap paper sketch a design about the size of the cardboard shape of some patriotic motif. Stars, stripes, an eagle, a dove, olive branch, the capitol are all great themes.
- Next transfer your completed idea to the foil form, but use your blunt tool instead of your pencil. Experiment in a corner first so that you can get the feel of the tool on the foil. Aluminum foil rips easily so you must remember to work with care.
- If there are places where you feel you should add an idea, do it, but once it is on the aluminum foil, it cannot be removed, so be wary. (See Figure 3–3B)

Figure 3–3B

Your finished product will be extremely worthwhile. A good place to exhibit the plaques would be in the auditorium. They will certainly enhance the room during a Veteran's Day Program.

Red, White and Blue Stabile

Paper Construction

Have you ever done a paper sculpture? It is such fun to do. By bending, twisting, turning, folding and cutting you can change a flat piece of paper into wonderful shapes. Why not make a non-moving construction called a Stabile for an art project? It is similar to a mobile; however, the mobile means moving, and the stabile means standing still.

Basic Materials: all types of red, white and blue paper, 6 by 9 inch cardboard, paper cement, stapler, scissors.

Procedure:

- Cut the red, white and blue paper into strips, circles, triangles, squares, rectangles, or any shape desired.
- Many changes can be made with a piece of flat paper. You can pleat the paper by folding it back and forth, curl it by taking a long strip and carefully rolling it around a pencil, fringe it by cutting parallel lines.
- The paper can be torn into a shape if you want fuzzy edges, and if you desire, you can use a hole puncher to get repeated holes in your shape. Experiment, you might produce a new paper form.
- When you are through experimenting, choose the shapes you want and start to glue them to your base.
- From time to time look at your stabile all around—can you see through it—are the colors arranged attractively? Be sure that your project pleases you at every angle. (See Figure 3–4)

Figure 3–4

A unique way to show off these wonderful creations would be to use them as centerpieces in the school cafeteria. It certainly would be a welcome treat for all.

My Favorite Character

Paint and Cardboard

Did you ever have a desire to be the main character in a favorite literary work? Children do, too. In fact a good deal of the time they dream imaginary dreams and live fantasy.

Book Week would be a wonderful time to suggest to the children that they become their favorite story book character. It will be an easy task, and everyone will enjoy the experience so much.

Basic Materials: rectangular sides of a large cardboard carton (cut by the teacher or custodian), white chalk, paste, scissors, paint, brushes.

Bonus Materials: yarn, fabric, buttons, cut paper, ribbons.

Procedure:

- Cut an oval shape the size of a head about 4 inches down from the top of the cardboard.
- About 12 inches down from the oval head hole cut out two smaller holes, one on each side of the cardboard shape for hands to poke through.
- When you have decided upon the character you want to become, lightly sketch it with white chalk on the cardboard.
- Next start to paint the areas of the character. Make sure one area is dried before you paint next to it. Wet paint runs.
- Start to add "goodies" to your painting as soon as it is dried.
- Perhaps a bit of yarn for belts or paper polka dots or stripes for clothing, a hat or bow would add interest. Continue to add materials until you are satisfied with your character. (See Figure 3–5)

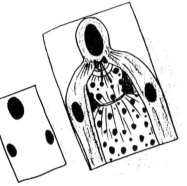

Suggest that the children put on their character, they will enjoy being someone else for a while. Perhaps your class could have a Book Week Parade, and the other students in your school could guess the book the character represents. Or your group can make up a spontaneous play and utilize the costumes they made for it. This would make a very dramatic assembly program.

Figure 3–5

Book Holder

Coat Wire Hanger and Mixed Media

Boys and girls love to make craft projects. Here is one that would be excellent for Children's Book Week.

Basic Materials: wire coat hanger, scissors, paper cement, colored paper, yarn, felt.

Procedure:

- Place the hanger on the floor.
- Step on one end of the hanger and pull it up so it is perpendicular to the basic shape.
- Repeat this process with the other end, so that the hanger forms the letter U.

- Next bend the hook up so you have three sections of the hanger turned up to form a substantial base for a book holder. (See Figure 3–6A)
- One way to decorate the holder would be to cover it entirely with colorful yarn.
- Another way to decorate it would be to decorate it with cut paper or felt.
- It could be a wonderful horse if a paper head was attached at one end, and a yarn tail at the other.
- Or it could be a bookworm holder if you constructed a paper worm head and attached it to one end, and added a partial worm tail to the other end. It is fun to experiment and make up a special idea. (See Figure 3–6B)

The final product will be a wonderful addition to the classroom book storage area. Several can be made and taken home as gifts. Every home needs an extra book holder.

Figure 3–6A   Figure 3–6B

Personal Book Marks

Felt

This is a wonderful project to make for Book Week. Every child loves personal items, and they will not only enjoy making the bookmark, but they will enjoy using it.

Basic Materials: felt strips in assorted sizes, assorted scraps of colored felt, paper cement, scissors.

Procedure:

- Cut a felt strip, top and bottom in a pleasing shape. The top can be squared, rounded, pointed, the bottom can be cut the same as the top or it can be fringed.

- Next cut pieces of scrap colored felt in any small shape and cement it to the book mark. Shapes like stars, flowers, circles, birds, leaves are nice to use.
- Add more than one shape or cut portions of the main part of the book-mark away so it appears holey—like Swiss cheese. Be careful not to make the project too fussy. (See Figure 3–7)

The bookmarks will be a favorite with the children. Suggest that they make extras for gifts. Before they are used, why not display them in the hall show-case? Everyone will want to see how your class commemorated Book Week.

Figure 3–7

Mobile Dioramas—Illustrate Your Favorite Story

Crayon

Suggest that your class become illustrators, and draw their favorite story.

Basic Materials: crayons, manila paper strips 9 by 24 inches, string.

Procedure:

- Sketch the scene from your favorite story on the long thin strip of paper. Make sure that the figures and situation depicted are kept large.
- Next crayon heavily all areas of your picture.
- When the picture is completed, bend it around into a large cylinder, and staple it at top and bottom. (See Figure 3–8A)
- Now take 3 pieces of string that have been cut in equal lengths and at-tach the string in 3 evenly divided spots at the top of the cylinder.
- Now tie all 3 strings together at the top. You have a round hanging diorama of your favorite story. (See Figure 3–8B)

This is a different way to illustrate a story, and should be a highlight of Book Week. They are light, so hang them from the light fixtures. Won't it be fun to see everyone's favorite story moving round and round?

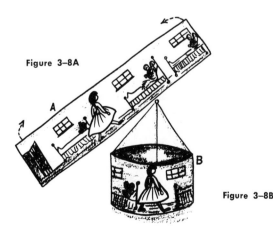

Figure 3–8A

Figure 3–8B

A Famous Character in Clay

Plasticine Etching

Figure 3-9A

Figure 3-9B

Figure 3-9C

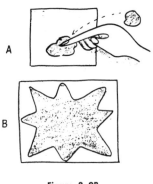

The topic sounds very impressive, doesn't it? Well, even if it is impressive the project is an easy one for your class to do, and, since it is the suggestion of a new use for Plasticine, the children will be excited and enthusiastic while participating on the project.

Basic Materials: 4 by 6 inch oaktag, Plasticine, pencil.

Procedure:

- Give each child a small piece of Plasticine, and have them play with it until it becomes pliable and soft. Now take the Plasticine a little piece at a time and rub it into the surface of the oaktag until there is a thin layer of Plasticine covering the oaktag. (See Figure 3-9A and 3-9B)
- Next take a pencil and start to etch into the Plasticine. Etch your favorite character, and if he does not please you, smooth over the clay, and your sketch disappears. A new type of eraser has been created!
- When you finally do like the sketch, mount the Plasticine etchings on black paper. (See Figure 3-9C)

A good way to display these projects might be on the library bulletin board. Why not cut out letters that have been coated with plasticene and say, *Your Favorite Character in Clay?*

Thanksgiving Section

Time of Plenty Rubbing

Crayon

Do you know what a rubbing is? It is a negative print of something engraved or carved that was copied by placing a piece of lightweight paper over it and rubbing this with crayon, pencil or other suitable materials. Now that I have talked about a "rubbing" you will probably remember that you rubbed pennies or ornamental hardware when you were a youngster. Did you?

In Great Britain it is a great hobby to make rubbings from the brass tombs of famous people who lived many years ago. Perhaps you can use this as a basis for introducing your class to this art project.

Basic Materials: assorted pieces of construction paper, scissors, paste, 12 by 18 inch manila paper, crayons, newsprint or lightweight paper.

Procedure:

- Begin by making a picture plate for the rubbing. Fruit and vegetables are abundant at this time of the year, use them for the subject.
- Cut all kinds of these foods out of the pieces of colored construction paper.
- Start placing the fruit and vegetables that you cut out on your background paper. Overlap some of them for interest—allow space in some areas, don't overcrowd.
- The foods may be strewn on a table, or you can cut out a bowl or dish to put under them.
- When the arrangement is satisfactory, paste it to the background. (See Figure 3–10A)
- Next take the newsprint and place it over the fruit and vegetable picture that has just been completed and hold it firmly, or secure it with paper clips. (See Figure 3–10B)
- Now very lightly with the side of a black crayon start to rub over the lightweight paper. Do you see what is happening? The picture you just completed is beginning to appear in almost magic form. Do not remove the newsprint until you have covered the surface of it with a black crayoned picture of the cutout food picture underneath. (See Figure 3–10C)
- Now remove the top paper, and try to make another rubbing. This time use more than one color crayon for your print. Any number of prints can be rubbed from the picture plate that you made.

Choose the rubbing that you like the best to mount on black paper.

A wonderful way to display the rubbings would be to cover a bulletin board with them and entitle it *Time of Plenty,* or you could mount the printing paper and the rubbing together on a large piece of paper, and write a short explanation of how the rubbing came about. People would be interested in discovering the rubbing trick.

Figure 3–10A

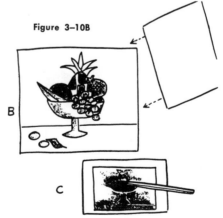

Figure 3–10B

Figure 3–10C

Paper Bag Pilgrims

Bag Construction

Have you ever figured out all the different things you could do with a paper bag? If you have, you are pretty intelligent. Most people consider it a sack to carry things in. Perhaps I can add to the list of things that can be done with a paper sack. Here is a project which utilizes the bag as a pilgrim. Your class will enjoy it!

Basic Materials: a rectangular bottomed paper bag, miscellaneous pieces of colored paper, newspaper, paste, scissors, 9 by 12 inch oaktag or cardboard.

Procedure:

- First open the bag and stuff it with crumpled newspaper.
- Next paste the bottom of the bag to the oaktag base. Concentrate on developing a head for a male or female pilgrim. (See Figure 3–11A, B and C)
- Cut out the features, hair, hat and collar for the pilgrim from bits of colored paper and paste them to the head.
- Add a hat, and soon it is difficult to tell that your base was once a paper sack. (See Figure 3–11D)

Place the Pilgrim people along the school window sill. What an impressive Pilgrim congregation to behold. Why not suggest that the children make up a name for their newly created person?

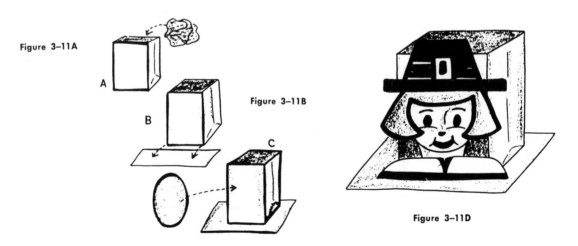

Figure 3–11A

Figure 3–11B

Figure 3–11C

Figure 3–11D

Tear a Pilgrim

Torn Paper Construction

If someone asked your students to take a piece of paper and tear it into a circle, square or a triangle, could they do it? I know they could if they had a little experience. They could become so good at tearing shapes that I am sure the next project would be simple for them. Let your class attempt tearing a pilgrim.

Basic Materials: assorted colored paper, 12 by 18 inch manila paper, paste, crayon.

Procedure:

- Allow the children time to experiment with the tearing of scrap paper in face, nose, hat and feature shapes.
- At first this seems like a difficult task, but soon the students will become adept at tearing the paper.
- When a child seems secure let him work with good paper.
- Start by tearing out the Pilgrim's face and pasting it to the background.
- Next tear out features and clothing. As you get a good shape paste it to the portion completed.
- The picture can be a male or female pilgrim, a full sized person or just a face. Let each child decide.
- The completed pilgrim picture has soft lines around the edges. This is an interesting change from the sharp lines created when scissors are used. Now add a crayon or paint background to the picture, or perhaps the picture can be torn out and pasted to a dark piece of paper. (See Figure 3–12)

Exhibit the pictures on the corridor bulletin board. A good title might be, *Can You Recognize Your Ancestors?*

Figure 3–12

Stage Is Set . . . Pilgrim's On

Finger Puppets

Everyone loves puppets. They are great friends. They keep you company whenever you need them. There are all kinds of puppets—funny, scary, silly, brave and even beautiful puppets, and there are many ways to create puppets. Here is a simple way that I am sure the children will enjoy.

Basic Materials: oaktag or cardboard, crayons, scissors.

Bonus Materials: yarn, fabric, paste, assorted colored paper.

Procedure:

Figure 3-13

- On stiff paper, sketch a character that the puppet will be. It can be anybody or anything. A person you know, someone imaginary, perhaps an animal.
- When the puppet is drawn, color it heavily with crayon and if you choose add a bit of yarn for hair and scraps of construction paper or fabric for clothing.
- Cut out the puppet, and decide on an area on the puppet where two small holes large enough for two fingers can be cut.
- Cut the two holes and try the puppet on to see whether or not he feels comfortable. If the holes are too small, cut them larger, if they are too big move your fingers further down the puppet shape. (See Figure 3-13)

It will be difficult to take off the new friend. The children will find out that before long the puppet takes on a new personality. It will do all sorts of things —sing, dance, hop, jump.

Suggest that the children make up a spontaneous play with one of their school friends. They can give it for the other boys and girls in the class. Have your students make a good stage by just turning a desk or small table on its side. The puppeteers can stoop down behind the table and hold their hand just high enough above the table not to be seen—the play can go on! Encourage other plays, perhaps another class can come in as spectators. This will undoubtedly be one of the hits of the year.

Transparent Thanksgiving

Cellophane Transparency

Most people think of a picture as something flat. Something that can be hung on a wall or must lean against something. Here is a transparent picture project for your class that can be hung in a window and be seen from front and back.

Basic Materials: cellophane, 9 by 12 inch manila paper, pencil, scissors, felt tip markers, black paper, paper cement.

Procedure:

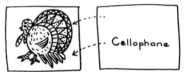

- Pencil sketch a scene with a Thanksgiving motif on a piece of manila paper.
- Now cut a piece of cellophane the same size as the trial sketch.
- Lay it on the sketch, and carefully go over the lines that you made before with a felt tip marker directly on the cellophane.
- When all the lines are traced with the felt tip marker, pick up the cellophane and you now have a transparent picture.
- Your cellophane picture is fragile. It can be made stronger and more attractive if you cut out black paper strips about 2 inches in width and cement them along the top, bottom and sides of the picture. (See Figure 3–14)

Figure 3–14

You now have a handsome window display. One way to display these transparencies would be to tape them side by side all over one window. The effect would be a transparent mosaic window. Another way to exhibit would be to space them in various windows in groupings of 2 and 3 for an entirely different effect.

Mosaic Indians

Paper Mosaics

Everyone loves to make a mosaic. It is a wonderful art experience and the reward you get with the finished product is really great.

Mosaic work means that you glue small pieces of clay tile, stones, paper, or other miscellaneous materials called tesserae on a base to form a picture. Mosaics are usually difficult for boys and girls unless they keep their subject simple, and work with a familiar medium. Here is a simple way to introduce mosaics to your class.

Basic Materials: assorted colored paper, 12 by 18 inch manila paper, scissors, paste, felt tip marker.

Bonus Materials: crayon, chalk or paint.

Procedure:

- On a piece of 12 by 18 inch construction paper lightly sketch an Indian head. This is the base. Do not add too many details. (See Figure 3–15A)
- Next gather together the pieces of construction paper that are needed. Use brown-red for skin, black for hair, and bright colors for the headdress and other decorations.
- Take one color at a time and cut it into different shapes about the size of a quarter. Paste these in the area designated for this color. Leave spaces between the tesserae or overlap the pieces when you paste. (See Figure 3–15B)
- Cut and paste the colors on the base until all the areas are filled with color.
- Now with a felt tip marker define the features of your composition. (See Figure 3–15C)
- The picture can be improved if chalk, crayon or paint are used to make a background behind the mosaic Indian, or the mosaic work can be continued in the background until all the paper area is covered.

When the mosaic is completed, why not use the picture as a cover for a Thanksgiving booklet? In the booklet could be a selection of stories dealing with Thanksgiving. Why not make the first story about the Indian, *Friend of the Pilgrim?*

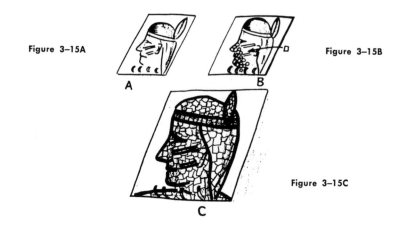

Figure 3–15A

Figure 3–15B

Figure 3–15C

Paper Sack Indian

Mixed Media

The Indian played an important part in the early development of the Pilgrim. We can never stress his role enough. Here is another good art project for November.

Basic Materials: paper bag with rectangular bottom, 9 by 12 inch cardboard, newspaper, assorted colored paper, paste, scissors.

Procedure:

- Open the paper sack and paste the rectangular bottom to the piece of cardboard.
- Crumple a sheet of newspaper and use it as an insert in the bag to help keep its shape. (See Figure 3–16A)
- Leave the bag open at the top as a part of the Indian headdress. Add paper feathers. (See Figure 3–16B)
- Cut features, hair, feathers, headband and paste them to the Indian head. (See Figure 3–16C)

A wonderful way to display the Indians would be to place them on the window sills in the classroom. Perhaps the children can have an Indian Day, and wear a headband during the class ceremonies that they have made for themselves.

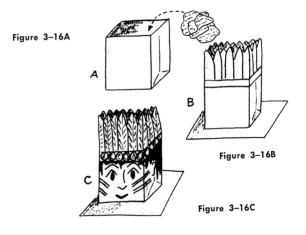

Figure 3–16A

Figure 3–16B

Figure 3–16C

The Many Shapes of a Turkey

Turkeys—they are synonymous with Thanksgiving! Here is a varied selection of many types of turkeys that can be developed for Thanksgiving projects. Choose one or all for your class to make.

Husky Turkeys

Crayon on Sandpaper

How can your class make a turkey husky? One way is to make him out of a material that I am sure you will consider tough and husky. The material is sandpaper, and it is a wonderful material to work with. The results are so vivid and exciting. Suggest that your class make a Husky Turkey, enthusiasm will be great.

Basic Materials: medium weight sandpaper, scrap crayons.

Procedure:

- First pencil sketch a picture of a turkey on a piece of sandpaper.
- Now fill in areas of the picture with heavy crayon. How vivid the colors appear on the sandpaper.
- Add color until the husky fellow is completed.
- Next mount the completed picture on a piece of black construction paper. (See Figure 3–17)

The finished product will look wonderful displayed as a border around the room. The pictures are so colorful and unique that they will give a wonderful aura of Thanksgiving to the classroom.

Figure 3–17

Pleated Turkey

Paper Construction

Basic Materials: 9 by 12 inch brown paper, 12 by 18 inch orange paper, assorted colored paper, crayons, paper cement, scissors, 12 by 18 inch black paper.

Procedure:

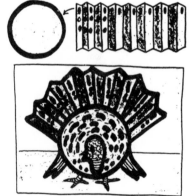

- Cut an oval from a 9 by 12 inch sheet of brown paper. Do this by rounding the corners of the brown paper.
- Pleat a 12 by 18 inch sheet of orange paper, decorate this pleated fan with crayon to show feather markings.
- Now cement this to the oval body.
- Next cut out a turkey head, wattle, feet and additional feathers from the assorted construction paper.
- Add these to the turkey construction. (See Figure 3–18)
- Now add crayon highlights or other cut out paper work to the turkey picture.

Figure 3–18

- Glue your completed turkey to a sheet of black paper and draw a suitable background with white, orange, yellow and green crayon.

The dramatic turkey pictures will look wonderful if they are displayed in the corridor of the school. They will certainly announce the coming of Turkey Day.

Roosting Cone Turkey

Paper Construction

Basic Materials: 9 by 12 inch brown paper, scissors, paper cement, assorted construction paper, crayon.

Procedure:

- Cut a circle from the 9 by 12 inch paper, use a pie plate for the pattern.
- Make a cut into the circle from the edge to the center of the circle similar to the cut into a pie or cake.
- Draw the one side of the cut paper over the other to form a flat cone, and staple this to become the turkey's body.
- Next cut out feathers, decorate them with crayoned feather markings and cement them under the cone body.
- Now cut out and add a paper head, wattle and features for the turkey body. (See Figure 3–19)

Figure 3–19

The roosting turkeys make wonderful centerpieces. I imagine they will be eagerly accepted by parents for the table decoration at the special Thanksgiving festivity.

Magic Hand Turkeys

Crayon

Children love to make things which appear magic in nature. Try this way of utilizing the hand for an art lesson.

Basic Materials: 12 by 18 inch manila paper, crayons.

Procedure:

- Have the children trace their hand in open position on the paper.
- The tracing becomes a great turkey when feet and wattle are added.
- Now that the symbol of the turkey is recognizable, continue to add other portions of the turkey body to the tracing with crayon.

- Feathers and features will immediately change the tracing to a new type of turkey. (See Figure 3–20)

Now add other turkey tracings. Perhaps a turkey farm can be made. Complete the picture by adding the necessary background. During Show and Tell time have the children tell about their turkey picture.

Figure 3–20

Group Turkey

Paper Construction

Basic Materials: mural paper, chalk, assorted construction paper, scissors, paste.

Procedure:

- The teacher draws a huge circle on the mural paper with white chalk and tacks it to the bulletin board.
- This is the basic outline for the turkey shape.
- Next the children cut out a variety of different feather shapes and paste them as they are completed to the turkey outline.
- Continue to have the feathers cut and pasted to the turkey body until it is completely filled with feathers.
- Now have one child cut a huge turkey head, and another feet, and wattle —fasten these to the feathered body. Voila, the turkey body is completed. (See Figure 3–21)

The class now has an excellent Thanksgiving bulletin board. Perhaps the November calendar can be inserted somewhere near the huge turkey. In this way days can be counted off prior to Thanksgiving festivities.

Figure 3–21

Cockey Turkey

Paper Construction

Basic Materials: 12 by 18 inch brown paper, 9 by 12 inch tan paper, crayons, scissors, paper cement, metallic paper.

Procedure:

- Fold a sheet of the brown paper in half.
- Start from the fold and make scalloped, pointed or wavy lines with a crayon to the diagonal corner.
- Cut it out and decorate it with crayon. This is the tail. (See Figure 3–22A)

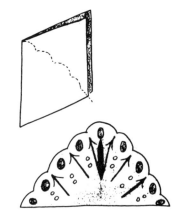

Figure 3–22A

- Next fold a piece of 9 by 12 inch tan paper in half and from the fold to the opposite two corners draw a turkey head. (See Figure 3–22B)
- Cut it out and fold the two loose edges in toward the middle and cement them to the tail background. The turkey will now stand up. (See Figure 3–22C)
- Enhance the turkey tail by cementing cut out chips of metallic paper on it.

These cockey turkeys will make a wonderful Three Dimensional bulletin board display. Just tack them on the bulletin board in a fan shape array, perhaps in the base of the fan arrangement you can tack large black letters announcing Thanksgiving Day.

People Turkeys

Craypas

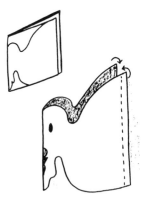

Figure 3–22B

Basic Materials: 18 by 24 inch manila paper, craypas, assorted cut paper, scissors, paste.

Procedure:

- Sketch a large turkey with crayons on a sheet of manila paper.
- Next draw people attire on the turkey. It can be dressed as a clown, fireman, policeman, dancer, painter, hippie, or any other person you want it to represent.
- Next add cut paper hats, belts, hair, shoes, jewelry to enhance the turkey person.
- Complete the background of the picture so it suits the turkey's clothing. (See Figure 3–23)

Mount the completed projects side by side on a large bulletin board. Entitle it, *Turkeys That Think They're People!*

Figure 3–22C

Hanger Turkeys

Mobile

Basic Materials: wire clothes hanger, old nylon stocking, scissors, paper cement, assorted construction paper.

Procedure:

- Pull a wire coat hanger so it forms a turkey shape.
- Slide a stocking over it, and fasten it to the hook end which is the face of the turkey. (See Figure 3–24A)

Figure 3–23

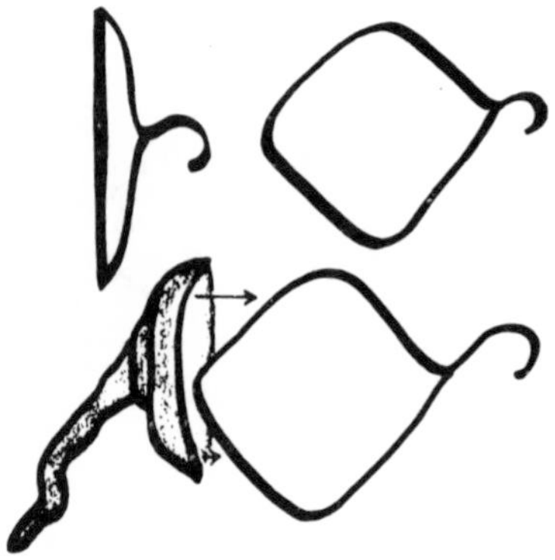

Figure 3–24A

- Cut off the excess stocking.
- Cut feathers from the construction paper and glue them to the stocking body.
- Add the wattle, feet and facial features to the turkey with more construction paper. (See Figure 3–24B)

Fasten a string to the top of the turkeys and hang them all at different levels in the classroom windows. They will look great inside and out.

Stuff Your Own Turkey

Newspaper Construction

Stuff your own turkey is precisely what we do in this lesson. The finished product is quite impressive; make them now, November is the time.

Figure 3–24B

Basic Materials: newspaper, scissors, a stapler, brown paint, brush, assorted colored paper.

Procedure:

- Take one complete sheet of large newspaper. Close it at its normal middle fold.
- Now cut the two parts into large circles. This will be the turkey's body.
- Keep the two circles together by stapling them all the way around, with the exception of an opening pocket about eight inches wide. (See Figure 3–25A)
- Now crumple newspaper pieces and carefully stuff them into the opening of the body.
- When the turkey is stuffed well, staple the body closed, and paint it brown.
- While the paint is drying make the head, feet and tail feathers of the turkey out of the colored paper.
- Now add the paper cutouts by stapling them to the stuffed turkey. (See Figure 3–25B)
- When he is finished you may want to accentuate body and tail feathers with felt tip markers.

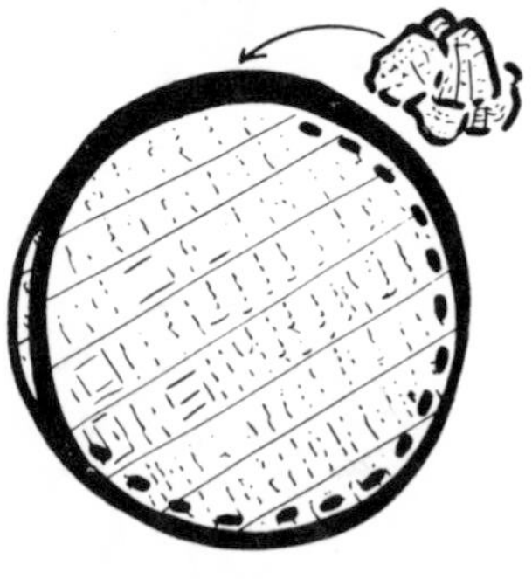

Figure 3–25A

A good place to display the turkeys would be to hang them from the light fixtures, or you might want to lean them along the window sills of the classroom. Both places would be fine.

Figure 3–25B

Food Turkey

Crayon

Here is a turkey which will provide a lot of thought. The project is composed entirely of a variety of foods that you think of for various parts of the turkey's body. Test the cleverness of your class.

Basic Materials: 18 by 24 inch manila paper, crayons.

Procedure:

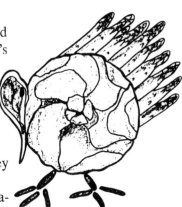

Figure 3–26

- Prior to the lesson suggest that the children name as many foods as they can, and list these on the blackboard.
- Your list in part will include things like carrots, spinach, cabbage, potatoes, oranges, pineapples, etc.
- Now suggest that the children take the list and compose a turkey utilizing the foods in the list.
- For example, the body could be composed of a cabbage, the head—a lamb chop, the wattle—radishes, the feathers—asparagus and rhubarb, and the feet—string beans. (See Figure 3–26)

It will be extremely interesting to see the type of bird the children will develop. No two will be alike. After the lesson have the children compose a story about their unusual turkey and mount the story and picture on one piece of paper. They would provoke a lot of interest on display in the hall corridors.

Vegetable Turkey

Vegetable Construction

If the children enjoy composing a turkey by drawing him from various foods, can you imagine how exciting it would be to construct one out of actual foods? Try this fun lesson.

Basic Materials: toothpicks, a variety of vegetables from home, assorted colored paper, scissors, nail file.

Procedure:

- Set a date for the children to bring to school a variety of vegetables, such as onions, radishes, potatoes, celery, carrots, spinach, beets.
- Also suggest that they bring with them a nail file, but make sure the tip is covered securely.

- Tell the children that they are to construct a turkey out of the materials they have brought from home plus the few items that can be used from the school source.
- Suggest that they start with a fairly large vegetable to be used as the body. A potato or onion might be good.
- Toothpicks are stuck into the chosen body for feet, and from there let the children take over.
- Caution them about the use of the nail file; it makes a good vegetable cutter, but must be used with care.

Actually the children will develop a wonderfully creative turkey with the materials from home. If necessary let them add cut paper pieces wherever they need them. (See Figure 3–27)

A good way to display these would be in the hall show case. You could call the turkey constructions, *The Grand Turkey Farm.*

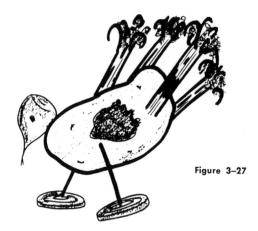

Figure 3–27

Why Are You Thankful?

Crayons

There are so many reasons why we are thankful, it would be hard to count them, wouldn't it? Here is a special way to record our reasons.

Basic Materials: 18 by 24 inch manila paper, crayons.

Procedure:

- Fold the manila paper in half.
- Now fold it in half again.

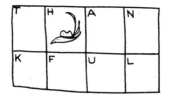

Figure 3-28

- Fold it once more, and press the fold with your thumb nail to make sure the crease is a good one.
- Open your paper. Now you have eight rectangles.
- Start with the top corner rectangle and write T, in the next rectangle write H, the next A, the next N. Then start in the next row of rectangles and continue writing K, F, U, L. (See Figure 3–28)
- When this has been accomplished, start with the letter T and in that rectangle draw a picture beginning with T that you are thankful for. The picture for T might be a trip, thought, toy that you are thankful for.
- The H rectangle might have a picture of a home, hat, or hobby that you are thankful for. Continue with the pictures until all the rectangles are completed.

You now have eight reasons why you are thankful. Compare the pictures with the others in the class. It will be interesting to see how many are similar.

GREAT THINGS TO DRAW THIS SEASON

1. Draw the Veteran's Parade.
2. Who is coming to your house for Thanksgiving?
3. Who is going to carve your Thanksgiving turkey?
4. Draw the way Mr. Turkey looks just before Thanksgiving.
5. Draw a part of an Election campaign you have seen on T.V.
6. Draw a book jacket of your favorite story.
7. Draw the contents of Mom's shopping bag at Thanksgiving.
8. Draw Mom preparing turkey.
9. Show us your ancestors in picture portrait.
10. Draw your family going to church.

December

December is one of the most festive months of the entire year. Adults and children both have a season spirit which involves participation in festivities and probably more display of artistic talent than at any other time. If you were to take a vote with a sampling of children this would probably be voted their favorite month. During December we celebrate Human Rights Day, Christmas and Chanuka. Following are some suggestions which may help to make December your favorite month.

Human Rights Day

Charcoal

What does this mean to the teacher and to the class? It would be interesting to have a discussion about this subject especially during December since it marks the time of Human Rights Day.

Basic Materials: charcoal, 12 by 18 inch gray paper.

Procedure:

- After a discussion about Human Rights Day, have the children draw with charcoal what they think it means to them.
- Utilize the charcoal in light, medium and dark tones.

- The charcoal smudges easily, work with care.
- The subjects may touch upon voting, the right to worship, free speech, choice to think freely. It will be interesting to see how creative the children will be in developing this theme.

By all means display the completed projects in the school corridor. This is a freedom, too, isn't it?

Gift Wrap—Designed

Happiness to me is receiving a gift. It doesn't matter how large it is, it can be very tiny. Most of the happiness comes from how the gift looks. How it is wrapped, the color and design of the paper. Do you feel this way? Making personal gift wrap is a great accomplishment. Let us experiment with a few different ways that you can help your class to produce nicely designed gift wrap. The designed paper can be used as an attractive art display, or to wrap presents. It will be up to the discretion of the teacher to use the project as she chooses.

String Prints

String, paint

Basic Materials: 12–15 inch pieces of string, paint, assorted sizes of paper.

Procedure:

- Drop the string into the paint, but make sure you are holding one end.
- Pull the string out, squeeze it between two of your fingers as you do.
- Place the string on a piece of dampened paper and drag it around until you have a trailway of patterns on your paper.

If you are pleased with the design, fine. If not, try trailing the string using another color paint. Experiment! (See Figure 4–1)

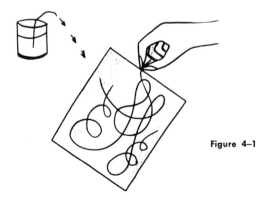

Figure 4–1

Drip Prints

Paint

Basic Materials: Paint, sticks, assorted paper.

Procedure:

- Dip the stick into the paint and drip the excess paint on pieces of paper.
- Try a variety of colors for an attractive piece of wrapping paper.
- You will notice exciting things happen when colors flow one into the other. (See Figure 4–2)

Sponge Prints

Paint

Basic Materials: paint, pieces of sponge, assorted paper.

Procedure:

- Dip the sponge into the paint, and then experiment.
- The sponge can be pressed onto the paper to form a design or you can twist and pull the sponge over the paper to make a design.
- Use various types and sizes of sponge.

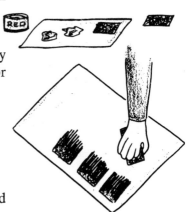

Figure 4–2

Perhaps you can create a new way to use the sponge as a printing tool. Why not combine the string, drip and sponge printing to form a new design for paper? (See Figure 4–3)

Stencil-Wrap

Crayon

Basic Materials: crayon, oaktag or shirt cardboard, scissors, tissues, assorted background paper.

Figure 4–3

Procedure:

- Cut out an interesting Christmas shape. A suggestion might be Christmas trees, candy canes, reindeer, angels, bells.
- Cut from the center of the stiff paper so you can use both stencils. The one you cut out is the positive, the remaining stencil is the negative.

Figure 4–4A

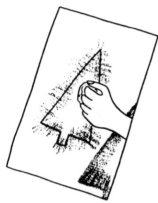

Figure 4–4B

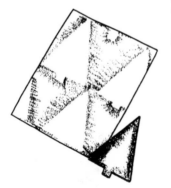

Figure 4–4C

- Next coat the cut edge of both stencils with a heavy layer of crayon.
- Now lay your positive stencil on your paper and using the tissue rolled into a ball, rub color onto the surface of your background paper. Pull the color from the center of your stencil outward. (See Figure 4–4A)
- Now take your negative stencil and pull the color from the oaktag into the cut out area. (See Figure 4–4B)
- Overlap the designs on the background paper so your composition is well balanced and has an all over pattern on it. (See Figure 4–4C)

Use assorted thicknesses of paper for your background paper. Tissue and rice paper are most exciting to utilize.

Holiday Banners

Mixed Media

What is a banner? How is it used? Why are they important? These are all questions you will discuss before your class creates banners of their own. If possible show the children an actual banner or a picture of one. Any history book is sure to have an illustration.

Basic Materials: mural paper, paint, yarn, scraps of assorted colored paper, paste, brushes, cardboard, scissors, felt tip pens, gold spray paint.

Procedure:

- First make a sample sketch of how you want your banner to look.
- When the idea pleases you, take a large sheet of mural paper and cut it into an interesting shape. Any size is fine—the bigger the better.
- Next decide upon the colors for your banner. It is a Holiday Banner, any colors will be fine, but restrict your choice to three basic colors. This will make your letters and designs more impressive, and lend continuity to the banner.
- Test the colors first so you can be sure you will enjoy them. Simple phrases or words like Joy, Peace, Noel, Greetings, are all excellent words on a banner. Creativity runs wild as the designed banner becomes a reality. Balls of yarn can be attached at the bottom of the banner.
- Scrap materials or simple geometric shapes can be cut from metallic paper and pasted on the background for another effect.
- A heavy strip of cardboard pasted at the top and bottom of the banner make it sturdy. (See Figure 4–5)
- Spray the banner with gold paint in areas for highlights.

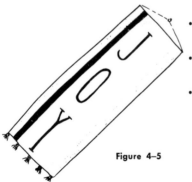

Figure 4–5

The banners are very impressive when completed. One excellent place to hang them would be in the main entrance hall of the school. During the medieval era this is specifically where they were hung—in the main halls. Extend them down from the ceiling at different heights. I'm sure the custodian would help you with this most noteworthy project. Everyone will remember your elegant display.

Crushed Foil Candelabra

Aluminum Foil Construction

Candles and candelabra seem to be synonymous with this season of the year. They are made of all kinds of materials, you may even have many different varieties to show the children. Why not have your class make this project? New materials are fine to work with—introduce the children to a candelabra that is different.

Basic Materials: aluminum foil.

Bonus Materials: paper cement, 12 by 18 inch colored oaktag, crayons, paint, chalk.

Procedure:

- Start with a piece of silver foil about two feet long.
- Crumple it, but don't crush it, into a shape that is firm and stands up well. This is the base of your candlestick holder.
- Next crumple smaller pieces into shapes which will become the holders for your candles.
- Attach these by folding pieces of the foil over one another to make them strong.
- Begin to sculpt the foil shape so it takes on an interesting form. (See Figure 4–6A)
- If you intend to make a candelabra that permanently stands, you will need to reinforce it with added pieces of foil.
- You may make it into an entirely different project by pasting the candelabra on its side to a piece of oaktag, and add a suitable background with crayons, paint or chalk. Perhaps a stained glass window, church scene, or home scene would be interesting behind the foil candelabra. (See Figure 4–6B)

In either case the result is very rewarding and fun to do. A display of the stand-up candelabra in a hall show case would be a wonderful way to announce Chanuka. A good way to display the candelabra pictures would be to line them

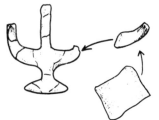

Figure 4–6A

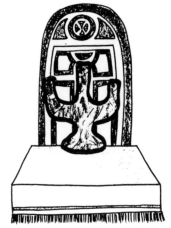

Figure 4–6B

on the cafeteria walls. Their three dimensional effect would be a nice display change.

Parchment Stained Glass Windows

Salad Oil and Crayon

Stained glass windows are one of the earliest forms of art work. Since most people prior to the Renaissance did not have a formal education they could not read, and biblical stories were depicted in churches in picture window form so that the people could understand them. Try this unusual experience with your class. Suggest that they draw a picture for a stained glass window that tells a story pertaining to this season. A surprise material will be used which makes this lesson an entirely different one.

Basic Materials: 12 by 18 inch manila paper, crayons, salad oil, Kleenex.

Procedure:

- Begin by sketching your picture story lightly with pencil on a piece of scratch paper. Try to work with an idea that has large forms. The window will not be attractive if you work tight and have small shapes. Try various ideas.
- When you are pleased with one, begin working on your large manila paper.
- Redraw the picture you have decided upon and crayon each portion heavily.
- When the picture is completed, outline each section heavily with black crayon, this simulates the solder in a real stained glass window.
- Next turn your picture over, and use the surprise material—salad oil, a product the children are familiar with in their homes.
- Very carefully begin to rub the oil on the back of your picture. Be sure that the surface of the whole area is rubbed with oil. Wipe off the excess oil with extra Kleenex, and you now have completed your stained glass window.

The windows are lovely and they are opaque—tape them side by side in a large window area. They will make a most unusual display inside and out. (See Figure 4–7)

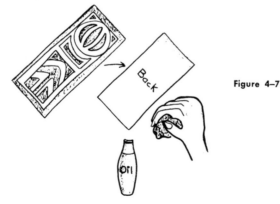

Figure 4–7

Madonna Triptych

Mixed Media

The Madonna and child have become a very important part of art history. Any number of great artists have attempted their individual portrayal of mother and child. Why not make this lesson serve a dual purpose? Have an art lesson and an Art Appreciation lesson. Show the children four or five famous art renditions. I might suggest the possible use of The Madonna of the Coronation by Botticelli, The Madonna Del Gran Duca by Raphael, The Sistine Madonna by Raphael, The Madonna of the Harpies by Del Sarto, or a Madonna by della Robbia.

Perhaps the children can tell the class about one they have seen at home or in a museum. Does the baby in any of the pictures look like a baby? How is the mother dressed? How is she holding her child? Do the mother and the baby look happy, sad, thoughtful? Suggest that each student imagine he is a famous artist, and is commissioned to compose a picture of his own original madonna for this art lesson.

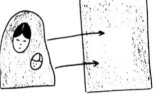

Figure 4–8A

Basic Materials: 12 by 18 inch manila paper, soft pencil, crayon, craypas, chalk, 12 by 18 inch black construction paper, scissors, paper cement.

Procedure:

- With pencil, sketch ovals for nicely shaped Madonna and child heads. Decide the position you would like the figures to take, and sketch the rest of the composition in lightly.
- When the picture is completely drawn, color it with crayon, craypas or chalk. Remember that the important things are colored heavily, less important things are colored lightly.
- Next cut out the Madonna and child and mount it on the black construction paper. (See Figure 4–8A)
- Take two more pieces of the same paper and holding them carefully together cut along the long side making a fancy triptych door. (See Figure 4–8B)
- Still holding the paper together fold the opposite long side about one half inch all the way down the side.
- Next paste one folded side under one side of the mounted picture, and the other corresponding side paste to the other side of the picture. (See Figure 4–8C) You now have doors which frame your picture, and are strong enough when opened slightly to make your project a standing triptych.

Figure 4–8B

Figure 4–8C

How gratifying the triptychs would be if they were placed standing along the window sills of your classroom. Perhaps one or two could be spared and placed at a strategic point like the principal's and secretary's desks.

Night Before Christmas Fireplace

Paper Fold

Even if the children in your class do not have a fireplace at home, wouldn't it be a nice experience for them to show how a fireplace might look if they had one?

Basic Materials: 12 by 18 inch manila paper, crayons, bits of fabric.

Procedure:

- Fold the 12 by 18 inch paper in half the short way. You have a tent fold which becomes your fireplace.
- Next on one side of the fold cut out a tunnel shape for the opening of the fireplace.
- Next show with crayon the type of material the fireplace is made of. Brick, stone, stucco, metal—show it.
- Then in the opening of the fireplace draw a fire, the andirons, the screen.
- Complete the fireplace scene by adding stockings which have been cut from the fabric and hung at the top of the fireplace.

Now stand it up and place the entire group on the window ledge. Why not have a vote on the fireplace that everyone finds most desirable? (See Figure 4–9)

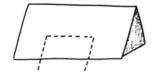

Figure 4–9

Paper Plate Carolers

Mixed Media

What would Christmas be like without some form of carol singer? Here is a wonderful project to try.

Basic Materials: paper plates, paper cement, scissors, assorted colored paper, crayons, 12 by 18 inch construction paper.

Procedure:

- Paste three 6 inch plates, plate side down on the construction paper.
- Next add cut pieces of colored paper for features, collars, and hair.
- Add a huge cut music book at the bottom, and a hodge podge of musical notes scattered around in the background.
- The pictures are great just the way they are, but if you would like, add your choice of a background with crayon or paint. (See Figure 4–10)

Figure 4–10

One of the best places to display the pictures would be in the music room, wouldn't it? Why not give the set to the music teacher as a special present?

Fluffy Plastic Wreath

Plastic Cleaning Bags

Here is a wonderful all weather wreath for the Christmas door. Have your class make them for very special presents. They turn out very professionally.

Basic Materials: plastic bags from the dry cleaners, scissors, wire coat hanger.

Procedure:

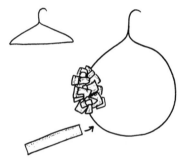

- Open the hanger so it forms as round a circle as you possibly can make. Leave the hook intact for later use.
- Now cut the plastic bags into strips 1 by 6 inches.
- Start to tie them on the hanger. An undetermined amount will be needed, so continue to tie and cut until the hanger is completely covered tightly with the plastic strips.
- The hanger will automatically become a fluffy wreath, and the hook remains just for hanging. (See Figure 4–11)

Figure 4–11

The wreaths could be hung very effectively on all the classroom doors in your school. On the day before Christmas closing, however, make sure they are returned for a special Christmas gift for Mom!

Wreath Montage

Magazine Cutouts

This wreath is an interesting way to utilize magazines in an unusual way.

Basic Materials: old magazines, scissors, paste, 12 by 18 inch red or green paper.

Procedure:

- Sketch with pencil the largest circle you can make on the colored paper.
- Draw a smaller circle within to complete your wreath.
- Thumb through the magazines and cut out the most colorful ads you can find. Cut these into pieces any shape, but no larger than one inch in size.
- Now start pasting the magazine cutouts within the wreath sketch. Overlap the pieces, so the montage becomes a colorful composition.

Figure 4–12

- Add a large metallic paper bow, and your wreath is completed. (See Figure 4–12)

A good place to display the wreaths might be on the walls of the corridor or cafeteria. These areas always need a cheery influence.

Paper Ring Wreaths

3-D Paper Construction

A simple way to make a three dimensional wreath would be like this.

Basic Materials: white or green paper strips cut 1 by 6 inches, 12 by 18 inch red construction paper, scissors, metallic paper, paper cement.

Procedure:

- Form and cement round paper rings; about 12 to 15 rings are needed.
- Now take the colored paper background and sketch a large round shape on it with pencil. This is the wreath outline.
- Next cement the rings turning them in various positions on the pencil outline. If more paper circles are needed, make them and add them to the wreath. (See Figure 4–13)
- Add round metallic paper berries to the completed wreath, and a big bow if you care to do so.

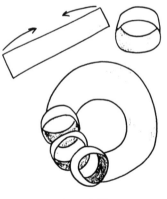

Figure 4–13

These wreaths can be used as a border above the chalk boards, or they might be taped to the back of each child's chair. At the bottom of the picture with felt tip marker—*Jane's Wreath* or *John's Wreath* could be written. At Christmas a little extra decoration is always welcome.

The Many Faces of Santa

It is always fun to make a Santa. There are so many ways he can be made that it is just fun to explore. Here are some suggestions.

Jolly Round Santa

Paper Construction

Basic Materials: 12 by 18 inch sheet of flesh paper, 12 by 18 inch white paper, assorted colored paper, 9 by 12 inch red paper, scissors, paste.

Procedure:

- Use a pie plate as a pattern and trace and cut out a circle of flesh paper for the face.
- The beard is half of a white circle with slits cut half way up and curled with a pencil.
- Santa's features are pieces of cut colored paper.
- His hair and mustache are made from the remaining white paper.

Don't forget to add his big red cap! (See Figure 4–14)

Yarn Santa

Yarn Painting

Basic Materials: 12 by 18 inch manila paper, yarn, paper cement, scissors.

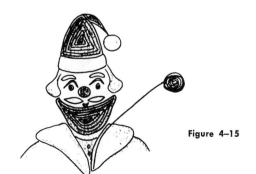

Figure 4–14

Procedure:

- Sketch Santa's face lightly with pencil on the manila paper.
- Paint the outline a small area at a time with the paper cement and carefully lay the yarn into it.
- Continue doing this until the entire Santa is painted in yarn. (Change yarn colors any time desired.)
- For a nicer designed Santa, cover in some areas solidly with the yarn, like Santa's beard or cap. (See Figure 4–15)
- Add a crayoned or chalk background of where Santa might be, or cut out the Santa and mount him on a contrasting piece of paper.

Figure 4–15

Polymer Santa

Polymer and Tissue

Basic Materials: polymer medium, brush, assorted tissue, 12 by 18 inch manila paper, felt tip marker.

Procedure:

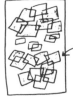

- Place pieces of torn tissue on a background of manila paper in the location where you would like Santa's features to be.
- When you are satisfied with the placement, paint over the tissue with polymer.
- The colors will blend into each other around the edges, but this makes the picture more interesting.
- When dry other details can be added with felt tip marker. (See Figure 4–16)

Experiment with polymer. Make tissue candles, angels, bells. There is no limit to the possibilities.

Figure 4–16

Geometric Santa

Paper Construction

Basic Materials: flesh construction paper, white construction paper, red construction paper, scissors, paste.

Procedure:

- Cut a triangle, rectangle, square or any other geometric shape that you desire out of a piece of flesh colored paper for Santa's face.
- Next, cut and paste a white beard cut into another geometric shape to his face.
- Add features and a hat cut from red paper to complete this gay fellow.
- If you choose, paste him on a sheet of background paper and add a crayon background. (See Figure 4–17)

Figure 4–17

Mr. and Mrs. Hand Santa

Hand Shapes

Basic Materials: 12 by 18 inch manila paper, crayons.

Procedure:

- Trace first one hand and then the other on your manila paper.
- Hold the paper with the fingers pointing down.
- Now draw Mr. and Mrs. Santa. (See Figure 4–18)
- Next complete the background.

Add Santa's helpers if you choose.

Figure 4–18

Santa Card Holder

Paper Construction

Basic Materials: 12 by 18 inch red paper, flesh paper, white paper, scissors, paste, assorted colored paper.

Procedure:

- Fold a 12 by 18 inch sheet of red paper up about 6 inches from the bottom.
- Staple it to form a pocket. (See Figure 4–19A)
- Next make a Santa head and attach it to the top of the card holder. (Use the Jolly Round Santa suggestion if you would like to do so.)
- Add letters cut from the assorted colored paper stating—CARDS.

This is a wonderful personalized card holder that could be tacked to each child's desk for holiday mail. (See Figure 4–19B)

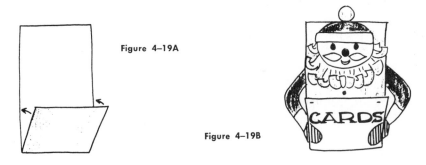

Figure 4–19A

Figure 4–19B

Santa Container

Jar Construction

Basic Materials: small baby food jar, pieces of assorted felt, yarn, paper cement, scissors, cotton.

Procedure:

Figure 4–20

- The glass jar is the Santa's face.
- Cut out features, beard, hair for the Santa and cement them to the jar.
- The hat is a piece of red felt which is wrapped around the jar top and cemented in place.
- Gather the red felt at the top of the hat, staple it and add a cotton tassel. (See Figure 4–20)

The jar becomes an effective holder for all sorts of goodies. It would make a very different party basket if it were filled with raisins, nuts and hard candies, wouldn't it?

An Angel Is an Angel

Everyone loves an angel—most people try to be one, don't they? Anyway, if they don't succeed perhaps the angels mentioned here will. Suggest that your class make one or all.

Angel Face

Paper

Basic Materials: 12 by 18 inch blue construction paper, paper plate, doilies, assorted colored paper, pipe cleaner, scissors, paper cement.

Procedure:

- Paste the paper plate on the blue paper.
- Cut out hair, either curl it, or style it the way you wish, and paste it to the paper plate face.
- Add features with bits of cut paper.
- Fashion the pipe cleaner into a halo and attach it to the angel head.
- Cut the doilies and paste them below the face for the angel collar. (See Figure 4–21)
- Now add crayon background to enhance the picture.

Did you ever have the children draw heaven?

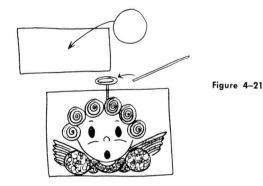

Figure 4–21

Hand Shaped Angel

Hand Used as Subject

Basic Materials: 12 by 18 inch manila paper, crayons, assorted cut paper, scissors, brad fastener, paste.

Procedure:

- Trace the hand shape so the thumb faces down on the paper.
- Add the head and features to the angel body with crayon.
- Cut a 3 by 5 piece of white paper, pleat it and paste it to the angel's shoulders.
- Next cut out an angel arm using one of your fingers for the shape.
- Attach this with a brad fastener to the angel shoulder under the wing. (See Figure 4–22)

Complete the picture with any background you choose using paint, craypas, crayons or cut paper.

Figure 4–22

Bell Angel

3-D Paper Construction

Basic Materials: 4 pieces of 9 by 12 colored construction paper, stapler, flesh paper, white paper, felt tip markers.

Procedure:

- Take four pieces of similarly colored construction paper about 9 by 12 inches.
- Round the two top corners of each with scissors.
- You now have four bell shapes, decorate them with felt tip markers.
- Next staple the four bell shapes together, two sides at a time. When joined, the four parts form a square and the shape stands up readily. This is the angel's robe.
- Cut an oval about the size of a lemon from the flesh paper and attach it to the top of the bell construction pulling two parellel bell shapes together for the neck.
- Next fold a piece of white paper 9 by 12 inches in half and lightly draw an angel wing on it.
- Cut the two pieces of paper at one time using the guide line you drew and you now have two identical wings.

- Attach these to the angel bell behind the head. (See Figure 4–23A)
- Now add features, hair, arms, collar to the angel with construction paper or felt tip marker. (See Figure 4–23B)

If you care to do so you can attach a cardboard stand to the angel. She makes a wonderful centerpiece, and pieces of evergreen placed on the stand will enhance her beauty.

Q Tip Angel

Q Tip Construction

Basic Materials: Q tips, glue, 12 by 18 inch colored construction paper, felt tip marker.

Procedure:

- On the construction paper arrange and glue Q tips about two inches from the bottom of the paper in an inverted fan shape.
- Start with an uneven number, nine would be fine!
- Work from the bottom up on the shape which is an angel robe. Add the Q tips between the spaces of the shape below.
- Work upward about five or six rows until you establish the robe pattern that pleases you.
- Next draw a head, features, wings and feet for your angel with felt tip marker. (See Figure 4–24)
- Add a background with colored chalk.

Figure 4–23A

Figure 4–23B

The pictures will be very outstanding if they are mounted side by side to the bulletin board and a sign shaped like a cloud is labeled *Are We in Heaven?* is attached underneath.

Dough Ornaments

Sculpting in Modeling Mixture

One most enjoyable Christmas project is one that is done with modeling materials that are common and easily obtainable. In fact, the mixture can be made at home and brought to school, or the dry materials can be brought to school and mixed in one large batch by some of the students.

Basic Materials: (Based on one child.) 1 cup of flour, ½ cup of salt, ½ cup or more of water, waxed paper, paint, brushes.

Figure 4–24

Procedure:

- Mix the dough to a pliable but firm consistency. Test it to see if it can be molded into shapes. If it is too soft, add more flour, too stiff—add more water. Now lay a sheet of waxed paper in front of you and start to create any interesting shapes you can make.
- If the dough is rolled into long thin pieces it can be looped like a pretzel into very nice abstract or geometric shapes. (See Figure 4–25A)
- You can also use solid shapes, and add pieces to this. For instance, a round face could have dough added for cheeks, chin, eyebrows, eyes, mouth, and these could be built up to make many dimensions.
- When an ornament is finished, set it aside to dry.
- Make sure you have included some type of opening or hole so it can be hung later.

The creations take about a week to dry. However, if the cafeteria manager is cooperative they can be baked at 400° until they are brown. If they are baked, interesting effects can be obtained by adding broken bits of hard candy like sour balls or lollipops to open areas of the dough. These become transparent colored areas when the baked pieces have cooled. (See Figure 4–25B) Painting will enhance the ornament greatly.

The ornaments are wonderful as a decoration for the Christmas tree, but they are also most beautiful if hung at various levels in a window.

Do not save the modeling mixture idea just for Christmas. Make Valentine shapes for Valentine's Day or various rabbit and egg shapes for Easter. This idea is good for any season—how will you use it?

Figure 4–25A

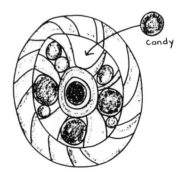

Figure 4–25B

Pipe Cleaner Ornaments

Pipe Cleaner Shapes

Here is a great way to decorate your class Christmas tree. Try this combination of pipe cleaners and tissue.

Basic Materials: pipe cleaners, colored tissue, paper cement, scissors, felt tip pen.

Procedure:

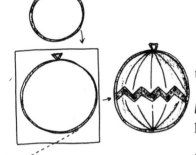

Figure 4–26A

- Bend and twist the pipe cleaners into various shapes for ornaments.
- One pipe cleaner shaped into a circle and cemented to tissue paper makes a Christmas ball.
- When the cement is dry just cut out the shape. (See Figure 4–26A)
- An angel is made by forming a circle with one pipe cleaner for a head, and a triangle for the robe with another pipe cleaner.
- Cement the circle on the tissue, and the triangle under it.
- When the cement is dry, cut out the shape and you have a great angel when you decorate it a bit with a felt tip pen. (See Figure 4–26B)
- A Christmas tree is made by forming a triangle with one pipe cleaner, and a small rectangle with another for a pot.
- Cement them on the tissue and when the cement is dry cut the tree and pot shape, and you have another wonderful ornament. (See Figure 4–26C)

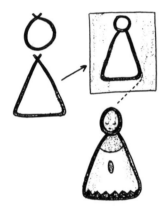

Figure 4–26B

Any number of ornaments can be made in this manner. Let the children experiment on the materials. Another good suggestion is to use various kinds of paper as a substitute for the tissue. Waxed paper, cellophane or clear plastic wrap are some sample alternatives.

Pom Pom Balls

Tissue Ornaments

A very inexpensive way to decorate a tree would be this suggestion.

Basic Materials: (for each ornament) six 4 inch circles of colored tissue, stapler, string.

Procedure:

- Fold each of the circles two times—in half, and then in half again.

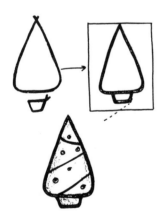

Figure 4–26C

- When you have six circles folded in fourths, staple the circles together at the point. (See Figure 4–27A)
- Now carefully open up the outer edges so the folded shapes open into a fluffy pom pom.
- Staple a piece of string to the pom pom and the ornament is ready to place on the tree. (See Figure 4–27B)

Make many, you will need them! (Don't forget this idea for decorations needed at a school party or fair.)

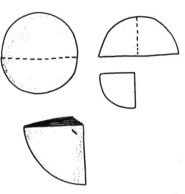

When Is a Tree Not a Tree?

, A list of Christmas goodies would not be complete unless the Christmas Tree were included in the list. Here are some of my favorites. Try them!

Figure 4–27A

Yarn Christmas Tree

Yarn Painting

Basic Materials: yarn, glue, 12 by 18 inch construction paper, assorted pieces of colored paper, scissors, crayon, paint, brushes.

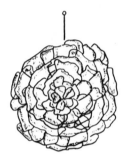

Figure 4–27B

Procedure:

- First sketch a simple Christmas tree shape on the large sheet of paper.
- Paint the outline a small area at a time with glue, and carefully lay the yarn into it.
- Continue until the entire tree is painted with yarn.
- Next add a cut paper container for the bottom of the tree, and little cut paper ornaments for tree decorations.
- A background of paint or crayons can be added if you choose.

Display the tree pictures on the walls of your room. They are attractive and will certainly announce the coming of Christmas. (See Figure 4–28)

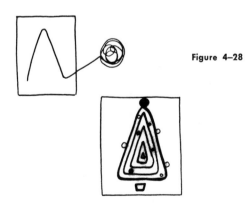

Figure 4–28

Christmas Ball Tree

Crayon and Felt Tip Pen

Basic Materials: 12 by 18 inch manila paper, crayons, felt tip marker, scissors, paste, 12 by 18 inch colored construction paper.

Procedure:

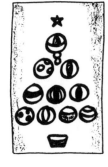

- Trace ten Christmas ball shapes approximately three inches in diameter on the manila paper.
- Decorate them heavily with crayon and design outlines with felt tip marker.
- Cut them out.
- Arrange and paste them in a pyramid shape about four inches from the bottom of the paper on the colored paper.
- Start with four balls at the bottom and keep on working up to the final one ball at the top.
- Cut and paste a container of colored paper for the tree holder and add a shiny metallic paper star to the top. (See Figure 4–29)

Figure 4–29

Arrange this display on a blank wall, and use the same format used for the tree. Place four pictures at the bottom and keep on working up the pyramid to the one at the top. You have a tree produced with tree pictures. Cut paper presents could be strewn under the giant tree, and why not add a giant star to the top?

Chain Link Tree

Paper

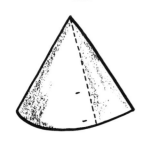

Basic Materials: oaktag, 18 by 24 inches, green construction paper, assorted colored paper, paste, scissors.

Procedure:

- Make a stand up oaktag cone out of half a circle that is 18 inches in diameter. (See Figure 4–30A) This is the base for the tree.
- Next cut strips of green paper 1 by 6 inches in an undetermined amount.
- Paste the strips into paper chains and start to drape and paste the chains around the cone starting from the bottom and working up.
- Keep cutting, pasting and adding the strips until you reach the top of the cone.

Figure 4–30A

- Now start to make and paste small ornaments to the tree.
- Add metallic paper chains, paper icicles.

The trees are really magnificent when they are completed. They make wonderful presents for Mom. How elegant they will look on the table during the Christmas season. (See Figure 4–30B)

Individualized Trees

Paint

Basic Materials: green paint, brushes (easel), 18 by 24 inch manila paper, assorted construction paper, scissors, paste.

Procedure:

- Work on the floor for this lesson.
- Paint the largest Christmas tree that can be painted on the 18 by 24 inch paper. While the paint is drying, start to make all sorts of cut paper ornaments and a base that can be added to your Christmas tree.
- Now paste these on the tree when the paint has dried.
- Cut out the tree.

They will look very chic on the walls of the hall corridor, or as a special treat they can be used as a School Library decoration. (See Figure 4–31)

Knitting Needle Christmas Tree

Mixed Media Construction

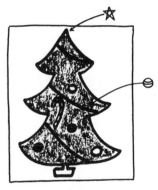

Figure 4–31

Did you ever hear of a knitting needle tree? That is precisely what we use as a Christmas tree base in this project. Try it, it will be a new way of using a familiar home material.

Basic Materials: an old knitting needle (brought from home), manila paper, scissors, crayons, heavy corrugated paper 6 by 9 inches, paint, brushes, masking tape.

Procedure:

- With the point of the scissor carefully puncture a small hole in the middle of the corrugated paper base.
- Then carefully stick the knitting needle through the hole until it has gone all the way up through the corrugated paper.

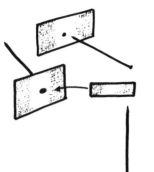

- Take a piece of masking tape and tape it over the head of the needle at the bottom of the base. (See Figure 4–32A) Now the needle stands up in its base.
- Next paint the base any color.
- While the paint is drying, cover the manila paper with an all over cray-oned abstract design.
- When this is done, cut the paper in strips of 1 by 6 inches.
- Now bend these strips, colored side out to form a loop and poke the knitting needle through both parts of the loop and slide the loop all the way down to the base. (See Figure 4–32B) You are making the tree with decorated paper loops.
- Continue to do this with other loops, fanning them out as you place them on.
- When you get closer to the top make the loops smaller so that the loops form a pyramid shape going up the knitting needle. (See Figure 4–32C)
- When all the loops needed are on the needle, cut out a decoration like a star, angel, or circle in duplicate.
- Paste one on one side of the needle and the other shape to the needle and its counterpart. This will prevent the strips from popping off. (See Figure 4–32D)

Figure 4–32A

Figure 4–32B

There can be many variations to this tree. Waxed paper, colored construction paper, old crinolines or even newspaper could be used for strips. Perhaps you can try groups of children making the various types in your classroom.

Giant Newspaper Christmas Tree

Group Paper Project

This idea is excellent for your December Bulletin Board. It takes very little effort, and allows participation from the entire class almost simultaneously.

Basic Materials: newspaper, gold spray paint, paste, any color paper strip, 1 by 6 inches long.

Figure 4–32C

Procedure:

- Cover the bulletin board with colored paper which will contrast with the paper strips you will be using.
- Next, the teacher tacks a huge triangular shaped Christmas tree on the bulletin board with large sheets of newspaper.
- Spray this carefully with the gold spray paint. Allow the newspaper print to show through for an unusual effect. (See Figure 4–33A)

Figure 4–32D

- Next suggest that the children make long chains from the paper strips for the tree. As the chains are made tack them from the top point of the tree down to the bottom. Keep on doing this until your tree is covered with vertical chains of color. (See Figure 4–33B)
- Now make a suitable container for the bottom of the tree and cut out the letters "December" from construction paper and put them either at the side or bottom of the tree. How do you like the joint endeavor?

Figure 4–33A   Figure 4–33B

Pastel Topiary Tree

Water Color

Be modern, suggest that the children make a different kind of tree.

Basic Materials: compass, watercolor paint, water, brushes, 12 by 18 inch white paper.

Procedure:

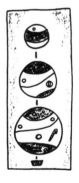

- With the compass draw 3 circles graduated in size from the largest to smallest. Use the paper the long way.
- Now paint your tree with a pastel color—pink, light blue, light yellow, pale green.
- When the paint has dried, start to decorate the tree with small interesting ornaments that you paint on the pastel areas.
- Add candles, chains, and the container under the tree. (See Figure 4–34)
- Complete the picture by adding a background of color behind the tree.

The trees are different, aren't they? They have a pale translucent quality, but they are still a Christmas tree.

Figure 4–34

MORE IDEAS FOR DECEMBER

1. Draw Mr. and Mrs. Santa.
2. Draw Santa's workshop and his helpers.
3. Show fat Santa going down a tight chimney.
4. Draw what you found on Christmas day.
5. Draw the Dreidel.
6. Draw the first night of Chanukah.
7. Draw and decorate a festive table.
8. How many ways can you draw Santa? (As a clown, baker, policeman, plumber, painter, fireman, etc.)
9. How does your front door look this season?
10. Draw how you felt on Christmas Eve.
11. Draw what you saw at the department store.
12. Draw how your Church or Synagogue looks during this season.
13. Draw Santa's embarrassing moment.
14. Draw your Chanukah presents.
15. Draw who you think Santa is.
16. Draw what you will do during the holidays.
17. Draw who will visit you on Christmas Day or Chanukah.
18. What do you see reflected in a Christmas ball?
19. Draw your favorite gift.
20. Draw a picture letter to Santa showing what you would like to receive.

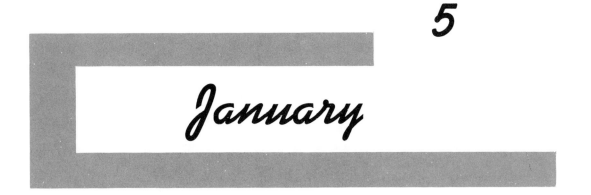

5

January

January, the mid winter month. Snow, ice and cold weather are to be expected. A white landscape is usual. The snow is beautiful and exciting, there is a new kind of outdoor fun.

Here are some seasonal art suggestions which may help to make January a Happy Time in your classroom.

The New Year—Have a Happy Time

Collage—Mixed Media

Art is a wonderful thing. It tells what you see, feel, hear, smell and know. Suggest that your class make a picture of the way they feel. Why not make a happy collage? This is a different kind of picture, it is one that is made by pasting paper and materials of all sorts to a background. It will be an easy task to show a *Happy Feeling* in a collage.

Basic Materials: assorted pieces of colored paper, cellophane, lace, doilies, seeds, feathers, string, yarn, sticks, wire, aluminum foil, 12 x 18 inch construction paper, rubber cement, scissors, staples.

Procedure:

- How can we draw a feeling? Here are a few suggestions:—A happy feeling can be simply expressed with favorite colors. Items may suggest a feeling. For instance, doilies may remind you of parties, fancy cake and candy, so the use of these would be repeating a happy memory. An ice cream stick or lollipop stick might remind you of "goodies"—this is a happy memory. Part of a fishing line, shells, or a piece of yarn might express a happy feeling for a hobby you enjoy.

· Think of things that express happy feelings that you have available among your art materials.

· Now choose a few of these materials from the collection that express a happy feeling.

· Cut or tear these items into shapes that you like.

· Arrange them on your paper base, where you think they look best.

· Overlap some of them, place others so they show through pieces of contrasting materials. Invent all kinds of arrangements. Do not add too much, leave open areas.

· When the picture is satisfying, glue or staple it to the background paper. (See Figure 5–1)

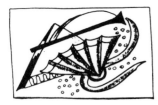

Figure 5–1

A collage is fun to make, and there are so many types that can be made. Examples might be a collage telling where you live, what you like to touch, hobbies, portraits of people you know. These all take a little thought, but they are a good type of art work for your class, and we have already discovered that picture making can be very different.

A good place to display the happy collage might be in the cafeteria. January starts the new year, and it should be a happy time for all!

Ben Franklin Sampler

Ball Point or Colored Pencil

Almost every female has at one time or another tried to show her skill with a needle in embroidering a sampler. In early times samplers were very common, perhaps even today your children may have one hanging on a wall at home. Suggest that your class make a sampler sans needle during art period.

Basic Materials: white graph paper with ¼ inch squares, ball point pen or colored pencils, scratch paper.

Procedure:

· On scratch paper sketch a simple drawing of a kite, feathered pen, a rolled Declaration of Independence, a lightning rod, spectacles, a silhouette of Ben Franklin—almost anything that would be reminiscent of Franklin.

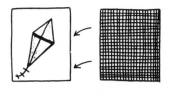

- Next take a sheet of graph paper and put it over the sketch. (See Figure 5–2A)
- If you hold the two pieces of paper together with a paper clip, you can lean them against a window and trace the sketch lightly with pencil.
- Now discard the first sketch and you are ready to begin work on your graph paper sampler.
- Put an X with the tool you have decided to use in every block where you find a part of a tracing. (See Figure 5–2B)
- As you work you will notice that the sketch that you did emerges with squared outlines. Nothing is rounded because you are working on squared paper.
- The sampler can be an outline of the sketch made, or you can fill in entire areas to form solid blocks of X shapes. (See Figure 5–2C)
- When the main picture is completed, work out an idea that will be interesting for the border. It may be a simple pattern like 3-X areas, and 1 blank area, 3-X areas, 1 blank area. It might be a border of X all the way around the picture. It is fun to see how creative you can be about developing a pattern, but once it is formed, it must be continued completely around the picture. (See Figure 5–2D)

Figure 5–2A

Mount the sampler on gray or black paper. They will make an excellent bulletin board display. Correlate this project with an Early Colonial Social Studies unit. It will be most successful.

When one sampler is completed, try others like a sampler of a family pet, house or a special holiday like Valentine's Day. A sampler heart or cupid would make a very different type of valentine.

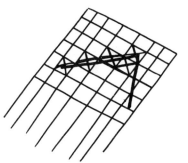

Figure 5–2B

The Frigid North

Paint—Aluminum Foil

Just the word frigid makes you feel cold, doesn't it? The word and its meaning describe something to us as an adult. How can we describe something with color? Here is an interesting way to introduce cold colors to your class, and this season is precisely the time to do it.

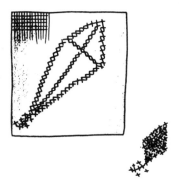

Figure 5–2C

Basic Materials: 12 inch sheet of aluminum foil, newspaper, white, blue, and purple paint, tissues.

Procedure:

- Discuss with the students what colors they would use if they were making a cold picture. White would certainly be used because snow and ice are

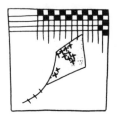

Figure 5–2D

white—but white is not a color. Blue and purple are cold colors because we see these in shadows of snow and ice.

- Suggest that the children create a frigid picture using white, blue and purple paint. The picture can tell a story. It may be a scene of an Eskimo village, or you sliding down an icy hill, or someone just playing in the snow. It can also be a picture showing cold colors arranged in an interesting design on your background.
- First cover your working area with newspaper.
- Next place a large dab of white, blue and purple paint in separate areas on the aluminum foil.
- Your finger is your paint brush in this lesson, so take color on your finger from the dabs of paint. In some areas mix the colors and in other areas have pure color. (See Figure 5–3)
- Work until you decide your picture is completed, then wipe your finger with the Kleenex. (Your brush is clean.)

Figure 5–3

Staple the completed pictures to blue construction paper and display them on a blank wall with tape. Perhape large icicles could be cut out of construction paper and taped above the pictures. Under the pictures paint a sign saying, *Pictures from the Frigid North.*

Light and Dark Pictures

Chalk and Charcoal

Here is an art lesson which is void of color. So much that is around us is in black and white—the newspapers, T.V., magazines, winter. It is interesting to see what the students can accomplish in the development of a light and dark theme using a bleak winter scene as a basis.

Basic Materials: 12 by 18 inch gray paper, white chalk and charcoal.

Procedure:

Figure 5–4

- Suggest that the children close their eyes and think of a snowy winter scene at twilight that they could draw.
- Have them develop the picture with charcoal. All the dark shapes in the picture will be done with the charcoal—buildings, trees, fences, vehicles, telephone poles, people.
- Next complete the picture with white chalk adding the light areas wherever they exist—snow, moonlight reflections.
- The gray paper background blends with the media used so do not cover all the paper. (See Figure 5–4)

Although void of color the picture produces a very interesting dark and light composition. Mount them on black paper and display them in the corridor. Label the exhibits—*What We See at Twilight*.

Imaginary Snow Vehicles

Crayon

Boys will love this lesson. Their creativity can run wild. It will be an opportunity to design a vehicle that has no limitations. We now have sleds, skis, toboggans, ice boats, snowmobiles. Let the class take off from here and develop a new vehicle.

Basic Materials: crayons, 12 by 18 inch manila paper.

Procedure:

- Suggest that the children develop a snow vehicle with crayon that can be utilized in snow or ice anywhere.
- There are no basic stipulations other than that its lines are made sleek and streamlined for speed and that it seat two passengers.
- Make the vehicle large.
- The children will create all sorts of unusual and exciting vehicles. When they are completed, cut them out and mount them on colored construction paper. (See Figure 5–5)

The class could have a Snow Vehicle Show. The projects could be displayed on the classroom wall with proposed price tags for possible sale. Each child could be a possible salesman. Invite a neighboring class to come in and visit as possible purchasers.

The enthusiasm can be furthered by a suggestion that the students carve their vehicle out of soap as a special project at home. There might even be a few courageous people who will build them in wood or cardboard. These would be an added treat to your show.

Figure 5–5

Laminated Snowflake Hangings

Waxed Paper and Tissue

A different art lesson is one which utilizes waxed paper in a laminating method. Your class will enjoy these artistic shapes long after they complete creating them.

Basic Materials: waxed paper, tissue, scissors, newspapers, an iron, string.

Procedure:

- Cut 2 pieces of waxed paper that are the same size. A suggestion might be two pieces 6 by 6 inches. Put them aside.
- Next cut a snowflake or flower shape from the tissue.
- Lay this between the two pieces of waxed paper, and laminate them by ironing them together.
- Make sure you are ironing on a thick pad of newspaper. (See Figure 5–6A)
- Now cut other designs from the tissue and place them on the shape already laminated.
- Cover this with a similarly cut size of waxed paper and laminate this to the original shape.
- Continue to repeat the process of cutting shapes, and adding them to the basic shape until you have sandwiched several layers of tissue and waxed paper together. The shape will become quite thick and stiff depending upon the layers laminated.
- When a shape is satisfactory, trim it carefully with scissors, puncture a hole through the top with a hot needle, and it is ready to be hung.

An ideal hanging is composed of 3 or more laminated shapes, so let the children make several laminations. (See Figure 5–6B)

The shapes are light, and can be hung from light fixtures or tacked to the ceiling. The designs appear opaque and almost illusive when they spin.

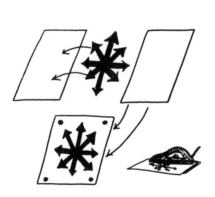

Figure 5–6A

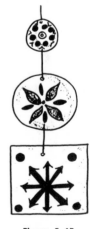

Figure 5–6B

Snow Roads

Paint, Crayon

This lesson produces dramatic results with very little effort.

Basic Materials: 12 by 18 inch pastel colored paper, crayons, white paint, easel, brushes.

Procedure:

- Everyone knows or has heard of snow roads especially if they live in the northern part of the United States.
- Take the easel brush and white paint, and use your imagination in creating a trail of snow roads on the pastel paper.
- When the roads are dry, start to fill in areas formed by your snow roads with heavy crayon. (See Figure 5–7)
- It will appear as if you are in an airplane and are flying over colorfully patched snow roads.
- Small buildings can be added to the areas of color for special interest.

Figure 5–7

Mount the pictures side by side covering an entire bulletin board. The scene made is a giant mosaic pattern of color surrounded by white outlines. Entitle the exhibit: *Snow Roads Everywhere.*

Paint Abstracts

Paint, Toweling

January—the cold month! Why can't we imagine through the media of art that we have warmth? This can easily be accomplished if you teach this warm color project to your class.

Basic Materials: paper toweling, white paste, 9 x 12 inch cardboard, water, paint, brushes.

Procedure:

- What are warm colors? Think of the sun and fire and the colors associated with them. Red, yellow, orange—these are the warm colors. Put them all in this project.
- Cover a sheet of cardboard with a layer of paste.
- Wet a paper towel, squeeze it damp dry and start to attach it to the pasted cardboard.

Figure 5–8A

- Do not lay it flat, but push it up into the paste. (See Figure 5–8A)
- When one towel is attached, add another until the cardboard is completely covered with crinkled toweling.
- Let the toweling construction dry, and then paint it with warm colors.
- Mingle the colors in some areas to produce exciting effects.
- You are painting a picture to show pure beauty of color. This is not a story picture. (See Figure 5–8B)

A good way to display the paintings would be to mount them en masse in one area of the classroom. The effect produced is an area of warmth. It will be a wonderful feeling to behold when coming in from the cold outdoors.

Tissue Painting

Tissue, Water

There are vast numbers of projects that can be done in an art class. This lesson has a new switch to it that may prove interesting to your students. Utilize this lesson during the winter slump.

Figure 5–8B

Basic Materials: 12 by 18 inch white paper, colored tissue, scissors, sponge, water, felt-tip pen.

Procedure:

- Cut about five snowflakes from squares of colored tissue. Make them as lacy as possible.
- Wet the white paper thoroughly with sponge and water and quickly lay the snowflakes in an interesting way on the paper.
- Make sure that the snowflakes are saturated by the wet paper. (See Figure 5–9)
- The color slowly bleeds from the tissue onto the white paper, transferring the tissue snowflake design. If additional snowflakes are needed, cut out more and add them to your composition.
- Lift the tissue shapes from the paper, and allow the paper to dry.
- Next add bold winter shapes like snowmen, stark trees and a huge snowflake over the colored designs with felt-tip marker.

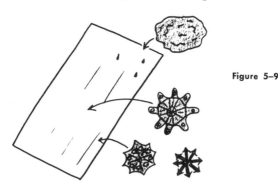

Figure 5–9

The pictures are colorful and unique. Fold them in half the short way and use them as a cover for January Homework Papers.

(Crepe paper may be used in place of colored tissue for a different effect.)

Detergent Snow Scene

Crayon, Detergent

A delightful three dimensional winter scene can be made this simple way.

Basic Materials: 12 by 18 inch light blue or gray construction paper, laundry detergent, water, paper cup, tongue depressor, crayons.

Procedure:

- Develop a farm, small town or city scene with crayon on the colored paper.
- Crayon heavily always leaving areas where there will be potential snow— blank. Complete the crayoned composition.
- Next mix a ½ cup of detergent with water in a cup until the mixture forms a consistency of whipped cream.
- Now apply the thick mixture carefully to portions of the picture where snow is desired. The ground, roofs, tree branches, telephone wires are all potential spots. (See Figure 5–10)
- When the picture is completed, lay it aside to dry.

Figure 5–10

Mount the dried pictures on black paper and display them in the school corridor. The three dimensional snow fools everyone. Label the picture display —*Snow Scenes from the Kitchen.*

The detergent can be used to produce a snowman. Why not make one during another lesson, and decorate the fellow with scrap materials and paper?

Mr. North Wind

Crayon Resist

This lesson in crayon batik will be fun for all! What better time for North Wind than January!

Basic Materials: 12 by 18 inch dark blue paper, blue crayon, white paint, easel brushes, newspaper.

Procedure:

- Draw your interpretation of Mr. North Wind on the blue paper with the

blue crayon. It will be a little difficult to see the blue crayon, because it is the same color as the paper, however, if you press hard with the crayon, you will manage.

- In some areas of your picture fill in whole areas of blue so your picture is more than an outline drawing. (See Figure 5–11)
- Areas that are not colored blue will be white when the picture is completed, so keep this in mind when you are drawing the picture.
- Now dilute the white paint with water using the ratio 2 paint to 2 water.
- Cover the painting area completely with newspaper, and with the easel brush and diluted white paint, cover the blue paper with white paint. The paint will adhere to the paper, but not the crayoned areas.

Figure 5–11

The picture becomes an eery rendition of a cold winter scene. What better way could you show North Wind?

Now bend the paper into a cylinder shape, stapling the ends. Attach a strip of blue paper from one side of the cylinder to the other for a handle. The children will enjoy carrying the project home this way, or you can hang the cylinders from the ceiling in clusters. When there is a breeze in the room, the shapes will spin with North Wind breezes.

Eskimo Puppets

Paint—Paper

Mid-winter is a great time for some creative showmanship. A puppet show featuring our friends from arctic regions would be a wonderful project at this time.

Basic Materials: 9 by 12 inch manila paper, assorted colored tempera paint, brushes, scissors, cotton, paper cement, tongue depressors.

Figure 5–12A

Procedure:

- On the manila paper sketch a large eskimo figure with pencil.
- When the sketch is pleasing, paint the eskimo. Limit the brightness of the painting.
- Use subtle colors for the fur habit.
- Allow the painting to dry.
- Next make a ring of cotton to fit around the eskimo's face and cement it in place to make a 3 dimensional fur parka. (See Figure 5–12A)
- Now cut out the figure and attach it to a tongue depressor. This makes a nice holder for your puppet. (See Figure 5–12B)

Do not stop with one eskimo, make arctic animals, igloos, other eskimos, and attach tongue depressors to them so you have a completed set of stick

Figure 5–12B

puppets. Put on a puppet show using a table turned on its side for a stage. Invite students from other classes to visit your Puppet Theatre.

Tree Silhouettes

Cut Paper

Trees are beautiful at all times of the year. For a January lesson show how they look when they are barren of leaves.

Basic Materials: black construction paper, scissors, paper cement, 12 by 18 inch blue or gray paper, white chalk, crayons.

Procedure:

- Sketch a large tree shape on the black paper, and cut it out carefully. (See Figure 5–13A)
- Now draw a winter background for the tree on the colored construction paper with crayon and white chalk for snow.
- When the scene is completed, add the tree silhouette with pop-out springs. (This is done by folding a small rectangular piece of scrap paper one time toward you, and one time away from you. The spring, if it is a good one, looks like a Z if it is held on its side.) The tree cutout may need several springs to attach it to the paper background. (See Figure 5–13B)
- The springs are attached by pasting one of the folded areas onto the tree, and the other to the background. You have added a third dimension to your winter scene.

The Library would be a wonderful place to exhibit the pictures. Perhaps the librarian can have available a copy of the poem *Trees* by Joyce Kilmer for those who want to expand their awareness of the beauty a tree has to offer.

Figure 5–13A

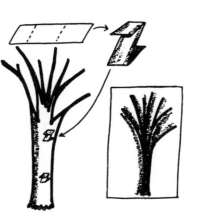

Figure 5–13B

Snow Man Glue Print

Glue Graphic

Glue printing is another fine form of Graphics. It will enable you to reproduce in numbers a delightful print.

Basic Materials: 4 by 6 inch cardboard, Duco cement, pop stick, water soluble ink, brayer, lightweight paper, spoon.

Procedure:

Figure 5–14

- Work directly on the cardboard which is the plate for your printing.
- Drip a trail of glue which takes the form of a snowman from the tube of glue.
- If additional textures or lines are needed, use the pop stick to pull the wet glue to areas that you desire.
- If the glue build up is not sufficient, redo the shape with glue again.
- It is not necessary but if a coat of shellac is painted over the dried printing plate, the design will be more durable. (See Figure 5–14)
- When the printing plate is dried thoroughly, roll on ink across the plate with the brayer. (If a brayer is not available, paint the ink on the plate with a brush.)
- Next, dampen a piece of lightweight paper and lay it on top of the inked plate.
- Rub the entire area of the paper with a bowl of a spoon or the side of your hand.
- Now lift the paper carefully from the plate, and the result will be a print of the glue snow man.

Try as many prints as you desire. Perhaps you can use the prints as an invitation for Parents' Council Meetings or you may want to make a batch of your very own winter stationery. The possibilities of using a print are endless.

Textured Snow Men

Plasticine and Mixed Media

Try this unusual snowman with your class. New experiences are always welcome!

Basic Materials: 9 by 12 inch cardboard, paste, Plasticine, scissors, scraps of miscellaneous materials like:—macaroni, pebbles, chips of old crayons, marble chips.

Bonus Material: 12 by 18 inch colored paper, crayon.

Procedure:

- Sketch a snow man lightly on the cardboard.
- Now take a small ball of Plasticine and soften it in your hands until it is very pliable.
- Next, pull off little pieces of the softened Plasticine and start to rub it into the sketched-in area of the cardboard.
- Continue to add pieces of the clay until the snowman shape is entirely filled in.
- Cut out the snowman, and mount him on colored construction paper.
- Now take the scraps of miscellaneous material and begin to press them into the Plasticine snowman. Immediately you have created a textured snowman. (See Figure 5–15)

Add a background to your picture with crayon or chalk.

Display these handsome fellows above the chalkboards of the classroom. They are just the right decoration for January.

Figure 5–15

Doily Snowlady

Mixed Media

Why not a female snow person? It would be a pleasant change, wouldn't it?

Basic Materials: paper doilies, assorted colored construction paper, scissors, paste, 12 by 18 inch pastel construction paper, crayons, chalk.

Procedure:

- Hold the paper the short way.
- Paste three doilies on the paper to form the head, body and torso of the snowlady.
- Next, cut bits of scrap paper into features and clothing for the snow person.
- Since it is a female, why not make her very feminine by adding cut paper hair, earrings, pocketbook, skirt, hat, and any items you can think of to make the composition interesting.
- When you think you have completed your figure, add a background to your picture with crayon or chalk. Make the background one that fits the subject. Show the snowlady walking on a city street, shopping for clothing, in a food market, at a launderette. (See Figure 5–16)

Figure 5–16

Now mount the pictures on contrasting paper and exhibit them in the Cafeteria or school corridor. Entitle the exhibit *The Ladies Snowflake*.

Cotton Snowman

Cotton Construction

The children will actually believe that they are building an honest to goodness snowman when they do this art lesson. Try it!

Basic Materials: cotton batting, paste, 12 by 18 inch black construction paper, white chalk, scrap pieces of construction paper.

Procedure:

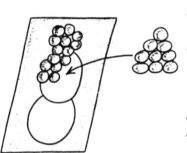

Figure 5–17

- On the black paper draw a snowman with chalk.
- Now pull pieces of cotton from a main wad, and roll it into snowball shapes the size of a nickel.
- Make a pile of snowballs, then begin to paste them into the chalk outline that was drawn previously. (Put the paste on the paper, and place the cotton snowball into it, otherwise there will be difficulty pasting the cotton to the paper.)
- Fill the entire snowman with the cotton snowballs. (See Figure 5–17)
- When the snowball snowman is completed, add eyes, nose, mouth, hat, broom with pieces of colored paper.
- Fill in the area behind the snowman with chalk—add snow falling.

Tack the snowmen to a bulletin board and add a title with large black cutout letters. Why not say: *Snowmen That Won't Melt!*

Cylinder Snow People

Paper Construction

Cylinder people are the most enjoyable creatures to make. They can be made for any season or at any time, but you will find that cylinder snow people are special fun!

Basic Materials: 9 by 18 inch white paper, scraps of assorted colored paper, bits of miscellaneous materials like: yarn, fabric, lace, doilies, fur, felt, buttons, scissors, paper cement and a stapler.

Procedure:

- First staple the white paper to form a cylinder that will stand. This is the body of the snow person.

- At this point begin to create.
- Cut paper into arms, feet, hair, features, clothing and start to cement them to the cylinder. Slowly the paper figure becomes alive.
- Is your snow person male or female?
- Does it have a muffler, gloves?
- Is it holding something?
- Add as much or as little as you want to the snow person. (See Figure 5–18)

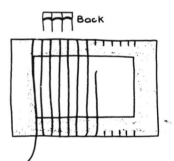

The nicest place to exhibit your new friends might be on the sills of the classroom window. However, they can also very effectively be tacked to the bulletin board in your room to form a vast clan of snow people. Ask the children to decide in which spot to place these frigid folk.

Figure 5–18

Weaving a Pattern

Weaving—Mixed Media

Your class will enjoy this weaving project because the project deals with the use of unusual materials.

Basic Materials: heavy cardboard with rectangle cut out of center, scissors, strips of fabrics, pipe cleaners, yarn, string, feathers, ribbon, wild grasses, rubber cement, assorted bits of paper.

Procedure:

- Cut an even number of slits at the top and bottom of your cardboard loom.
- Use string to form the warp, looping it on one side of the loom. (See Figure 5–19A)
- The looped side is the back of the loom.
- Start to weave strips of ribbon across the warp in 3 or 4 places on the loom.
- Cement these at each end of the loom as they are woven.
- Next weave some of the other collected materials—pipe cleaners, wild grasses, yarn, the feathers.
- Each time an addition is made to the pattern, fasten each side with cement.
- Weave until the entire warp has been filled.

Figure 5–19A

Frame the rectangle loom with a contrasting sheet of construction paper. The easiest way to do this would be with paper strips pasted along the sides, top and bottom, to cover the woven portions on the sides of the loom. (See Figure 5–19B)

Display the Pattern Weaving in a corner of the room devoted to various types of weaving. Perhaps various types of industrial patterned fabric could

Figure 5–19B

be displayed at the same time. What a wonderful way to correlate art with a social studies unit.

Weave a Blanket

Paper Weaving

A weaving project is an excellent lesson for January. The children are cognizant of cold and warmth, and it would be a good way to introduce them to the basic method of how our blankets and fabrics are woven.

Basic Materials: 12 by 18 inch colored construction paper, scissors, 1 by 12 inch colored paper strips, paper cement.

Procedure:

- Fold the paper in half the short way.
- With pencil start at the fold and draw 4 or 5 wavy or zigzag lines across the paper parallel with the top and bottom to about 1 inch before the open edges of the paper. (See Figure 5–20A)
- Next, continuing to hold the paper folded, start from the folded edge and cut along the lines.
- Now open the paper; this is the weaving mat. (See Figure 5–20B)
- Take the paper strips and start to weave using this pattern: First row: over, under, over, under; second row: under, over, under, over.
- Repeat alternate first and second rows until the weaving is finished.
- Make sure the strips are pushed together closely.
- To complete the weaving, paste the loose strips on each side of the mat both front and back. (See Figure 5–20C)
- Added decoration can be applied with crayon or bits of construction paper.

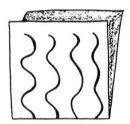

Figure 5–20A

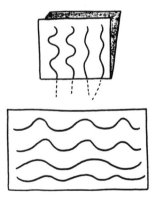

Figure 5–20B

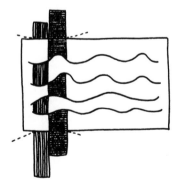

Figure 5–20C

The woven paper blanket is very handsome when completed. Cover an entire bulletin board with them. You will have one large blanket pattern. Entitle the display: *Woven Materials Keep Us Warm*.

WONDERFUL SUBJECTS TO DRAW

1. How did you spend New Year's Eve?
2. What did you do on New Year's Day?
3. Draw what you think Ben Franklin looked like when he experimented with electricity.
4. Draw "you" in your snow outfit.
5. Draw a family of snowmen.
6. How would a snow lady look in funny clothes?
7. Draw how you think snow feels.
8. How does Dad look when he shovels snow?
9. Draw where you would rather be during winter.
10. Draw a set of mittens and a muffler that you would like.

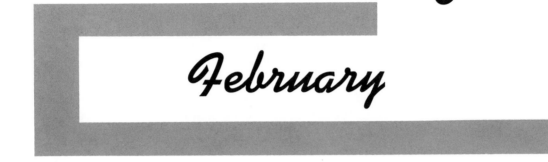

6

February

February is a colorful month. Some of the greatest personalities of our history have birthdays at this time. Thomas Edison, Abraham Lincoln, George Washington are but a few of the important February celebrities.

Valentine's Day only less important than Christmas and Easter in the minds of children is also a special February Day.

Following are suggestions which will help to make the month of February a memorable time.

Edison Abstract

Water Color

Edison contributed greatly to the American culture; commemorate his birth with this interesting art lesson. Suggest that your class make an abstract of an electric bulb. An abstract lets you see all sides and parts of a subject at the same time, until ofttimes the shape portrayed loses its identity.

Basic Materials: 6 by 9 inch manila paper, scissors, 12 by 18 inch gray paper, box of water color paints, paint brush, newspaper, cup of water.

Procedure:

- With pencil sketch the shape of a light bulb on the manila paper.
- Cut the shape out, and trace it 5 to 7 different ways on the gray paper,

125

overlapping whenever possible, and keeping the shapes parallel with the edges of the paper.

- If additional shapes are needed to complete the composition, add them, but do not overcrowd the picture.
- Discard the cutout shape.
- Now cover the working area with newspaper, and get the paint, brush and water ready for the next step.
- Use only yellow, white and black paint, and begin to fill in enclosed areas of your bulb abstract. (See Figure 6–1)
- A good idea would be to paint all the white areas first, yellow areas next, and black areas last. In this way you will minimize the number of times water must be changed.
- When the abstract is completed, mount it on a sheet of black paper for the most effectiveness.

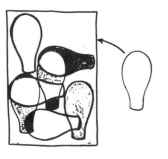

Figure 6–1

If your school plans to have an Edison Day Program, display the pictures on the walls of the auditorium or all-purpose room. Another good suggestion might be to use them folded—book style to use as an art portfolio for February.

Lincoln's Home—In and Out

Paper, Crayon

For a wonderful art experience, have your students build a house—Lincoln's house. It sounds difficult, I know, but this method will be very simple, and the material used is at a minimum. Try it!

Basic Materials: 12 by 18 inch manila paper, paste, crayons, scissors, scraps of construction paper.

Figure 6–2A

Procedure:

- Fold a piece of manila paper in half the short way, and your shape becomes a tent fold. (See Figure 6–2A)
- Hold the paper with the open ends toward you, and begin on the front cover of the tent fold to draw the type of log cabin Lincoln lived in when he was a youngster. It was a simple basic cabin.
- Lightly sketch the window, door and chimney, and when the composition is pleasing, fill in the areas heavily with crayon.
- Complete the exterior of the cabin, and then open the tent fold and begin to sketch the interior of the cabin. (See Figure 6–2B)
- Design the inside of the house with the stand-up fold becoming a fireplace and wall.

Figure 6–2B

- The floor and furniture can be drawn on the lower flap of the fold.
- Incorporate as many Colonial ideas as you can think of for possible use in your drawing. Think about how the floor was covered, what hung over the mantel, what type of material the wall was made of. All these ideas can be checked in your history or library books.
- Another suggestion would be to draw pictures of people and furniture on the scrap construction paper. Crayon and cut them out. They can be added with a little paste for 3-dimensional detail.

Display the Log Cabins on a bulletin board. Tack them so the tent fold will open. (See Figure 6–2C) When people look at the display they can peek inside the house. Label the exhibit: *Lincoln's Home—Inside and Out!* on a sign under the mass of Log Cabins.

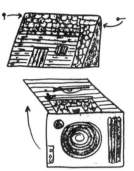

Figure 6–2C

Lincoln Clay Plaque

Plasticine

Commission your pupils to sculpt a head of Lincoln. The reaction at first will be one of surprise and anxiety—the task sounds difficult, but the method used is simple and will delight everyone.

Basic Materials: 9 by 12 inch sheet of oaktag, Plasticine, pencil, scratch paper.

Procedure:

- Sketch the side view or profile of Lincoln's head. If you have difficulty remembering what he looks like, refresh your memory by looking at a penny. However, do not copy the likeness—sketch the face from memory.
- When the sketch is pleasing, transfer it to the oaktag.
- Next soften the ball of Plasticine by playing with it in your hands. The heat of your hands will make it pliable and soft.
- Break off bits of the clay and begin to spread it with your fingers inside the lines sketched of Lincoln's head.
- Continue to do this until you have completed the silhouette of Lincoln in clay.
- Now build up some areas of the head to form the beard, cheekbones, hair. This will give the head a 3-dimensional appearance. (See Figure 6–3)
- The clay shape can be cut out and mounted on another piece of paper, or the oaktag background can be filled in with a thin layer of another color Plasticine.

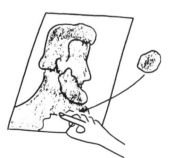

Figure 6–3

A good suggestion would be to make this lesson the beginning of a classroom *Hall of Fame*. Now that the Lincoln head is completed, have the class sculpt other great men for the collection.

Lincoln Construction

Cut Paper

A cylinder shape of Lincoln's head makes a wonderful way to commemorate his birthdate.

Basic Materials: 9 by 18 inch sheet of flesh paper, 12 by 18 inch sheet of black paper, assorted pieces of colored paper, rubber cement, scissors, stapler.

Procedure:

- Staple the flesh paper into a cylinder shape.
- Now cut and cement the eyes, nose, ears and mouth on the cylinder for the face.
- Cut the black paper into a hat and beard, and attach them to the cylinder shape. (See Figure 6–4)
- Now cut and cement bits of paper hair under the hat and over the ears of the Lincoln head.
- Add a collar of white paper at the bottom of the cylinder for finishing touches.

The most effective way to display the Lincoln heads would be to tack them from inside the cylinder to a bulletin board. They could be labeled *Lincoln—Many Men in One,* or *Lincoln—Man Liked by All.* Make sure they are available prior to the great man's birthdate. Parents will enjoy using them as a centerpiece on Lincoln's Day.

Figure 6–4

Washington Coin

Aluminum Foil

A wonderful art lesson is designing a coin commemorating a famous person's birthdate. Try it with your class as a special February treat!

Basic Materials: cardboard, scissors, pencil, aluminum foil, rubber cement, compass, scrap paper.

Procedure:

- Have available an assortment of coins for the class to view. Discuss them —what they look like, the size and shape, types of material used in composing them, what is on the coin. The one common aspect to most coins is the denomination written on it. When the discussion has exhausted itself, and enthusiasm is high, suggest that the class design a coin especially in honor of George Washington.

- First on a piece of scrap paper draw a circle with the compass at least 9 inches in diameter.
- Now start to sketch a design for the front of the coin, the back can be planned later. Washington led such a colorful life that there are any number of ideas that could be used on the coin. Consult the librarian for books on the subject if there is difficulty with the development of an idea.
- When the basic composition of the coin is completed, decide whether words or numbers are to be added, then incorporate them in the design.
- Next cut a cardboard disc to match the trial sketch, and an aluminum foil disc which is slightly larger than the cardboard shape. This is necessary so the aluminum foil can overlap the cardboard, and make it easier to work on when it is etched. (See Figure 6–5)
- Now transfer the trial sketch to the foil mounted cardboard with a dull pencil. Do not press too hard or a hole will form in the foil.
- Complete the entire coin by repeating the process used on the front of the coin.
- Now glue the back and the front of the coin together.

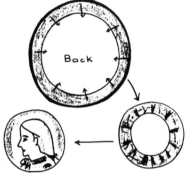
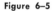

Figure 6–5

Mount the coins on large sheets of cardboard—3 or 4 to a display and hang them on the walls of your classroom. A few explanatory sentences can be placed under each coin with felt tip pen.

Invite other classes in the school to visit your Classroom Mint.

Washington Tree

Mixed Media

Everyone has heard the fictitious story about Washington and the famous cherry tree. Here is an art treatment using the idea that your class will enjoy.

Basic Materials: 12 by 18 inch gray or light blue paper, crayons, red tissue or crepe paper, cotton, scissors, rubber cement.

Procedure:

- Draw a huge tree on the colored paper.
- Add Washington as a boy preparing to do his hatchet mischief.
- Now cut the red paper into small squares and place a small piece of cotton in the square.
- Twist the ends of the stuffed red paper, and paste the little round shapes on the tree.
- Keep adding the cherry shapes until the tree is covered with them. (See Figure 6–6)

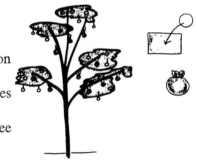

Figure 6–6

Use the pictures for a George Washington Week bulletin board. Cut out large red letters and tack them above the display with a tricky title like: *Please Don't Eat the Cherries.*

Commemorative Stamp

Design in Monochromatic Scheme

Suggest that your class create a picture stamp with a theme involving Lincoln, Washington or Edison. Make them huge—poster size. They will be most impressive. The outcome may be the beginning of the hobby, Philately, in your class.

Basic Materials: 18 by 24 inch manila paper, crayons, scissors, pencil.

Procedure:

Figure 6–7

- Ask the children to create a mental picture dealing with one of the famous men in February.
- Next sketch the idea on the paper lightly with pencil.
- Incorporate the price of the stamp in the composition.
- Now choose one color crayon and complete the sketch in lights, darks and medium tones of the color. (Working with shades of one color is called a Monochromatic scheme. It is a good term for the children to be familiar with.)
- Complete the coloring and then proceed to cut points or scalloped edges all the way around the stamp. (See Figure 6–7)

Mount the stamps on black paper. Display them in the auditorium or all-purpose room during February. The stamps will probably be the largest that anyone has ever seen.

Patriotic Shield

Crayon Batik

Muster the call for Patriotism with this great art lesson. Use the noted shield as a basis for some stirring national themes.

Basic Materials: 12 by 18 inch manila paper, red and white crayons, scissors, diluted blue tempera paint, easel brushes, newspapers.

Procedure:

- Fold the manila paper in half the short or long way.

- Draw half a shield on the folded paper. (See Figure 6–8A)
- Cut out the shield and decorate it heavily with red and white crayon using National or Patriotic themes for the drawing.
- Good symbols are: The Statue of Liberty, Liberty Bell, the Eagle, Uncle Sam, stars, stripes, the flag.
- Borders can be added around the shield or across the top.
- Areas not crayoned will be blue when the shield is painted, so leave areas uncrayoned.
- Now spread newspaper on the floor and dilute the blue paint—2 parts paint to 2 parts water—to make a blue wash.
- Place the shield on the newspaper, and cover it entirely with blue wash.
- The paint will adhere to the paper, but will roll off the waxy crayon. (See Figure 6–8B)

Figure 6–8A

When the paint is dry, mount the shields on red paper. The shields are most effective if they are displayed en masse grouped together in a shield formation on an empty wall or huge bulletin board. The exhibit might be entitled: *Our Proud Bearings.*

Patriotic Vaseline Prints

Vaseline Graphics

A Vaseline print? Who ever heard of such a thing? Vaseline is a commodity used for medicinal purposes—how can it be used in art work? Here is an interesting way to use a familiar material in a new way. So, raid the medicine chest, and try a Vaseline print with your students.

Figure 6–8B

Basic Materials: 2—12 by 18 inch sheets of manila paper, Vaseline (ask the children to bring some from home), red or blue powdered paint, newspaper, pencil, colored pencil.

Procedure:

- Plan a picture with a patriotic theme. A parade, a national landmark, a design utilizing stars and stripes.
- Sketch the idea on the manila paper and reserve it for future use.
- Now mix the paint and vaseline together. Add paint for a darker hue.
- Next spread a thin layer of the mixture on the clean piece of manila paper.
- Be sure that the mixture is spread to the edges of the paper. Your hand makes a good spreader.
- Now cover this with the manila paper that has been sketched on.
- The Vaseline is between a sandwich of paper, the sketched side up. (See Figure 6–9A)

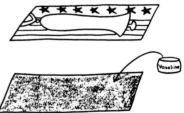

Figure 6–9A

Figure 6–9B

- Take a colored pencil with a blunt tip and carefully resketch the pencil lines in the preliminary drawing.
- Draw in color quickly over all the lines you made previously.
- Work fast, the paper sandwich has a tendency to absorb the oil from the Vaseline; if this occurs you will have difficulty separating the paper.
- Complete the entire sketch and then carefully pull the two sheets of paper apart. The results will be a pleasant surprise. There will be 2 prints —a positive and a negative. (See Figure 6–9B)

Mount the two prints on a large piece of black paper, and exhibit the project on the walls of the school corridor. Entitle the display: *The Mysterious Prints,* and be prepared to answer the many inquiries about them.

Patriotic String Painting

String, Paint, Mixed Media

This painting technique is an excellent one for the teacher. It involves very little effort, and yet the results are quite exciting.

Basic Materials: 12 by 18 inch blue paper, white paint, 15 inch string length, red and blue crayons.

Procedure:

- First decorate the blue paper with patriotic symbols using the red and blue crayons heavily. Use stars and stripes in a cluster burst so the composition appears as a firecracker explosion. Scatter the clusters on the blue paper, but leave lots of free area for the next step.
- When the crayon composition is completed, fold the paper in half the long way with the crayon inside.
- Take the folded paper to a table which has been covered with paper in preparation for the next step which is string painting.
- Have the string and paint available on the table.
- Now open the crayoned paper.
- Dip the string into the bottle of white paint, and as you pull it out hold a ruler or tongue depressor between the string and the jar as you take it out. This will eliminate an excess of paint on the string.
- Now lay the string on one side of the folded paper, leaving a portion of the string hanging out at the bottom. (See Figure 6–10A)

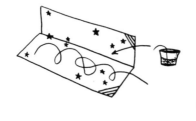

Figure 6–10A

- Refold the paper with the string inside.
- Hold your hand on the folded paper so you can feel the string underneath.
- Next take the tail of the string and start to pull it out slowly moving the string back and forth as it is pulled.
- Open the paper when the string has been completely pulled from it. The shape the string painting has taken will be a great surprise. (See Figure 6–10B)

A fine way to display the work might be to cover an entire bulletin board with the pictures tacked side by side. Just the huge mass of red, white and blue will be a stirring sight.

Figure 6–10B

Valentine's Day Projects

A time for love, hearts and flowers. Try some of these unique art experiences with your students.

Valentine Mobile

Paper and String in Motion

Here is a wonderful type of valentine to receive—a message in motion.

Basic Materials: 4 by 6 inch foilboard or oaktag, scissors, red, gold and white paper, rubber cement, string.

Procedure:

- Cut the foilboard or oaktag into a circle, rectangle or triangle. Walk with the scissors from the outside of the shape into the middle. (See Figure 6–11A) This is the base for the mobile.
- Next cut a variety of different valentine shapes out of cut paper and decorate them with bits of contrasting paper. Nice shapes to use might be hearts in all sizes, cupids, doves, flowers, letters, ribbons, arrows.
- When there are several shapes made, start to tie the strings to the pieces and attach them to the base of your mobile.
- Place them in various locations so they will not be hanging at the same level.
- Attach several shapes to one string to produce interest.
- Decorate the shapes on both sides—there is no back or front to a mobile.
- Stop to look at the construction of the mobile from time to time. Too many additions will make the mobile too fussy.
- When the mobile is pleasing, attach a string at the top for hanging. (See Figure 6–11B)

Display the mobiles in the cafeteria for a wonderful February decoration.

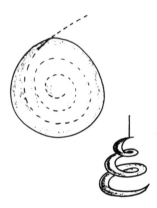

Figure 6–11A

Figure 6–11B

Valentine Posters

Mixed Media

Let your class proclaim that Valentine's Day has arrived with a spectacular poster. Use untraditional colors, phrases and size to make the poster truly unique.

Basic Materials: 18 by 24 inch construction paper in light blue, pink, orange, red; assorted tempera paint, brushes, scraps of colored paper, scissors, rubber cement, assorted pieces of metallic paper.

Procedure:

Figure 6–12

- Suggest that the children make a way-out poster for Valentine's Day. Proclaim Love, Be Mine, Your Valentine, Sweetheart, in a new way. Use unusual color combinations, cut paper shapes and paint in a bold manner.
- Start with one word or phrase and paint or paste cut paper letters forming the word on the large poster size paper. The word can be placed vertically, horizontally or on a slant. (See Figure 6–12)
- Next decorate the remaining part of the poster. Paint or cut and paste circles, stripes, spots of color in valentine shapes wherever they are needed to complete your composition.
- Do not clutter the poster, leave areas free for interest.

When the posters are completed, let the class decide where the posters should be placed. Put rings of tape on the back of each poster, and let each child choose his own exhibit spot. It will be a pleasant surprise to discover the fine locations chosen.

You See Through My Heart

Crayon—Waxed Paper Transparency

The laminating process is an exciting experience. Every child can share this happening no matter the age. Why not introduce your students to crayon lamination?

Basic Materials: waxed paper, scrap crayons, an iron, a pad of newspaper, scissors, rubber cement, 12 by 18 inch red paper.

Procedure:

- Cut 2 pieces of waxed paper 6 by 9 inches in size.
- Put one aside.
- Open a pair of scissors and hold them so the cutting edge of one is in your hand, and use the cutting edge of the other to start shaving bits of crayon off onto one sheet of the waxed paper. (See Figure 6–13A)
- Continue shaving the crayons using assorted colors, and scatter the shavings in various places on the paper.
- When there is a good supply of shavings on the paper, carefully cover it with the piece of paper previously put aside.
- Take the paper and crayon sandwich to an ironing area which has been covered with a pad of newspaper.
- Iron the paper sandwich quickly. The heat of the iron will immediately melt the crayon shavings and the waxed paper together—lamination has taken place.
- Put the newly made lamination aside.
- Now take the red paper and fold it in half the short way to make a folder.
- On the front of the folder lightly draw a large heart shape.
- Stab scissors through the 2 thicknesses of paper, and cut out the heart shape. (See Figure 6–13B)

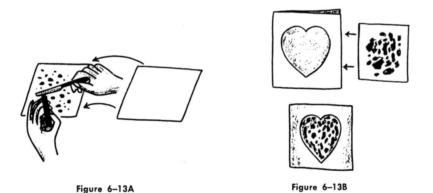

Figure 6–13A   Figure 6–13B

- The folder now has a back and front cover with a heart shape cut out of it.
- Open the folder and place the laminated paper inside, secure it closed with rubber cement. The see-through laminated heart shape is completed.

A great place to display them would be to tape them in the windows of the classroom. They can then be appreciated by everyone inside and out.

Valentine Bouquets

Mixed Media

A Valentine Bouquet for each child's desk would be a special treat, wouldn't it?

Basic Materials: a small aluminum foil container, Plasticine, pipe cleaners, assorted scraps of construction paper, rubber cement, scissors, scraps of metallic paper, tissue.

Procedure:

- Fill the container with Plasticine, and set it aside.
- Now cut out heart shapes from the construction paper, and decorate them with tissue and metallic paper.
- Attach the shapes to the pipe cleaners, and put the bottom end in the Plasticine.
- Continue to make the heart shapes and leaves until the entire bouquet is completed. (See Figure 6–14)

Display the Valentine Bouquets as personal arrangements at each child's desk. Here is a unique way to exhibit this very different kind of Valentine.

Figure 6–14

Sandpaper Valentine Graphic

Sandpaper Print

Texture in graphics can produce interesting effects. Here is a graphic technique that uses a familiar material. Introduce your students to sandpaper prints.

Basic Materials: 6 by 9 inch sheet of sturdy cardboard, fine-medium-coarse sandpaper, rubber cement, scissors, lightweight white paper, red water base ink, brayer, aluminum foil, newspaper, spoon.

Procedure:

- Cut the various coarsenesses of sandpaper into valentine symbols. Shapes like hearts, flowers, cupids, arrows, doves and ribbons would be fine.
- Arrange the shapes on the cardboard, and when the arrangement is pleasing, glue the sandpaper shapes to the cardboard. (See Figure 6–15)
- Next spread newspaper on a table in one area of the room.
- Tear a sheet of aluminum foil and use it for an inking surface.

Figure 6–15

- Put ink on the foil; run the brayer through it and then roll it over the sandpaper composition.
- When the sandpaper plate is covered with ink, place a piece of white paper over it.
- Next rub the entire surface of the paper with the bowl of a spoon.
- Now carefully lift the paper from the plate, and a print has been made. Repeat the process as many times as you choose.

The prints would make wonderful valentines for the children to send to each other. Paste them on a folded sheet of 12 by 18 inch white or pink paper. A message can be written within the fold with felt tip marker.

The Broken Heart

Cut Paper

The children are oriented to space because of recent happenings. This lesson will aid them in developing space in art.

Basic Materials: 12 by 18 inch red paper, 9 by 12 inch white paper, scissors, rubber cement.

Procedure:

- Cut a large heart shape from the white paper.
- Now start to cut the shape into pieces.
- As each piece is cut place it in basically the same shape on the red paper. When the heart is entirely cut out it will look like an assembled jigsaw puzzle.
- Now carefully separate the pieces so there will be spaces of red paper showing between the white pieces. (See Figure 6–16) The spaces can be wide or narrow—no matter—space is being added to a solid shape, and this is an interesting art experience.
- Now pick up each piece and cement it back to its original spot. The broken heart will be completed when all pieces are cemented.

The pictures are quite exciting to behold. Display them in the school corridor. Find one large empty wall and tape the pictures in the form of a huge heart. Entitle the exhibit: *Our Class Is Broken-Hearted.*

Figure 6–16

Valentine Garden

Cut Paper Bulletin Board Display

The children will enjoy working on this joint valentine project. Use it for your February Bulletin Board.

Basic Materials: assorted colored construction paper, scissors, paper doilies, metallic paper, paper cement, staples.

Procedure:

- At the bottom of the bulletin board put a strip of cut grass.
- A simple way to do this is to take strips of green paper 6 by 18 inches in size.
- Cut the paper in grass teeth the entire length of the paper. (See Figure 6–17)

Figure 6–17

- When finished there are 2 grass strips to place on the bulletin board.
- Continue cutting and stapling the cut strips until grass covers the bottom of the proposed display.
- Now suggest that the children cut and paste heart shapes into flower shapes for the valentine garden. Hearts can be made into faces with bits of cut out paper, doilies can be added around hearts, 4 hearts can be pasted with points in to form a heart flower, a rosette can be made by pasting small heart shapes into a ring—let the children experiment with all types of heart flower creations.
- Each time a flower is completed, let the child staple it to the garden.
- Add flowers, leaves and vines until the project actually looks like a blooming garden.

You will all enjoy your efforts for the entire month of February.

Valentine Silhouettes

Cut Paper

A silhouette is usually associated with a profile or figure. Here is a unique treatment with a valentine in mind.

Basic Materials: 9 by 12 inch white paper, scissors, rubber cement, 12 by 18 inch red paper, white string, white crayons.

Figure 6–18A

Procedure:

- Fold the white paper in half and draw half a heart on it.
- Now sketch valentine symbols in the heart shape.
- Areas that are being drawn will eventually be cut out so make sure the fold and the frame of the heart remain intact.
- It will help if you color in areas that are to be cut out. In this way you are protecting the frame and fold from being cut too much. (See Figure 6–18A)
- Cut the heart shape out along with the portions designated to be cut.
- Make the shape as lacy as possible.
- Now cement the shape to the red paper.
- Take the string and cement it around the heart in loops, wavy or pointed designs. (See Figure 6–18B)
- Other decorations can be added with white crayon or scraps of white paper.

Figure 6–18B

The silhouettes are lovely when they are finished. They would be eagerly accepted by the librarian for display in her room. Ask her.

Daguerreotype Portraits

Cut Paper

For a change from the traditional hearts and flowers, this is a new twist.

Basic Materials: 12 by 18 inch manila paper, crayons, paste, red and black construction paper.

Procedure:

- Suggest that the children cut red hearts which will eventually become people's faces. The people might be grandparents or great grandparents; and the valentine picture created will be a daguerreotype of them.
- After a discussion about the appearance of these heart people, give

Figure 6–19

the class the manila paper background, crayons, paste and the red and black construction paper.

- Make the heart faces first by cutting them on the fold of a piece of red paper.
- Decorate them with a crayon face and paste them to the manila paper.
- Next make the body and background on the manila paper with crayon. (See Figure 6–19)
- When the pictures are completed, cut them in an oval shape and paste them to a black background frame.
- Cut or decorate the frame with crayon.

The daguerreotypes are quite a change from the ordinary valentine. Display them on a bulletin board in the school corridor. A good title for them might be: *My Make Believe Ancestors.*

Valentine Wiggly Waggly

Paper Construction

Children will love making this unique paper construction. It is simple and fun to construct.

Basic Materials: red construction paper, scissors, paste, staples, bits of assorted colored paper.

Procedure:

- Cut a heart out of a 6 by 9 inch piece of red paper.
- Now cut a 12 by 18 inch piece of red paper into 4—3 inch strips.
- Cut away ¼ of 2 strips, these are the arms of the wiggle waggle.
- Fold all the strips into fan folds and staple them to the heart shape for arms and legs.
- Cut eyes, nose and mouth out of the scrap paper and paste them to the heart head for the face.
- Now cut out feet and hands for the construction. Cut the hands like mittens, and the feet in oval shapes; paste these to the wiggle waggle. (See Figure 6–20)

Figure 6–20

- Attach hair, hat, ears or any other desired shape to the construction.
- When it is completed, attach a piece of elasticized string to the top.

When hung from a light fixture in the classroom, the Wiggle Waggle makes a delightful addition to the valentine decor.

WONDERFUL SUBJECTS TO DRAW DURING FEBRUARY

1. Draw what you want the groundhog to do when he comes out of his hole.
2. Draw Edison in his laboratory.
3. Draw one of Lincoln's experiences.
4. Make a valentine card for Mother.
5. Draw a Mother heart with her family.
6. How would you look if you lived during Washington's era?
7. Draw Washington as a president.
8. Draw a Minuteman.
9. Draw a ballroom during colonial time with people doing the Minuet.
10. Draw the person who is your favorite valentine.

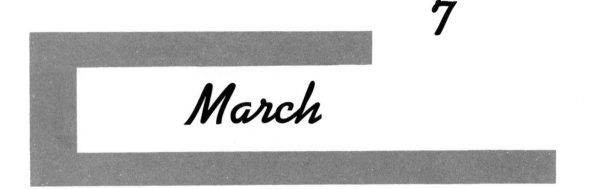

7

March

March, the unpredictable month. Spring is officially welcomed, but cold weather is determined to linger. Pussy Willows and Forsythia are common sights. Alexander Graham Bell is the famous man of the month, and St. Patrick's Day, the time for Leprechaun activity, is probably the highlight for the children. Experiment with some of the following March ideas.

Individual Telephone Books

Mixed Media

March commemorates the birth of Alexander Graham Bell. His invention is such an important part of our everyday existence, isn't it fitting that we create a project in celebration of his special day? What could be more appropriate than a personalized Telephone Book?

Basic Materials: 14 pieces of 6 by 9 inch typing paper, 1 piece of 6 by 9 colored paper, 12″ yarn, crayons, felt tip marker, stapler.

Procedure:

- Take the colored paper, fold it in half and on the outside cover decorate it with crayon and felt tip marker. Any idea dealing with the telephone will be a good one to use. Suggestions might be—picture of Alexander

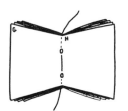

Figure 7–1

Bell working in his laboratory, people talking on the telephone, a large drawing of a telephone, picture stories telling why the telephone is important.

- Now fold the 6 by 9 inch typing paper in half. This will make 28 pages in the booklet.
- Put them into the completed cover, and either staple the pages together or with scissors pierce 2 holes in the midsection of the booklet.
- Next string the yarn through the holes and tie the booklet together on the outside.
- Skip the first page of the book, and start to alphabetize the pages. This will make it easier for you to use the book. (See Figure 7–1)

When the telephone books are completed, have them passed to each child in the classroom. Let every child put his own name and telephone number in the book. What a wonderful way to record a class.

Sculpt a Lion or Lamb

Sawdust Sculpture

Three dimensional sculpture is a great treat for the students. If you are in a school system where clay and a kiln are not available, it is advisable to round out the program with homemade sculpturing recipes. Here is one that is easy to prepare, and is always a success.

Basic Materials: 2 cups sawdust, 1 cup wallpaper paste, ¼ cup plaster of paris, water to moisten mixture. (Recipe for 1 child can be prepared in empty coffee tin.)

Procedure:

- Mix all the dry ingredients together.
- Now slowly add the water, mixing as it is poured. When the material is moistened and has the consistency of clay, start to sculpt it into a desired shape. A good suggestion would be to make the veritable lion or lamb figures for March. (See Figure 7–2)

Figure 7–2

- Dry them thoroughly for at least a week. They are nice in their natural state, but they can be painted with tempera. The texture of the sawdust mixture gives the sculptured figure an authentic appearance.

Display the work in a hall showcase for all to see! A title like: *March Comes in Like a Lion and Goes out Like a Lamb,* would be very appropriate.

Raining Cats and Dogs

Crayon

March is a peculiar month. No one is sure whether winter is over and spring has come. At any time during this month, the weather can play tricks on us. Here is a lesson that ridicules this unusual month for weather.

Basic Materials: 12 by 18 inch manila paper, crayons.

Procedure:

- Suggest that the children draw a picture showing a storm during the month of March that is so bad that it rains cats and dogs. But—instead of raindrops, make little cats and dogs falling in a variety of ways—on their heads, backs, upside down, sideways.
- Make the animals a variety of species and colors for a most exciting effect. (See Figure 7–3)
- Complete the picture by showing where the storm is taking place.
- Is it in the country, city, on a farm, on the way to school?

Mount the pictures on black paper and display them on a bulletin board in your room. Cut out large black letters and tack them above the exhibit saying: *Raining Cats and Dogs!*

Figure 7–3

Potato Prints

Graphics

The potato is one of the easiest materials with which to print. It is a vegetable that is common to all and is readily available. Suggest on Potato Printing Day that each child bring his own potato for the project.

Basic Materials: potato, nail file or scissors, 12 by 18 inch manila paper, sponge, tempera paint, newspapers.

Procedure:

- Cover the work area with newspaper.
- Cut the potato in half and gouge out portions of the fleshy white part of the potato with a nail file or the point of a pair of scissors to make a design.
- Saturate a small flat sponge with paint.
- Press the potato cut out on the painted sponge and then on paper.
- If the potato design is not pleasing, gouge out more areas.
- Now cover the paper with the potato prints forming an overall design on the paper. (See Figure 7–4)

Figure 7–4

To make another picture change the pattern of the potato any time by cutting the used portion of the potato away and carve a new design.

The Potato Prints are wonderful used as a folder. On the cover of it write with felt tip pen the subject the folder will be used for.

Potato Heads

Craypas

The Irish are noted for their splendid potato crops. Use the potato as a take-off for a St. Patrick's Day project.

Basic Materials: 18 by 24 inch manila paper, craypas, a potato shape cut from from brown paper, paper cement.

Procedure:

- Have available to the children the manila paper, the brown paper potato shape and the craypas.
- Suggest that the children make use of their potato shape in any way they desire. The potato could be used as a potato person, animal, bird, fish, or just a potato!

- Next cement the shape on the paper in the position desired.
- Now draw the picture with craypas. The background must fit the potato subject. (See Figure 7–5)

The varied uses of the potato subject will be interesting and quite unique. Use the pictures as a hall display. They are so large and impressive that this would be the best spot for them.

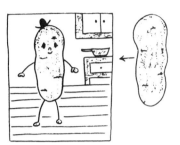

Figure 7–5

March Bulletin Board

Cut Paper

A wonderful bulletin board for March can be made as a joint project in the classroom. It involves the shamrock and Leprechauns.

Basic Materials: 3 pieces of 24 by 36 inch green paper, 9 by 12 inch manila paper, crayons, scissors, stapler.

Procedure:

- The teacher prepares the shamrock background of the display by cutting the 3 huge pieces of green paper into circles.
- Attach them together in pyramid shape, and then from the center outward tear the paper so 3 open areas are made. (See Figure 7–6A)
- Attach a cut out green paper stem to the bottom, and the result is a giant shamrock.
- Suggest that the class draw little Leprechaun people on the manila paper in any position possible. They can be running, sitting, climbing, skipping, jumping.
- Crayon them heavily and cut them out.
- When they are completed, staple the wee Leprechauns to some area of the huge shamrock. They can be under a portion of it, on top of it, climbing on one side of it.
- Try to attach them so they fit the position they were drawn in.
- Keep adding the little fellows until it is decided that no more are needed.
- Add small cut out shamrocks in the empty areas of the bulletin board for added interest. These can be made from the scraps left over from the giant shamrock. (See Figure 7–6B)

Figure 7–6A

Figure 7–6B

Add a calendar for March in one area of the bulletin board. Cut out letters for March from green metallic paper, and put them above the display. The bulletin board for March is complete.

String Designs in Green

String Weaving

This lesson combines a mathematical principle of drawing patterned straight lines to make a curve, with an art lesson. It sounds like a monstrous task, but is quite easy if the directions are followed. The children will really enjoy making String Designs. Use green for the theme of the lesson, and the project will become a wonderful addition to your St. Patrick's Day color scheme.

Basic Materials: green thread, 6 by 9 inch pieces of shirt cardboard, masking tape, scissors, pencil, ruler, 12 by 18 inch green paper.

Procedure:

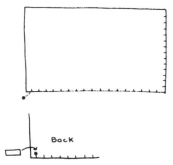

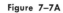

Back

Figure 7–7A

- Along the edges of the four sides of the cardboard place a pencil dot mark at ½ inch intervals.
- Next, with scissors cut ½ inch slits at each dot around the entire piece of cardboard.
- Now take a spool of thread, put a knot at the first slit to the left of the cardboard as it is laying in front of you. (See Figure 7–7A)
- Then carefully place a little piece of tape over the knot to make sure it stays in place. The taped area will become the back of the design.
- The thread is anchored so begin the design. Extend the thread to the second notch on the right side. The design is formed from left to right.
- The pattern is first notch at bottom left, second notch at right, second notch at bottom, third notch at right, third notch at bottom, fourth notch at right. (See Figure 7–7B)
- Continue weaving going to the next notch at bottom and the right until the notches are all used at the bottom.
- Cut the string and fasten it to the back with tape. Notice that the design was made with straight lines, but the repeated line pattern forms a curve.
- Turn the cardboard so the curve is at the top of the cardboard. (See Figure 7–7C)
- Now repeat the identical process used for the first curve until you have formed another curve, see *.
- The double curve forms an ellipse. Boys and girls are always thrilled when this happens.

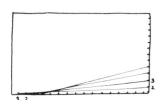

Figure 7–7B

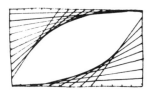

Figure 7–7C

- Now take the large piece of green paper and cut a 5½ by 8½ inch rectangle out of the center of it. This makes an ideal frame. (See Figure 7–7D)
- Lay the String Design front side down on the frame, and tape the 4 sides of the cardboard to the frame.

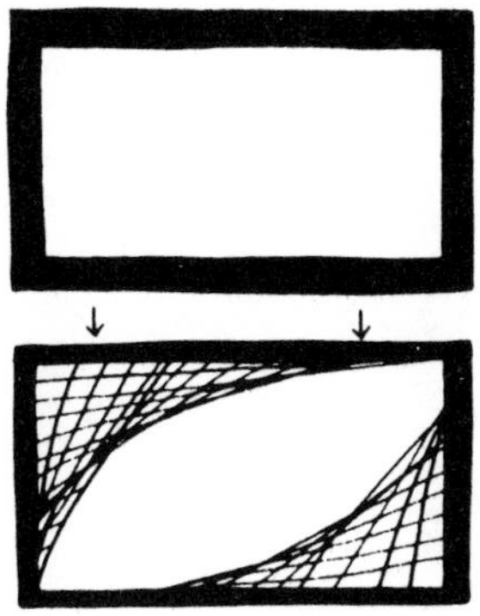

The green Ellipse String Designs are quite impressive in their frame. Another good suggestion might be to make a string design in a flat box lid for a very exciting 3 dimensional appearance.

Display the projects on the walls of the school corridor. Entitle the display: *Making Straight Lines into Curves.* Be ready to answer any questions pertaining to the riddle you will frequently be asked—how can you make a curve out of straight lines?

Figure 7–7D

Line Designs

Colored Pencil or Ball Point Pen

Line Designs are another outgrowth from the String Design projects. The lines are drawn lines instead of string.

Basic Materials: 9 by 12 inch paper, ruler, ball point pen, colored pencils.

Procedure:

- When doing this type of design start by marking a piece of construction paper with pencil dots at ½ inch intervals.
- Then use the ruler to draw lines with either ball point pen or colored pencils from point to point using the pattern mentioned previously, see* preceding project.
- When the line designs have developed into an ellipse, an interesting way to add to the design would be to use the colored pencils to decorate portions of the small rectangular shapes that were made when the lines cut one another. (See Figure 7–8)

Try displaying the Line Designs as a border above the chalk sill. They make a handsome exhibit.

Figure 7–8

Lacy Shamrock

Cut Paper

This cut paper project is not only an excellent St. Patrick's Day lesson, but it also is a great aid in giving the student much needed practice in scissor cutting.

Basic Materials: 18 by 24 inch green construction paper, scissors, green cellophane, paper cement.

Procedure:

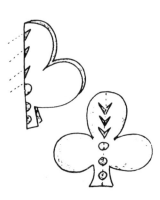

Figure 7–9

- Cut the largest shamrock possible from the green construction paper.
- Now fold the shamrock in half lengthwise.
- Start to cut chips and pieces from the fold. (See Figure 7–9)
- Do not cut too much of the fold, or the shamrock will break in half.
- Open the fold and the shamrock has a variety of nice cut out shapes down the middle.
- If the cutting does not seem lacy enough, close the fold, and again cut portions away until the decorations cut are pleasing.
- When the center cuts are completed, fold one of the shamrock petals and again cut portions of the paper away until you are satisfied with the design.
- Now fold the shamrock petal on the opposite side and repeat the same kind of cutting so you form an interesting symmetrical cutout design.
- When the shape is lacy, but not too busy looking, cut a piece of cellophane and paste it behind the cutout shamrock. The results—an interesting see-through shape.

Look for the largest windows you have in your school building and tape the shamrock cutouts to them. People from inside and outside will then be able to enjoy this St. Patrick's Day Project.

Shamrock Plant Scroll

Ink, Cut Paper

Here is a technique which employs blowing ink on paper with a straw instead of applying it with a brush or pen.

Basic Materials: India Ink, brush, straws cut in half, 6 by 18 inch white paper, 9 by 12 inch green construction paper, scissors, paste, 2—7 by 1 inch black paper strips, scraps of construction paper, newspaper.

Procedure:

- Cover the working area with newspaper.
- First make the branches and stalk of the proposed plant.
- Use the brush to place a blob of ink at the bottom of the white paper.
- Suggest that the children stoop down and, using the piece of straw, blow behind the blob of ink.
- Blow until the ink starts to move, and then follow it up blowing constantly until the ink refuses to move anymore.
- When this occurs, start at the blob again, or at another point where the ink still seems wet. (See Figure 7–10A)
- Continue to blow the ink until there are no more wet areas.
- If the shapes already made are not high enough on the paper, or have not branched out sufficiently, add another blob of ink to areas of the stalk and start the blowing process again.
- When the stalk and branches of the plant are satisfactory, set the paper aside to dry.
- Now take the green paper and scissors and cut shamrocks for the branches of the plant. An easy way to cut a shamrock is to remember that the shape is really 3 circles attached in pyramid form with a tail at the bottom.
- Start to paste the cut out shamrocks to the plant. Scatter them so the composition is interesting.
- Keep cutting the shamrocks until the plant is well supplied.
- Now take a scrap of colored paper and cut and paste a container to the bottom of the shamrock plant.
- Next paste the black strips at the bottom and top of the scroll. The picture has an oriental quality to it. (See Figure 7–10B)

An excellent place to display the shamrock scrolls might be taped as a border above the chalk sills in the classroom. They certainly help to announce the coming of St. Patrick's Day!

Figure 7–10A

Figure 7–10B

Clover Gems

Tissue Paper

A very splashy decoration can be made for St. Patrick's Day out of just paper. Your class will enjoy making these giant Four leaf clovers.

Basic Materials: 12 by 24 inch green construction paper, shades of green and white tissue paper, scissors, paste.

Procedure:

- Cut the largest clover shape possible from the 18 by 24 inch green paper. This is easy if the clover is thought of as 4 large circles together with a tail at the bottom.
- Next take the tissue and tear it into little pieces, crumple each piece and paste it to the clover shape.
- Continue to add tissue to the clover leaf in any design desirable.
- The shape can be entirely filled in with tissue, it can be made with a border of tissue, or with circles of tissue.
- Design a shape that is pleasing. (See Figure 7–11)

Figure 7–11

When the clovers are completed, they are large and gay. The best place I can suggest for their display might be the school cafeteria. Scatter them helter-skelter all over the walls for a wonderful St. Patrick's Day decoration.

Crayon Glazed Shamrocks

Crayon

Crayon glazing is a wonderful skill that is seldom employed in art. Introduce your class to this exciting technique.

Basic Materials: crayons, 12 by 18 inch manila paper, oaktag or lightweight cardboard, scissors, dull knife.

Procedure:

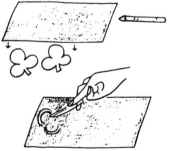

- Cover a sheet of 12 by 18 inch manila paper heavily with green crayon.
- Now cut various sizes of shamrocks from the oaktag or cardboard.
- Place the shamrocks one at a time under the crayoned paper.
- Hold the shape in place with one hand, and with the other hand start to scrape around the outline of the shamrock with the dull knife.
- Scrape away the crayon until an outline of the shamrock appears. (See Figure 7–12)

Figure 7–12

- Now place another sized shamrock under the green crayoned paper and repeat the scraping process.
- Do this as many times as is necessary to make an interesting overlapping composition. The picture takes on a glossy, glazed appearance.

The finished project makes a wonderful cover for a March Homework folder. Fold the glazed paper in half and on the cover in felt tip marker print —*Homework for March!*

Mosaic Shamrocks

Paper

A paper mosaic picture for St. Patrick's Day makes a different type of art project for March. Materials are at a minimum and the final product is quite impressive.

Basic Materials: pieces of green paper in all shades, light, medium, dark, 12 by 18 inch white paper, paper cement, green crayon.

Procedure:

- Draw the largest shamrock possible on the white paper.
- Now take the shades of green paper and tear them into pieces about the size of a quarter.
- Start to cement the pieces within the lines of the already drawn shamrock.
- Scatter the shades of green so that one shade is not clumped in one area.
- When the mosaic shamrock is completely filled with torn pieces of green paper, decorate the area around the shamrock with crayon lace. (See Figure 7–13) This will enhance the project.

Display the mosaic shamrocks in the foyer at the school entrance. The Irish are not the only people who will be pleased to see them.

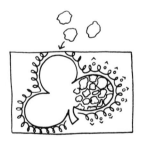

Figure 7–13

Shamrock Folk

Mixed Media

People are very important beings. There are all different kinds. Why not introduce your class to Shamrock Folk?

Basic Materials: 12 by 18 inch manila paper, 9 by 12 inch green paper, scissors, paste, crayons.

Procedure:

- Cut shamrock shapes out of the 9 by 12 inch green paper. The number of shapes depends upon the size of your cut shamrocks.
- If two shapes are cut it can be a shamrock couple. Three or more shapes may be a shamrock family.
- When it is decided whether it is a family or just one or two Shamrock People paste the shapes to the manila paper and with crayon draw the faces and stick figures for the bodies.
- Next draw the clothes and background for the picture. (See Figure 7–14)

Figure 7–14

- If it is a family perhaps it could be mother and father walking along with their child. If it is a couple, perhaps it could show them shopping, going to church or traveling.

The Shamrock People when incorporated into a picture make a very unique type of project. So many varied ideas can be interpreted from each drawing.

When the pictures are completed why not ask the children to display them to the group along with a short resume of their picture? This is a wonderful way to get spontaneous reaction from each child. The vocal delivery they will give will equal a stage performance.

Green Pictures

Paint

Nothing could be more Irish than to paint a green picture. Suggest that the class close their eyes and imagine that everything is green and white for St. Patrick's Day. Now ask them to open their eyes and paint in green a picture they imagined. The results will be quite interesting.

Basic Materials: 12 by 18 inch white paper, paper cup of green paint, paint brush, newspaper.

Procedure:

Figure 7–15

- Cover the working area with newspaper, then distribute the paper, brush and green paint.
- Now immediately begin to paint an idea dealing with Leprechauns on the white paper.
- Remember, only green color is used.
- The suggested possibilities could be a Leprechaun Village, Leprechaun's hiding the pot of gold at the end of the rainbow, or a Leprechaun playing a trick on someone. (See Figure 7–15)

The green and white pictures are an unusual outgrowth for St. Patrick's Day. Mount the pictures on a darker shade of green paper, and exhibit them in the school corridor. Perhaps the display could be called *Looking Through Green Colored Glasses,* or *Green Means St. Patrick's Day.*

Leprechaun Trickster

Crayon

Leprechauns are appealing to the young and the old. The children especially delight in the stories about the tricks and escapades performed by Leprechauns. Why not use the Leprechaun pranks as a basis for a March art lesson?

Basic Materials: 12 by 18 inch manila paper, crayons.

Procedure:

- Hold the manila paper the long way on the desk and draw a Leprechaun face and a portion of his shoulder at the bottom of the paper with crayon.
- When the face has been completed draw a thought bubble from the face

Figure 7-16

to the top of the paper similar to a cartoon illustration. (See Figure 7–16)

- Now draw a picture in the thought bubble of some prank or trick the Leprechaun could possibly be conjuring up to play on an unsuspecting mortal.
- The prank can take any form. It can be a Leprechaun tripping a person, hiding a piece of someone's apparel, painting a house a hideous color, almost any trick drawn would be acceptable.

When the pictures are completed, an interesting way to use them would be to line them on a bulletin board or a wall and have the children vote on the Leprechaun picture which they thought portrayed the best trick.

An explanation of what you plan to do with the pictures prior to their drawing would create much motivation.

Leprechaun Puppets

Envelope, Mixed Media

Children love all kinds of puppets. Here is an unusual type of puppet that can be made by everyone.

Basic Materials: white paper envelope, crayons, scissors, paste, assorted colored construction paper.

Procedure:

- Cut an envelope in half the short way.
- Draw the face and a portion of a Leprechaun on the half-envelope.
- Color the picture heavily with crayon.
- Now add a body and paper clothing to the bottom of the envelope. (See Figure 7–17)
- When the puppet is completed, a hand inserted into the pocket of the envelope will make the puppet come alive.

Have the youngsters create a short play about St. Patrick's Day and perform it behind a table which has been turned on its side. A creative hour will fly by quickly with the play acting of these little envelope fellows.

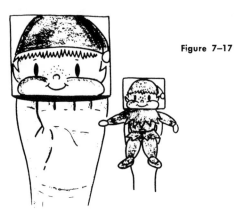

Figure 7-17

Leprechaun Masks

Cut Paper

Everyone usually associates mask making with Hallowe'en. Here is a wonderful Leprechaun mask for St. Patrick's Day.

Basic Materials: 9 by 12 inch oaktag, pencil, scissors, crayons, 9 by 12 inch green paper, assorted scraps of colored paper, paper cement.

Figure 7–18

Procedure:

- Cut the oaktag in an oval shape at least the size of an average face.
- Next place the oval on your face and very carefully with pencil put a mark where the eyes, nose and mouth are.
- Now cut out these areas. (See Figure 7–18)
- Next add cut paper to the mask for the beard, eyebrows, hair, lips, hat or any decoration required.
- Attach a piece of elasticized string on either side of the mask and it is ready to be worn.

A fun way to use the masks would be to have the class make up a short skit about Leprechauns, and have them enact the skit for each other. This is an excellent way to correlate art and English in your classroom.

Funny Kiddie Kites

Cut Paper

Kite decorations are always fun to make and display during the month of March. Here is an idea for very decorative Kiddie Kites.

Basic Materials: 12 by 18 inch assorted colored paper, scraps of colored paper of all sorts, scissors, paste, yarn, fabric, string, crayon.

Procedure:

- Cut the 12 by 18 inch paper into large diamond shapes. This is the kite base.
- Decorate the shape as a funny person or clown.
- Do this by cutting and pasting the cut paper on the kite for the features of the person.
- Make comical eyes, nose, mouth, hair and hats—exaggerate and contort the features into funny, ridiculous shapes.

Figure 7–19

158   MARCH

- Add crayon highlights where needed.
- Now add a string to the bottom of the kite for a tail. On it tie bits of fabric into bows to complete the kite. (See Figure 7–19)

The nicest way to display the projects would be to tape them helter-skelter at high levels on the classroom walls. The kites exhibited like this appear as if they are flying high. How gay the room will appear with this fine March project.

Fish Kite

Tissue Construction

March, the windy month, is an excellent time to make a kite. There are many types. Here is one fashioned after the Japanese that the children will enjoy making and flying!

Basic Materials: 24 by 36 inch assorted colored tissue paper, scissors, paper cement, strips of lightweight cardboard, paint, string.

Procedure:

Figure 7–20A

- On the 24 by 36 inch tissue paper sketch a large fish shape with pencil and cut it out.
- Lay this shape on another piece of tissue.
- Trace the shape already made, but allow a 1 inch margin all around the cutout fish. (See Figure 7–20A) Cut out this shape also.
- Now lay the smaller fish shape on the larger shape and start to fold and paste the larger shape to the smaller shape. (See Figure 7–20B)
- Do this to every portion but the mouth and the tail. The ends must remain open.
- Next measure the opening of the mouth.
- Cut a 1 inch strip of cardboard the mouth length, and form it into a circle.
- Staple it together.
- Now place it at the mouth of the fish and carefully paste the tissue around the mouth to the cardboard circle. (See Figure 7–20C)
- Cut a piece of string into three 12 inch lengths and attach it to different areas of the cardboard circle mouth, and tie the loose ends together.
- Tie this to a ball of cord, the kite is ready to be flown.
- If additional color or decoration is desired, add it now.

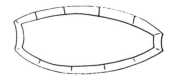

Figure 7–20B

Figure 7–20C

A wonderful suggestion for this lesson would be to have a Kite Flying Contest in your class. Use the Japanese styled fish kites, and give prizes to the children who can keep their kites up longest, and highest.

Forsythia Bouquet

Cut Paper

Brighten your classroom with cheery Forsythia pictures. The children will enjoy this cut paper project. Suggest that they make a bouquet of Forsythia.

Basic Materials: 2 by 18 inch strips of yellow paper, crayons, scissors, paste, assorted construction paper, 12 by 18 inch pastel paper.

Procedure:

- Draw a stalk bouquet on the pastel paper with brown crayon.
- Next cut out and paste a container at the bottom of the stalk bouquet. (See Figure 7–21A)
- Now draw with crayon a background for the proposed Forsythia arrangement. Perhaps the teacher can suggest that the background be someplace in the child's home, at school, in a store window.
- When the drawing is complete, have the children set them aside and begin to cut the yellow paper strips into pieces approximately ½ inch by 2 inches.
- Cut until all the yellow paper is in pieces and then start to paste the strips in cross fashion on the crayoned stalks.
- Paste only the middle portion of the crosses so the ends can be turned up to create a 3 dimensional effect to the blossoms.
- Paste abundantly so the stalks really have the look of bursting blossoms. (See Figure 7–21B)

Figure 7–21A

A good way to display these colorful spring pictures would be to arrange them in a border above the chalk sills. The bright yellow flowers almost say, *Welcome, spring!*

The Many Ways with Pussy Willows

The ubiquitous Pussy Willow is a sure proclamation of springtime. Here are a variety of ways the subject can be used for March art lessons.

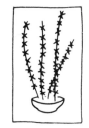

Figure 7–21B

Fuzzy Pussy Willows

Cotton

Basic Materials: cotton batting, 12 by 18 inch construction paper (any color), crayons, paste.

Procedure:

- On the construction paper draw with brown or black crayon stalks for the proposed Pussy Willows. (See Figure 7–22)
- Now take the cotton batting, and make little cotton balls the size of Pussy Willows.
- When many have been made, put dabs of paste on the stalks and place the cotton shapes into it.
- Keep adding cotton pussys until the stalks are filled.
- Now make a crayon background for the Fuzzy Pussy Willows.

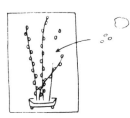

Figure 7–22

Pastel Pussy Willows

Pastels

Basic Materials: 12 by 18 inch black or gray construction paper, box of pastels.

Procedure:

- With brown pastels draw Pussy Willow stalks on the construction paper.
- Next blend the white and gray pastels into little pussy willow shapes on the brown stalks. (See Figure 7–23)
- When the stalks are covered with the pussy willow, make a colorful container under the stalks, and if you care to do so, a background showing where the Pussy Willow container is located.
- Spray the completed pastel drawing with fixative or hair spray to set the color.

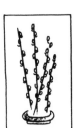

Figure 7–23

Real Pussy Willows

Crayon

Basic Materials: 12 by 18 inch manila paper, crayons.

Procedure:

- Draw 3 stalks on the manila paper with brown crayon.
- In place of the usual Pussy Willows now draw small kitten shapes on the stalks.
- The real pussy cats become the pussys on the picture.
- Have the cats drawn in all positions, sizes, shapes and colors. (See Figure 7–24) This adds an entirely new dimension to the typical willow pictures.

Figure 7–24

- Put a little brown cup under each cat to show his position on th
- Crayon heavily and when finished draw a suitable background
  picture.

Cereal Pussy Willow Bouquet

Puffed Rice

Basic Materials: 12 by 18 inch pastel construction paper, box of Puffed R
paste, crayons.

Procedure:

- With crayon draw a vase with a bouquet of Pussy Willow stalks comin
  from it.
- Next draw a background for the bouquet. This could be a living room
  scene, a scene of the vase in a window, it might even be a scene with the
  vase in a hospital room.
- When the drawing is complete, put a dab of paste on the stalks where the
  Pussy Willows are to be placed.
- Put a piece of Puffed Rice into each pasted spot.
- Continue until your Pussy Willow Bouquet is filled with Puffed Rice
  pieces. (See Figure 7–25)

The pussy willow pictures, whether you use one of the ideas or all of them,
are always a pleasant addition to your room during the month of March. Why
not display the Pussy Willows on the bulletin board and label the exhibit *A
True Sign of Spring*.

SUGGESTIONS FOR PICTURE DRAWING DURING MARCH

1. Draw how you feel when Spring is on its way.
2. Draw a Leprechaun Village.
3. Draw the saying, "March comes in like a lion and goes out like a lamb."
4. Draw how you think Alexander Graham Bell looked in his laboratory.
5. Draw as many things as you can think of that the telephone has done
   for us.
6. Draw a farm scene in winter—in spring.
7. Draw your School Nurse.
8. Draw a scene outside your class window.
9. Draw yourself coming to school.
10. Draw the funniest trick you think a Leprechaun might perform.

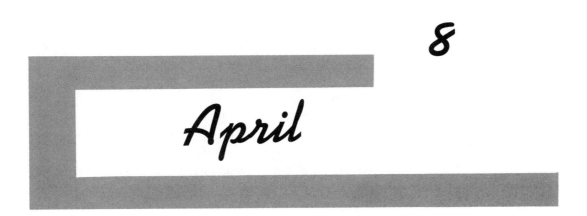

8

April

April—spring is busting out all over. Less than three months remain before the school year ends. Many exciting things are celebrated this month. The first day of April commences with All Fool's Day—a time for pranks and such fun. Then there is Easter—a special day for children. Two of our Presidents—Thomas Jefferson and Ulysses S. Grant, are commemorated in April along with a famous incident that occurred in our history—Paul Revere's ride.

All in all, it appears that April is a busy month. Make good use of the following suggestions when planning your art lessons.

Crowded Pictures

Crayon

A crowded picture is exactly that. It is a picture with so many things in it that it becomes crowded.

Thomas Jefferson, one of our great presidents, is commemorated during April. Use one of the incidents in his career in this unusual art lesson.

Basic Materials: 18 by 24 inch paper, crayons, felt tip pen.

Procedure:

- Suggest that the children make a crowded picture to commemorate Jefferson's Day. He was the author of the Declaration of Independence, and a scene showing the signing of it would certainly be the basis for a crowded picture, perhaps his Inauguration which is also a scene which lends itself to a crowded picture could be used, or Monticello (his home) swarming with visiting tourists would make a wonderful crowded picture.

- Research may have to be done in order to produce the picture in the correct setting. Perhaps time could be set aside during a social studies lesson for a correlation discussion about precisely what could be shown of the period he lived in the picture to be drawn. This extra enlightenment will produce added stimulus to the lesson.
- When the discussion about Jefferson is ended give the children crayon and paper and let them draw a scene of their choice.
- This will take considerable time because the picture involves so much detail.
- Again stress that important things in the picture are colored heavily with crayon, while background and unimportant things are colored lightly.
- Highlight portions of the picture by outlining them with felt tip pen.

Figure 8–1

The library would be the ideal place to exhibit the Crowded Pictures. Mount them on black paper and present them to the librarian for display.

Crowded pictures make unique pictures. At another time in the school year ask the children to make crowded pictures showing: animals, birds, fish, people. You will be quite pleased with the interpretations. (See Figure 8–1)

Paul Revere Has Nothing on Us

Crayon

Did you know that Paul Revere planned the first Continental bills? He was skilled in copper plate work so it is no wonder that he was given this special honor. Why not use this idea as a basis for an art lesson? Suggest that the children design a bill for present use.

Basic Materials: 12 by 18 inch manila paper, crayons.

Procedure:

- Introduce the lesson by suggesting that the children draw a design for new paper money just as Paul Revere was asked to do.
- Suggest that the designs should not counterfeit our present bill—create a new and original money design. Think of new faces and scenes in our history that could be utilized as a part of the design.
- First make a trial sketch on scrap paper. When an idea is pleasing and adaptable for the final drawing, transfer it to the large manila paper.

- The idea will be best shown if the drawing fits the size of the 12 by 18 inch paper.
- Next decide upon a color that you think you want your paper bill to be.
- Use a monochromatic scheme and use the color of choice in light, medium and dark for the entire composition. (See Figure 8–2)

Mount the bills on black paper for the most advantageous appearance and display them on a huge bulletin board tacked side by side. A good title cut out of black paper letters would be: *A New Way with Money* or *Money Makers*.

Figure 8–2

Paul Revere's Adventure

Charcoal

Paul Revere's famous ride from Boston to Lexington on April 18, 1775 was one of our history's greatest adventures. Use the idea in an April art project.

Basic Materials: 18 by 24 inch gray paper, charcoal, yellow crayon.

Procedure:

- A night scene is special fun to portray and it is quite easily done when the materials used are gray paper and charcoal.
- First, very lightly sketch some phase of Paul Revere's trip. It could be: Revere waiting in the darkness for the signal to be off for Lexington; a scene showing the actual signal—one lantern in the Old North Church tower if the British moved by land, two if they came by sea; a scene showing the two lights with Paul Revere riding off to call the Minutemen to arms; a scene showing the surprise of the British the next day when the Minutemen were there in Concord to greet them.
- When the sketch has been lightly developed, go back to portions of it and start to work on the development of light, medium and dark shades with the charcoal.
- Use the charcoal with smooth even strokes.
- Continue working until there is an even, firm tone to the desired value.
- Allow areas of paper to show in the composition, it gives balance and movement to the subject.
- Keep the composition simple, and try when possible to represent textures wherever they appear in the picture.
- If the picture includes a lantern, put a spot of bright yellow crayon in that area. It gives the picture an exciting effect.
- When the composition of the picture is pleasing, spray it with fixative or hair spray and mount it on a contrasting sheet of construction paper.

The pictures are large and quite remarkable in appearance. A wonderful place to display them would be in the corridor of the school. Let all see—*Paul Revere's Adventure.*

A Monument for Ulysses S. Grant

Box Construction

Grant's Tomb is a famous historical attraction on Riverside Drive in New York City. It is said to be a monumental masterpiece. Geographical distances stop us all from visiting some of the famous sights in our country, but pictures in encyclopedias and magazines can give us vicarious experiences. Use a picture and briefing about Grant as a take-off on a good April art lesson.

Basic Materials: small sized boxes of various shapes supplied by the children, paper cement, scissors, felt tip markers, white construction paper, shirt cardboard.

Bonus Materials: tempera paint, brushes, green construction paper.

Procedure:

Figure 8–3A

- Suggest that the children build a monument for Grant using an idea of their own origin. This can be done by experimenting with the placement of the boxes* in various positions until a desirable arrangement has been made.
- When this occurs, cement the boxes in place and start to embellish the monument with felt tip marker and additions of white construction paper columns, porticos and porches.
- Grant's Tomb on Riverside Drive actually says: "Let us have peace"— Grant's own famous words—painted above the entrance. Perhaps you can put the saying somewhere on the construction that was created.
- Upon completion, the monuments can be mounted on shirt cardboard and landscaped with tempera paint and green construction paper shrubbery. (See Figure 8–3A)
*- If boxes are not available, they can be made with squares of white construction paper in this manner.
- Fold the square in half and in half again the long way.
- Open the paper, and hold it so the fold is perpendicular to the body.
- Now fold the paper once, and then a second time the long way.
- Open the paper, there are 16 squares.
- Make slits at the 4 inside points illustrated, and then paste the flap over the center outside squares. (See Figure 8–3B) A wonderful box is formed.

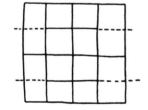

Figure 8–3B

A contest for the most beautiful construction made would be a wonderful outcome of the lesson. Why not display the monuments on worktables in the hall, along with a ballot box? The children could vote on the monument they liked best, and drop their opinion in the ballot box. After a period of time set by the teacher, the ballots could be counted to establish the winner. A certificate of merit, or a blue ribbon would be a most appropriate award.

Easter Projects

Easter lends itself to a wide variety of art subjects. Here are a number of ideas that you may want your class to try during this season.

Mock Stained Glass Windows

Paper Construction

Stained glass panels are a wonderful project for the Easter season. These are only made of paper, but when viewed from afar, they are most impressive.

Basic Materials: 18 by 24 inch black construction paper, colored cellophane or tissue, scissors, paper cement.

Procedure:

- Fold the black paper in half.
- With chalk draw a design on one side of the fold.
- Make the design bold and simple, the pieces holding the design together must be thick.
- Cut the design segments out of both pieces of the folded black paper.
- Now cut pieces of tissue or cellophane and fit them behind each opening.
- Repeat colors in some areas of the symmetrical design to add interest to your composition.
- Cement the colored paper on the side used for sketching. (See Figure 8–4A, B, C)

A wonderful place to display the windows would be in the auditorium or library windows. Mount them in blocks so they simulate large stained glass windows.

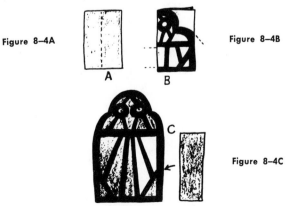

Figure 8–4A

Figure 8–4B

Figure 8–4C

Easter Mobile

Mixed Media

Mobiles are always a treat to make. Here is a wonderful one that the students will enjoy long after they have completed them.

Basic Materials: 2 by 10 inch strip of lightweight cardboard, manila paper, scissors, crayons, string, felt tip marker, staples.

Figure 8–5

Procedure:

- Decorate the strip of cardboard with crayon and felt tip marker.
- Staple the strip into a circle shape.
- On the manila paper draw a number of eggs and decorate them with crayon and felt tip marker.
- Cut them out and attach them with various length pieces of string to the cardboard circle. (See Figure 8–5)

The mobiles make a wonderful display if they are attached to the various light fixtures in the classroom. Another suggestion might be to ask teachers in your wing or area to duplicate the lesson with their class. The many mobiles then could be used as a wonderful display on the light fixtures in the hall corridors.

How Do You Draw a Rabbit?

Crayon and Mixed Media

Here is a wonderful way to teach the children a few rudimentary ideas about drawing.

Basic Materials: 12 by 18 inch manila paper, crayons, scissors, 12 by 18 inch pastel construction paper, paste.

Figure 8–6A

Procedure:

- A simple rabbit drawing is made by drawing a large oval shape for the body, and a smaller oval shape for a head. (See Figure 8–6A)
- If it is the front view of the rabbit, draw his 2 upper legs and his 2 lower legs.
- If it is the side view add 2 side view legs to the rabbit with just a suggestion of his legs on the opposite side. (See Figure 8–6B)

Figure 8–6B

- If it is a back view, attach the 2 upper legs, and 2 lower legs showing their back view, and sketch in a tail. (See Figure 8–6C)
- A rabbit face is made easily if a V is put in the head oval for the nose. (See Figure 8–6D)
- Now suggest that the children draw a picture of a rabbit or rabbits and fill in the ears, eyes and whiskers.
- Next crayon the rabbit, cut it out and paste it to a piece of pastel construction paper.
- Decorate the picture with a background of flowers and Easter Eggs for a gay spring picture.

Figure 8–6C

Now mount the pictures on a larger background paper and exhibit them on a bulletin board. A good title might be *The Many Ways with a Rabbit*.

SPECIAL NOTE TO TEACHERS: Children may be shown how to sketch something that is not familiar to them. However, after it is shown, the teacher must erase the sketch she uses as a demonstration immediately. Never allow a child to copy work. His power of observance is great. Make sure he uses it to advantage.

Figure 8–6D

Funny Bunny

Paint

Have each child in your class become a funny bunny. Everyone will enjoy this lesson.

Basic Materials: 12 by 24 inch pieces of oaktag, cups of assorted tempera paint, brushes, scissors.

Figure 8–7

Procedure:

- Hold the oaktag the long way and about 6 inches up from the bottom of the paper cut an oval the size of a face shape.
- Now start to paint the area around the cutout area like a rabbit head. (See Figure 8–7)
- Add pouchy cheeks on the side of the oval shape, above the oval add huge rabbit ears, and below the oval paint a girl's collar or a boy's tie and shirt.
- When the rabbit is completed paint a background for it. It can be any type of background—a field, the inside of a rabbit hutch, a farm scene.

The Funny Bunny project is best displayed by the creators.

Why not have the class form a line wearing their props and visit another grade close by to show off their handiwork? Everyone will enjoy this different concept in art shows.

Rabbit Centerpiece

Cut Paper

A unique centerpiece can be made with this 3-dimensional rabbit idea.

Basic Materials: 12 by 18 inch gray, brown or white construction paper, scissors, crayons, staplers, cotton.

Procedure:

- Draw a rabbit in a lying-down position on the colored paper of your choice. (See Figure 8–8)
- Make sure he fits the paper the long way.
- Now decorate him with crayon and cut him out.
- Staple the front legs of the rabbit to his tail.
- Add a cotton tail to the stapled area.

Figure 8–8

The rabbit ring shape makes a wonderful centerpiece for a table. A small container can be filled with jelly beans or colored eggs and placed in the opening of the ring. Another suggestion would be to use the rabbit rings as covers for plant holders or other containers in the classroom. They add to the spring aura of the room.

Stand-up Rabbit

Mixed Media

Three dimensional projects make most desirable art lessons. This idea utilizes a rabbit cutout in a delightful way.

Basic Materials: 12 by 18 inch brown paper, crayons, scissors, cotton, paste.

Figure 8–9A

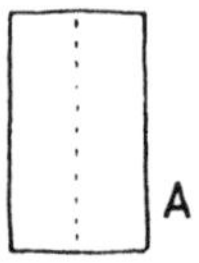

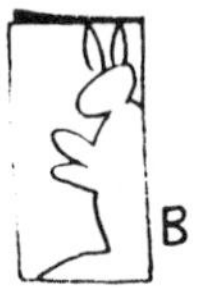

Procedure:

- Fold the brown paper in half the long way.
- Suggest that the children draw the side view of the rabbit, but make sure the back of the rabbit is drawn toward the fold.
- Next cut the rabbit with the paper still folded.
- Now, using heavy crayon, decorate the rabbit with people clothes both front and back.
- Add a cotton tail for finishing touches. (See Figure 8–9A, B, C)

Figure 8–9B

Stand the rabbit clan along the window sill for display. Since the rabbits stand by themselves, group them uniformly—talking, walking, or just standing aloof. A different way to display an art project is always fun!

Figure 8–9C

Stone Rabbits

Stone Construction

A stone is a very important object. It is found almost everywhere, and it can be used in so many interesting ways. Here is one good art idea that can be done with an ordinary stone.

Basic Materials: stones of all sizes and shapes, felt tip markers, assorted colored scraps of felt, scissors, Duco cement.

Procedure:

- Ask the children to bring interesting shaped stones to school. Wash them and have them available for use on the day of the art lesson.
- First let the children choose a stone from the initial group.
- Suggest that they examine the stone from all angles, and try to imagine the stone becoming a rabbit shape of some form. It could be a rabbit sitting, standing, hopping, lying down.
- Use the felt tip marker to accentuate the rabbit shape.
- Draw the portions of the body, ears and features.
- If the stone shape lends itself readily to the ink drawing, stop here. (See Figure 8–10A)
- If not, cut and paste pieces of felt on the stone for the ears or other features of the rabbit for easy recognition. (See Figure 8–10B)
- Another type of rabbit can be made with 2 or more stones glued on top of one another. The stones can be parts of the body.
- Add legs and features with felt tip marker.
- Ears can be cut from felt scraps and glued in place for a very realistic rabbit. (See Figure 8–10C) Suggest that the children make several rabbits of various types.

Figure 8–10A

Figure 8–10B

Figure 8–10C

The best place to display the rabbits would be in a hall showcase. Make a sign saying *Stone Rabbits on Parade* and place it behind the exhibit.

Burlap Rabbits

Burlap Texture

The texture of burlap is nubby and nice. It would be a wonderful material to use for a rabbit body. Suggest that your pupils make burlap rabbits.

Basic Materials: burlap about 9 by 12 inches, assorted colored paper, felt tip pens, scissors, paper cement, 18 by 24 inch yellow or pink paper, crayons.

Procedure:

Figure 8–11

- Cut the burlap into a rabbit shape.
- With felt tip pen add the features, legs and arms to the burlap.
- Next cement the rabbit to a large piece of colored paper.
- Now with crayon and cut paper make a different kind of background.
- Make the background with an occupational theme. Imagine that the rabbit could be at a circus, in a police station, in a department store, in a school, in a doctor's office.

When the picture is completed, it would be fun for the children to show their pictures and tell a little about the occupation they chose for their burlap rabbits. (See Figure 8–11)

Wallpaper Rabbit

Wallpaper

Different materials and textures are always fun to use in an art lesson. This idea utilizes wallpaper in an unusual way. Try it for a special Easter treat!

Basic Materials: wallpaper sample book, crayons, assorted pieces of scrap construction paper, scissors, paste, 18 by 24 inch light blue or yellow construction paper.

Procedure:

- Choose a page from the wallpaper book.
- On the back of the wallpaper (which is solid in color), sketch a large rabbit in pencil.
- Cut it out and paste it on the colored paper background wallpaper side up.

- Now use crayons and cut paper to decorate the rabbit.
- Use heavy crayon to draw the rabbit's features and cut and paste colored paper clothing on the rabbit.
- If it is a lady rabbit make sure she has a fancy Easter bonnet on her head.
- If it is a gentleman rabbit, make him a high-hat or a derby.
- Dress the rabbit as much or as little as you care to do, but let a lot of the wallpaper remain showing.
- When the rabbit is completed start to work on the background. Use crayon, cut paper or both to complete the pictures. The background could be almost anything—the rabbit in church, on Main Street, in his home, or in school. Stress originality when completing the picture. (See Figure 8–12)

Figure 8–12

The Wallpaper Rabbits would make wonderful hall displays. Mount the pictures on black paper and tape them to the walls outside your room. Label the display with a sign that might say: *There Are All Kinds of Rabbit Folk* or *A Different Rabbit in Our Midst.*

Egg Diorama

Cut Paper

Here is a different way to make an Easter Egg. It is reminiscent of the very nice sugar peep-hole eggs that you see during the Easter season.

Basic Materials: 18 by 24 inch white paper, scissors, crayons, assorted colored scraps, scraps of tissue, paper cement, 1 by 9 inch strip of cardboard.

Procedure:

- Fold the 18 by 24 inch white paper in half.
- Cut a large egg with the fold intact. (See Figure 8–13, Steps A, B, C, D, E)

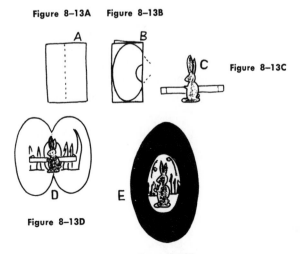

Figure 8–13A   **Figure 8–13B**

Figure 8–13C

Figure 8–13D

Figure 8–13E

- Now cut half a circle out of the fold for the peep-hole.
- Open the egg and decorate it with crayons, cut paper and tissue.
- When the egg is completely decorated, set it aside.
- Now take a scrap of colored paper and cut out a little rabbit.
- Fasten the rabbit to the center of the cardboard strip. (See Figure 8–13, Step C)
- Next turn the egg to the inside, and carefully place the rabbit over the peep-hole.
- Paste the cardboard strip to each side of the egg. (See Figure 8–13, Step D)
- When the paste is dried, close the egg and staple the back and sides. (The cardboard should keep the egg puffed out.) When you look into the peep-hole there is a nice three-dimensional scene. (See Figure 8–13, Step E)

The children will be so enthusiastic about their handiwork that they will want to take them home immediately for their parents' appraisal—let them!

Giant Conglomerate Egg

Crayon—Group Project

Group projects are excellent learning experiences. This idea involves groups of six children working together as a team. The lesson is basically simple but the results are quite impressive!

Basic Materials: mural paper, scissors, crayons, 24 by 36 inch colored construction paper, paper cement.

Procedure:

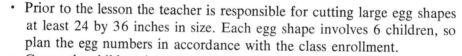

Figure 8–14A   Figure 8–14B

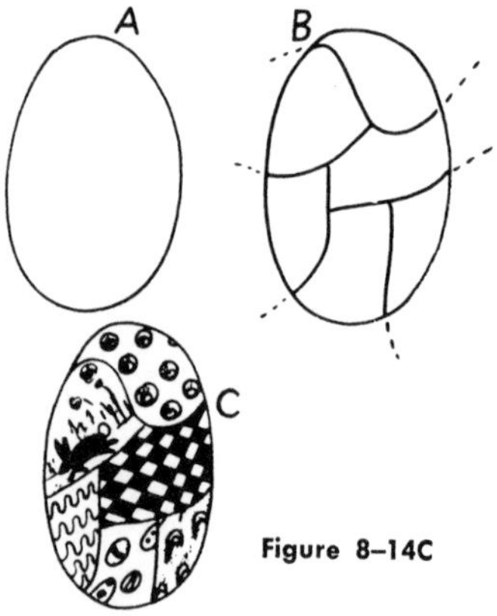

Figure 8–14C

- Prior to the lesson the teacher is responsible for cutting large egg shapes at least 24 by 36 inches in size. Each egg shape involves 6 children, so plan the egg numbers in accordance with the class enrollment.
- Group the children in teams of 6 in various parts of the room. Choose one child as the captain of the group.
- Now give each group an egg, but not in its original form. Cut the egg in 6 pieces like a jig-saw puzzle and each of the 6 children will receive one of the pieces. (See Figure 8–14, Step A, B, C)
- Next have the children decorate the egg portion that they have heavily with crayon in any way they choose.
- Allow a designated amount of time for work on the egg design, then suggest that the groups form to assemble the egg parts. (See Figure 8–14, Step C)
- The captain of the group can assign duties to his team.

- Two children paste the egg puzzle together on the 24 by 36 inch colored paper; one cuts grass and cements it under the egg; and the other 3 can draw and cut out rabbits, chickens, ducks or small decorated eggs for placement on the assembled picture.

When the Egg projects are completed, they make wonderful large decorations for the cafeteria or hall.

Another way to display the eggs would be to assemble them after they are crayoned, cut them out as large cracked egg shapes and group them together in piles on a large bulletin board. Under the pile of huge eggs tack lots of grass, and many small cutout eggs. Cut letters in bright yellow or purple that say: *Eggs—by the Dozen!* or *Eggs Mean Easter!*

Egg Shape Hangings

Plaster of Paris and Glass

Here is a unique twist to the usual Easter Egg project. Have the class make plaster of Paris Egg hangings decorated with bits of broken colored glass.

Basic Materials: plaster of Paris, aluminum foil oval tins, scraps of broken colored glass bottles.

Procedure:

- Place the pieces of the broken glass in an attractive arrangement in the bottom of the aluminum tin.
- Now mix the plaster of Paris to the consistency of whipped cream and pour it into the tin mold.
- Before it dries put a hairpin or wire hook at the top of the shape for hanging.
- Let the plaster dry thoroughly and then remove the cast from the mold. Wipe the glass portion clean. See Figure 8–15, Steps A, B, C)

These shapes are most attractive hanging at various levels in a school window.

(As an alternative, the plaster can be changed to any color by just adding color before mixing the material.)

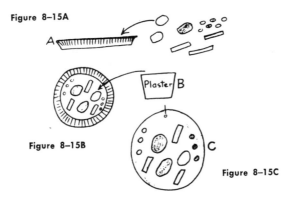

Figure 8–15A

Figure 8–15B

Figure 8–15C

Stuffed Eggs

Paint

These are not the kind you eat, but they certainly will be appealing to the children. Use Stuffed Eggs as an Easter art lesson.

Basic Materials: two sheets of 12 by 18 inch manila paper, cups of assorted tempera paint, brushes, stapler, newspaper.

Procedure:

Figure 8–16A   Figure 8–16B

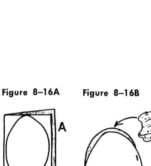

- Cut 2 identical egg shapes the largest possible from the manila paper.
- Start stapling the 2 shapes together at sides and bottom.
- Let the top remain open for stuffing.
- Now crumple newspaper and carefully stuff your egg pillow. (See Figure 8–16, Steps A, B, C)
- When more paper cannot be added, staple the top closed.
- Now decorate the egg with designs. When one side is painted, and dry, turn the egg shape over and repeat the painting on it.

A piece of string can be attached to the Stuffed Eggs and they can be hung at various lengths in a window. Another idea would be to stack them in corners of the room or in a display case on green excelsior grass for a totally different treatment.

Figure 8–16C

Easter Egg Melange

Paint

A melange of Easter Eggs will make an exciting art lesson for your class.

Basic Materials: 12 by 18 inch manila paper, water color paints, brushes, cups of water, pencil.

Procedure:

- With pencil sketch egg shapes of all sizes—helter-skelter on the manila paper. Overlap some eggs, but do not crowd the paper. Arrange the medley of eggs in an interesting way.
- Next paint the eggs with all kinds of nice designs and color.
- When the eggs are completed, fill in the spaces and areas that are not colored.

- Fill in these spaces with a solid dark color of paint. (See Figure 8–17) This will make the melange very impressive.

The best suggestion for the melange would be to use it for the cover of some type of school work. They might most successfully be used to carry home the art projects for the month of April.

Figure 8–17

Easter Egg Card

Paper, Felt Tip Marker

A personal card is always a treat to receive from someone. Suggest that the children make a card for their parents, and during an English period perhaps a verse can be created to insert in the card.

Basic Materials: 12 by 18 inch pastel colored construction paper, crayons, scissors, felt tip pens.

Procedure:

- Fold the colored paper in half the short way.
- Draw a large sketch lightly with pencil of a huge egg shape. Make sure the fold of the paper becomes the hinge of the card. (See Figure 8–18, Steps A, B, C)

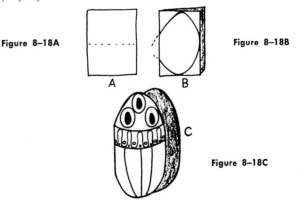

Figure 8–18A

Figure 8–18B

Figure 8–18C

- Cut the egg shaped card and begin to decorate it with the felt tip marker and crayon.
- When both front and back of the card are completed, create a verse for the written portion inside the card.
- Now very carefully print the verse with felt tip pen.

The day before the Easter vacation have the children deliver their project. The parents will enjoy this personal message.

Self-Styled Easter Egg Hunt

Stone Decoration

Here is a new twist to the Easter Egg Hunt. Have the children make the eggs for the hunt. This art project plus fun idea will make the lesson a joyous one.

Basic Materials: stones, cups of assorted tempera paint, brushes, newspapers, felt tip pens.

Procedure:

- The appointed day for this lesson suggest that the children bring 3 stones to school for the project.
- Cover the working area with newspaper, and let the children decorate their stones with paint.
- Advise them to cover the stone completely with color, let it dry and then decorate it with felt tip pens.
- When the eggs are completed put them aside until the day of the egg hunt.

If the weather is satisfactory, the hunt is most enjoyable outdoors. The stones should be placed by the teacher or a parent in hidden spots in the playfield at a time when the children are busy with their lessons.

At the appointed time, the children should be taken outdoors for the Egg Hunt. Suggest that each child carry a paper bag during the contest. The winner is the one who collects the most eggs. It is fun to include a special gold or silver egg in the hunt, and the one who discovers this egg wins a bonus prize. No one really does not become a winner because everyone will be able to keep the stone eggs that he finds.

(If weather should be inclement, use the gymnasium or auditorium for the Egg Hunt.)

Three Dimensional Egg Tree

Miniature Egg Stabiles

This is a wonderful way to utilize natural material and man made materials in an art lesson.

Basic Materials: small dead tree branch, Plasticine, aluminum foil containers, assorted colored construction paper, scissors, crayons, string.

Procedure:

- Fill the foil container with Plasticine, and anchor the small branch in it. (Small pebbles or stones can be used in place of Plasticine.)
- Set the small tree shape aside.
- Now draw many egg shapes on the colored paper and decorate them on both sides with crayon.
- Cut them out and tie them to the branches of the tree shape.
- Add as many of the cutout eggs that are needed to make the tree a true egg tree. (See Figure 8–19)

The egg trees make wonderful centerpiece decorations. They make excellent Easter presents to take home to Mom.

Figure 8–19

Easter Egg Tree

Crayon

A nice way to make an Easter Egg Tree is with crayon and paper. Try this idea for an Easter art lesson.

Basic Materials: 12 by 18 inch manila paper, crayons.

Procedure:

- On a large piece of manila paper held the long way, suggest that the children draw a huge tree with their black or brown crayon.
- Now suggest that they make the tree into an Easter Egg Tree by drawing eggs on the many branches.
- Color the eggs with crayon, make some of them solid colors, others can be highly decorated with design.
- Make the composition as colorful as possible.
- Add as many eggs as are needed to make the tree look like an Egg Tree. (See Figure 8–20)

Figure 8–20

- Now draw a crayoned background for the picture. It could be a scene with children picking up the fallen eggs, a gay spring scene with a medley of flowers and grass, or it could be a make believe scene of some sort.

When the picture is completed, mount them on black paper and display them on a wall in the classroom. Entitle the display—*A Forest of Egg Trees* or *Many Species of Egg Trees*.

Stand-up Easter Basket

Cut Paper

This is a wonderful way to use the Easter Basket idea in an art lesson.

Basic Materials: 12 by 18 inch yellow construction paper, 9 by 12 inch manila paper, crayons, scissors, paste.

Procedure:

- Fold the 12 by 18 inch yellow paper in half the short way.
- Draw a basket on the paper with the fold at the top as the handle of the basket. (See Figure 8–21, Steps A, B, C)

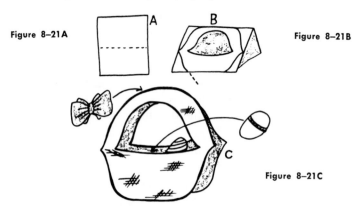

Figure 8–21A

Figure 8–21B

Figure 8–21C

- Cut out the basket and put it aside.
- Now make many egg shapes on the manila paper.
- Decorate them with crayon, cut them out and paste them tucked inside the 3-dimensional basket.
- Cut a bow out of a piece of scrap construction paper and attach it to the handle top to complete the project.

A good place to use the baskets might be in the cafeteria during the week before Easter. They might be grouped in threes or fours on the tables in an interesting arrangement. They certainly make a wonderful addition to the Easter spirit of the school.

Easter Basket

Paper Bag

A basket is an Easter essential. Here is an idea which involves almost no expense, and produces a wonderful project.

Basic Materials: small paper bag with rectangular bottom, scissors, crayon, staples, tissue.

Procedure:

- Cut the bag so that the ears become the handle of the rabbit basket. (See Figure 8–22)
- Then make features for the rabbit face with crayon.
- Add bits of black paper strips for whiskers to complete the basket.
- Staple the ears together to make the basket more sturdy.
- Fill the basket with tissue straw. This is done by cutting the tissue into very fine shreds.

Figure 8–22

Display the baskets on the sill of the classroom window. Who knows what will happen to fill the contents of the basket during the week prior to Easter. Time will tell!

Cereal Box Easter Basket

Paper Construction

A wonderful sturdy Easter basket can be made with a round or square cereal box that is donated by Mom.

Basic Materials: cereal box (round or square), paper confetti, paste, cardboard handle 1 by 6 inches.

Procedure:

- Cut the cereal box away so a portion of about 4 inches is left as a base.
- Using a paper punch, punch assorted colored scrap paper into piles of paper confetti.
- Now cover the outside base of the cardboard basket with paste and roll it into the paper confetti for an unusual decoration.
- Staple the cardboard handle on the basket, cover it lightly with paste and roll it also in a pile of confetti to complete the basket.
  (See Figure 8–23, Steps A, B, C)

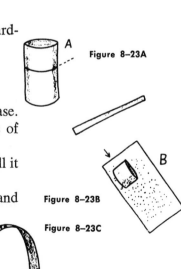

Figure 8–23A

Figure 8–23B

Figure 8–23C

In Your Easter Bonnet

Mixed Media

The Easter bonnet has become a great tradition at Easter. Most times the joy is limited to the female adult. Why not expose everyone to the bonnet craze?

Basic Materials: paper plates, paper doilies, assorted scraps of construction paper, tissue paper, pipe cleaners, yarn, paper cement, scissors.

Procedure:

Figure 8–24

- Give each child a paper plate, scissors, paper cement and have the other material readily available for them to use.
- Suggest that the class create personal hats of their own styling.
- The paper plate is the base, and the yarn is needed to tie the hat on each child.
- Suggest that a theme be used when planning the hat. It could be a nautical, spring, flower, bird, household, hobby or toy theme. Stress original themes! (See Figure 8–24)
- The construction paper and tissue can be used to cut shapes representing the theme.
- Pipe cleaners can be shaped into ornaments for the hat.
- Doilies can add to hats which have a feminine appearance. It will be exciting and quite interesting to survey the results of the children's efforts.

The best way to display the bonnets would be to have an Easter Parade. The children love to participate in such a function and it will be a real treat if other classes join you in this project.

Ask the Principal, Nurse and Librarian to act as judges for the Easter Bonnet contest. Perhaps you can have a prize for the prettiest, funniest and most original hat. The experience will be one you will want to repeat.

Jelly Bean Skyscraper

Jelly Bean Construction

Here is a wonderful new idea that utilizes the toothpick and leftover jelly beans (that the children supply), in a great after Easter art lesson.

Basic Materials: jelly beans, toothpicks, compass.

Bonus Materials: wood or cardboard base, tempera paint, brushes, Duco cement.

Procedure:

- A construction means to build something, and that is precisely what is done in this lesson.
- Give each child a compass, a pile of toothpicks, the jelly beans—and the creation can start.
- Make a base by putting a jelly bean on each end of a toothpick. (If the toothpick does not readily go into the jelly bean, pierce it first with a compass point.)
- Continue to add toothpicks and jelly beans until you see a definite pattern forming. Try to build the construction up high with many open spaces. Avoid tight closed areas. (See Figure 8–25)

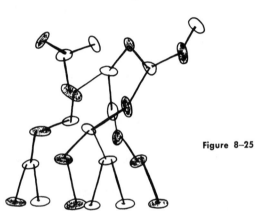

Figure 8–25

- The construction can be as large or as small as the builder would like it to be.
- When they are completed, they are handsome just as they are, however, they may be glued to a wood base or sheet of cardboard with Duco cement for more durability.
- If more color is desired, they can be painted with tempera paint.

Three dimensional material like the Jelly Bean Constructions are shown to their best advantage in a display case. When exhibiting them, attempt to put prop boxes in the showcase so the constructions can be shown at different elevations. A good title for the display might be: *Anyone Can Be a Builder with Jelly Beans,* or *Jelly Bean Skyscraper.*

Live Bunnies

Cut Paper

Send your class home dressed as live bunnies the day before the Easter Recess.

Basic Materials: cardboard strips, brown or white paper 9 by 12 inches, stapler, cotton, safety pin.

Procedure:

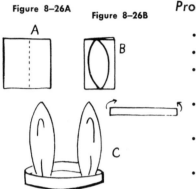

Figure 8–26A   Figure 8–26B

Figure 8–26C

- Cut the cardboard strips so they fit around the children's heads.
- Staple them to form a circle.
- Fold the 9 by 12 brown or white paper in half the long way, and cut out 2 rabbit ears.
- Staple them to the circle where the ears should be. (See Figure 8–26— Steps A, B, C)
- Just before the children leave for home, have them put on the rabbit ears, and pin a big cotton tail to their clothing in the back.
- The bunnies won't be complete unless you use an eyebrow pencil to make little whisker shapes right above the mouth.

The parents will be delighted to see their little bunnies arriving home.

WONDERFUL THINGS TO DRAW DURING APRIL

1. Draw an April Fool's trick that someone played on you. Also draw one that you played on someone.
2. Draw how you think the blue and gray uniforms looked during the Civil War.
3. Draw what makes you happy.
4. Draw a picture of some silver objects that Paul Revere might have created in his youth.
5. Draw a silly rabbit dressed in clothing.
6. Draw a rabbit just using dots.
7. Draw your Easter outfit.
8. Draw what you did on Easter Sunday.
9. Draw a rabbit delivering Easter eggs.
10. Draw how you want your Easter basket to look.
11. Draw a rabbit family.
12. Draw your Mom's Easter hat.
13. Draw a dozen eggs—decorate them.
14. Draw a picture of how you look when you have eaten too much candy.
15. Draw the Easter present you liked best.
16. Draw a picture of Monticello.
17. Draw a placemat for Easter.
18. Draw your Church during Easter or Passover.
19. Draw an Easter rabbit's home.
20. Draw a rabbit's egg factory.

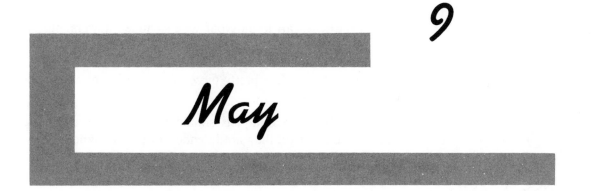

9

May

May . . . we are finally liberated from cold breezes for another winter. Nature has again proven her wonderful powers. The trees have bright green leaves. Flowers are blooming everywhere. It is good to be alive!

This month commemorates three important occasions: Loyalty Day, Mother's Day and Memorial Day. Experiment with some of the following May Ideas for your art lessons this month.

Miniature May Day Bouquet

Mixed Media

Scrap material supplied by Mother can be utilized in such fine projects. Ask her to raid her sewing box for this May Day idea.

Basic Materials: empty wooden thread spools, scraps of felt, bits of wire, beads, fancy buttons, bits of ribbon, Plasticine, scissors, tempera paint in pastel colors, brushes, paper cement.

Procedure:

- Fill the hole of the thread spools with Plasticine, paint the wood area, and set the spools aside to dry. These are the flower containers. They are in miniature, so the flowers made for it must be tiny and dainty.

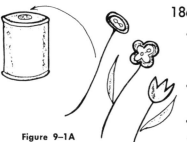

Figure 9–1A

- Cut pieces of wire about 2 or 3 inches long, fasten beads, fancy buttons or felt flowered shapes to the wire stems. (See Figure 9–1A) These are the flowers for your bouquet.
- Cut pieces of green felt leaves and attach them to the wire flowers with paper cement.
- Make many flowers.
- When the spool is dried, start to put your wire stemmed flowers into the Plasticine.
- Add flowers until the bouquet is satisfactory in size.
- Then for a finishing touch tie a pretty piece of scrap ribbon around the spool. (See Figure 9–1B)

On May Day these Miniature Bouquets should be placed secretly on a table, desk or shelf for the person they are intended to please. Who will the person be?

Figure 9–1B

Milk Carton Basket for May Day

Mixed Media

Use the school milk containers for this very fine basket idea.

Basic Materials: milk containers, strips of 1 by 6 inch cardboard, scissors, pastel shades of tempera paint, liquid soap, brushes, stapler, newspaper.

Procedure:

- Rinse the milk container well, and then cut the top off the carton to make a little square basket.
- Attach the cardboard strips to the sides of the basket with the stapler.
- Next add liquid soap to the tempera paint so the surface of the waxed container can be painted. (Without the soap the paint will not adhere to the waxy surface.)
- Cover the work area with newspapers and then paint the entire basket with a solid color paint.
- When it is dried, decorate it with designs in other colors.

The basket is a sturdy, gay container for a May Day Basket or a basket for a future party. (See Figure 9–2)

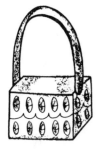

Figure 9–2

May Day Baskets

Paper Construction

This basket is frilly and very elegant to behold.

Basic Materials: 12 by 18 inch yellow, pink or light blue construction paper, large paper doilies, scraps of metallic paper, paper cement, scissors.

Procedure:

- Cut the large colored paper into half a circle and form it into a cone shape. (See Figure 9–3, Steps A, B, C)

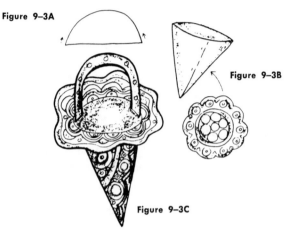

Figure 9–3A

Figure 9–3B

Figure 9–3C

- Out of the scraps remaining cut a strip of paper for a handle and paste it to the cone.
- Now very carefully roll and paste the white doily around the cone shape. Bend some of the doily back in some areas to make it frilly.
- Now cut the metallic paper scraps into little circles, squares, triangles or star shapes and cement them in a scattered fashion all over the lacy cone and handle. The cone basket is ready for use!

Pouch Basket

Paper Construction

This May Day Basket is easy to construct and makes a delightful holder. Notice that no scissors or paste are necessary for this project.

Basic Materials: 9 by 9 inch pastel colored paper, pipe cleaners, felt tip markers, scotch tape, paper punch.

Procedure:

- Fold the 9 inch square of paper in half, then fold each side into the middle fold. (See Figure 9–4A)

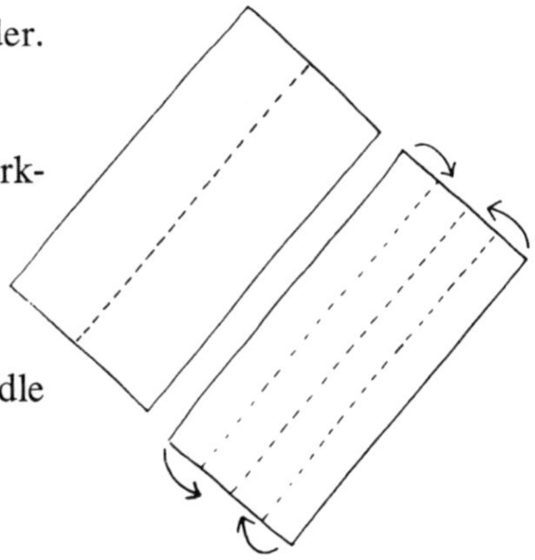

Figure 9–4A

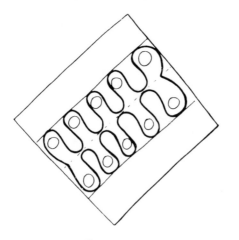

Figure 9–4B   Figure 9–4C   Figure 9–4D

- Open the paper and decorate the indicated area with felt tip marker designs. (See Figure 9–4B)
- When the designated section is completely decorated, refold the paper and then fold this in half so that the open areas are together.
- Now carefully put a piece of scotch tape over the 4 corners of the holder. This fastens the holder together. (See Figure 9–4C)
- Punch a little hole with the paper punch through the area where the tape has been fastened, and loop and attach the pipe cleaner through it. (See Figure 9–4D) The pouch basket is completed.

May Day Baskets are wonderful gifts to give people that you especially like. Fill the baskets with tulips, daffodils, and violets or any other flowers the children are able to supply.

The procedure is to slip the baskets on the door of the recipient's house— ring the bell, and quickly disappear. A lovely May Day gift is always such a wonderful treat for the lucky person who receives one! Revive this old-fashioned ritual with your class. You will be pleased if you do!

The May Pole

Mixed Media

May would not be complete unless the children had an opportunity to participate in a May Pole dance or an art lesson dealing with the much celebrated May Pole. Here is a new and unusual way to introduce a May Pole art lesson. In the lesson we will use props. These are things which are added to a picture to create more interest and authenticity to a drawing.

Basic Materials: ice cream or lollipop sticks, Duco cement, 12 by 18 inch manila paper, crayons, bits of thin ribbon or yarn.

Procedure:

- Glue the stick toward the middle of the manila paper. This is the May Pole.

- Then with crayon proceed to draw figures of children around the May Pole. (See Figure 9–5)
- Draw both boys and girls dancing around the pole. As many or as few children as desired can be drawn.
- When the dancers are completed, draw a suitable background for the May Pole dance. Is the dance being performed indoors, on a lawn outdoors, or in a school yard?
- When the background is completed, cut pieces of the yarn or ribbon and attach them with cement to the May Pole top at one end, and to the hands of one of the children in the picture at the other end. This completes the May Pole picture.

Figure 9–5

What a wonderful way to use this May subject in a very special way. Mount the pictures on a large piece of black paper and tape them to a wall near the gymnasium. It will be interesting for the children to compare the dance they may do in the physical education period with the pictures that the children create about the May Pole.

Special Projects for Mother's Day

Design a Set of Dishes for Mother

Colored Pencil

Art surrounds us. It is manifested in the clothes we wear, the furniture we surround ourselves with, the way we fashion our hair, the house we choose to live in, the way our food is arranged when it is served, the patterns on our china and silverware. Literally, everything we touch or see has had the touch of a craftsman—sometimes good, sometimes bad. Regardless, it is important that we as teachers make the children aware of how important art and design is in their everyday lives. Here is a wonderful lesson that can be utilized for a Mother's Day art project.

Basic Materials: 12 by 18 inch white paper, compass, scissors, scrap paper, colored pencils.

Procedure:

- Prior to the lesson, show the children a variety of different dinner plate designs. Discuss why some are more attractive than others, and what makes them better in design than others. Then suggest that the children design a plate for a set of dishes for Mother's Day.
- First with the compass draw the largest circle possible on the white paper for a plate shape.

- Make a smaller circle within this for the rim of the plate.
- Cut the plate shape out and put it aside.
- Now on scrap paper make some designs which might be desirable to use on a plate—for the reasons discussed earlier in the lesson.
- Experiment with designs until one is pleasing, next make a trial sketch of where it is to be used—around the plate, in the center of the plate, or as an overall pattern on the plate.
- When the idea is finalized, begin to draw it on the white paper shape with colored pencil.
- Sketch it lightly first, and make portions darker as you go along so the design simulates a real china pattern.
- If a rim is desired, add it also with the colored pencil. (See Figure 9–6)

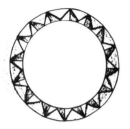

Figure 9–6

Now display the plates in an exciting way—on a large bulletin board put strips of brown paper across the entire board in a horizontal fashion to give the appearance of shelving. At the top of the bulletin board tack brown paper which is cut in the shape of a China closet top. Next arrange the plates on the mock shelves. Tack large cut paper letters at the bottom of the display saying: *We Only Have Originals in Our Closets,* or *Designing China Is Fun!* There will be a multitude of favorable comments about this unusual display.

Place Mats for Mom

Crayon on Textile

Place mats for Mom! This is a wonderful art lesson and take-home project, made with fabric.

Basic Materials: discarded white sheeting cut into pieces approximately 12 by 18 inches in size, crayons, an electric iron, pad of newspapers.

Procedure:

- Suggest that the children draw designs on the textile with heavy crayon.
- The design can be an all-over variety depicting a scene; it could be designs or pictures in the middle of the place mat with a design in the corners; it could be an all-over repeated design.
- Apply the crayon heavily with the strokes going in one direction for easier application.
- Do not design too close to the edge.
- When the place mat has been designed, the next step is to permanentize the color in the cloth. This is done by placing the cloth, crayon side down on a pad of newspapers.
- Iron the back of the designed cloth until the heat of the iron melts the

crayon color into the fabric. Now the mat can be washed without hindering the design. (See Figure 9–7A)

· Next start to fringe the four sides of the place mat.
· Make the fringe at least ¾ inches wide all around the cloth. This enhances the appearance of the mat. (When fringing the cloth, a straight pin can be an invaluable help when a stubborn thread refuses to budge in the fringing process.) (See Figure 9–7B)

Figure 9–7A   Figure 9–7B

The fringing is tedious, but it can be a happy affair if the teacher offers a prize to the pupil who collects the largest ball of fringe thread. A piece of fruit or a small box of raisins is all that is needed for a prize.

When the place mat is completed, carefully fold it up and wrap it in a piece of tissue paper. The present is ready for Special Delivery to Mother.

Fancy Foibles

Felt-tip Markers—Doilies

Art is made exciting and is a true learning process if the children work with various materials and tools. Try utilizing two commercial products—a paper doily and colored felt tip markers for a Mother's Day treat.

Basic Materials: large white paper doilies, colored felt tip markers, paper cement, 12 by 18 inch black paper, newspaper.

Procedure:

· Cover the working area with newspaper.
· Visualize a colored design on the doily.
· Start with the center of the doily and a colored marker.
· Color a portion of the doily in an enclosed lacy area, and as the lacy design proceeds in the pattern change colors from time to time until the entire doily is covered with colored ink. (See Figure 9–8)

Now mount the designed doily on black paper. The doily designs are bright and quite attractive. A bulletin board display of them is quite impressive. Mount the pictures side by side to form a huge all-over design. Entitle the display: *Fancy Foibles for May!* or *Design a Doily!*

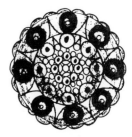

Figure 9–8

Mom's Shopping Bag

Paper Bag Design

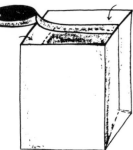

Figure 9–9A

May is the month to really fete Mother. Here is a wonderful idea for a special project in art, just for her.

Basic Materials: large brown paper bag, cups of assorted tempera paint, brushes, heavy yarn, stapler, masking tape, paper punch.

Procedure:

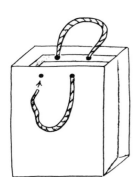

Figure 9–9B

- Fold the edge of the paper bag down about 3 inches toward the inside of the bag, and fasten it all around with a masking tape seam. (See Figure 9–9A)
- Now punch two holes with a paper punch in the front and back of the bag along the masking tape seam.
- Fasten 2 handles of yarn one in front, and one in back using the holes that were punched. (See Figure 9–9B)
- Now decorate the bag with paint. A picture of Mom's favorite flower, animal, or bird would be a good subject to use on the front of the bag.
- Use a color or a portion of the design in your picture to repeat in a painted border around the top of the bag. (See Figure 9–C)

When the bag is complete, set it aside to dry. Now carefully wrap it in tissue paper and tie it with a piece of yarn.

The day before Mother's Day have the pupils take the gift to Mom for her special treat. It will be a handsome, usable present that will please Mom immensely.

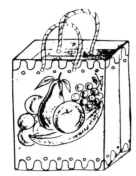

Figure 9–9C

Wall Hanging

Water Color on Fabric

Applying crayon to a textile is quite a common occurrence, but here is a technique that involves painting fabric with water color paint. Try the idea for a Mother's Day project.

Basic Materials: pieces of discarded sheeting approximately 9 by 20 inches, box of water color paints, pointed brush, cup of water, scrap soap, trial paper, pencil, newspaper, felt tip marker, white tissue paper.

Bonus Materials: ribbon scraps, medium 9 inch dowel, needle, thread, scissors.

Procedure:

- On trial paper draw a sketch of large splotchy flower designs.
- The fabric pieces are long and narrow, so keep this in mind when arranging the flowers. Use an uneven number of flowers, 3, 5, 7, in the design and arrange them in a curve. (See Figure 9–10A)
- Complete the sketch and then carefully transfer the idea to the sheeting with light pencil.
- Now carefully cover the work area with newspaper and begin to paint the sheeting with water color.
- Before each application of paint, rub the wet brush over the scrap soap. This is necessary or the paint will spread on the fabric.
- Use bright showy colors in the painting.
- When it is completed, either outline the design with black paint and a pointed brush or cover the picture with white tissue paper and outline the picture with black felt tip marker right through the tissue. (The tissue will absorb the extra ink and prevent the marker ink from spreading.) (See Figure 9–10B)

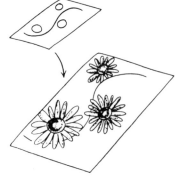

Figure 9–10A

The wall hanging is bright and very grand when finished. Enhance its appearance by hemming the sides and attaching pieces of looped ribbon at 4 places at the top of the hanging. Slip a dowel through the loops and the project takes on a very professional quality. Mother will enjoy it for a long time. (See Figure 9–10C)

Figure 9–10B

Tools Mother Uses

Magazine Picture Prop

The children are in their home environment a good part of their lives. Do they really know about the daily happenings in their habitat? Are they aware of the tools that are used to make a household function? Here is a little test in awareness that can be used as a most provocative art lesson. It is the utilization of a magazine picture in a creative drawing.

Basic Materials: old magazines, 18 by 24 inch manila paper, paste, crayons.

Figure 9–10C

Procedure:

- Prior to the lesson the teacher peruses through magazines and clips out all types of common household electrical appliances and tools. Pictures of electric irons, toasters, brooms, ovens, refrigerators, washing machines, sewing machines, vacuums, brushes, pails are some of the cutouts that can be used. Duplicates are all right to use because each child will approach the subject differently.

- Tell the children that the picture that is being given them is a very special one and when they see it they must think of a way they can incorporate the picture in a drawing of their own. Suggest that the idea used be based on how the object in the clipping is used by their parent in the home.
- Supply each child with the picture, paste, paper, and crayons.
- When the idea for the drawing has been formulated, suggest that the magazine clipping be pasted to the manila paper and that the child proceed with a crayon drawing around the pasted picture.

Figure 9–11

Teachers are always pleasantly surprised and very pleased at the creativity of the class with this project. Wonderful things seem to happen on the paper. (See Figure 9–11)

Mount the completed pictures on gray or black construction paper and display them tacked to a bulletin board in the classroom. Entitle the display: *How Mom Keeps Busy,* or *Tools Mother Uses.* Use large black cutout letters.

What a unique way to portray "Mother's Day"!

Personalized Mosaic Hand or Foot

Plastic Bottle Mosaic

Mothers are always anxious and delighted to receive a memento from their offspring. A simple tracing of a foot or hand will make this idea a new art experience.

Basic Materials: large plastic coated paper plates, Duco cement, plastic bottles of all colors cut into small pieces, scissors, pencil.

Bonus Materials: tempera paint, brushes, pipe cleaners, masking tape.

Procedure:

- If a hand is used, just lay the hand in the center of the paper plate and trace it with a pencil.
- If a foot is used, remove the shoe, place the plate on the floor, trace the foot in the center of the paper plate with pencil.
- Next, start to fill in the tracing in mosaic form using the pieces of plastic bottle for tesserae.
- Use scissors whenever necessary to add pieces of plastic to stubborn areas.
- Continue to add pieces until the entire tracing is filled in mosaic form. (See Figure 9–12)

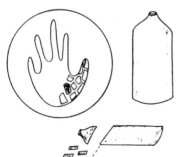

Figure 9–12

- Now add mosaic pieces in the area surrounding the foot or hand in another color, or fill the area by painting it with tempera paint.
- If the paint is used, add a small quantity of liquid soap to the paint; otherwise it will not adhere to the plastic coating.
- Next attach a pipe cleaner loop on the back of the plate with masking tape if the plate is to be hung.

Before sending the mosaics home to Mom, why not exhibit the plates as a border above the chalk boards? It will be quite unique to see the various sizes of hands and feet on display in the classroom. Have a class contest to see if the children can identify what hand or foot matches each pupil in your room. It should evolve into a humorous undertaking.

Crackle Designs

Water Color and Crayon

Children love new materials and different approaches to a project. Here is an idea which is quite unique and will make an exciting art project for Mother's Day.

Basic Materials: 12 by 18 inch manila paper, crayons, water, box of water color paints, brush (shellac, floor wax or tan shoe polish), electric iron.

Procedure:

- Draw a design on the manila paper leaving the background uncolored.
- Make the design bold, but simple. It could be a design of flowers, birds, fish or animals. Choose a subject which is Mother's favorite, and color it heavily with crayon.
- Now immerse the paper in water for a short time—do not let it become soaked.
- Next crumple and crush the paper until it has a multitude of creases.
- Open the paper, smooth it carefully, and drop water color on the surface of the crumpled paper. (See Figure 9–13A) Notice how the paint runs into the crossed lines of the paper.

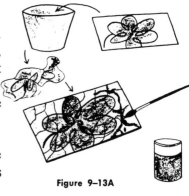

Figure 9–13A

- When the paper is dry, press it between two pieces of paper to make it smooth.
- Then apply a coat of either shellac, floor wax or tan shoe polish to preserve the crackled picture.

Figure 9–13B

- Now make a frame for the crackled picture by cutting a rectangle 10 by 16 inches out of the center of black construction paper.
- Place the picture front side down on the black frame and tape it with masking tape. (See Figure 9–13B) The results will be a handsome antique-type design.

A good place to display the pictures before they are brought to Mother would be on a large bulletin board in the classroom. Tack the pictures side by side for a grand exhibit. Entitle the display: *Antiqued Designs—Reminiscent of the Past* or *Designs with an Antique Appearance*.

Bird Stabiles

Mixed Media

A wonderful stabile can be made with paper, a piece of Plasticine and a paper towel roll. Try this great spring idea with your class.

Basic Materials: 12 by 18 inch colored construction paper, 9 by 12 inch manila paper, crayons, scissors, string, paper towel roll, stapler, piece of Plasticine.

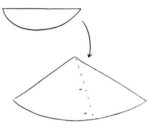

Figure 9–14A

Procedure:

· Draw and cut out half a circle from the colored paper.
· Bend it into a wide cone, and secure it with staples. (See Figure 9–14A)
· Now make a small ball of Plasticine, stick the towel roll into it, and balance the wide cone on the top of the towel roll. (See Figure 9–14B)
· Next take the manila paper and with heavy crayon draw a variety of different sized and shaped birds.
· When many birds are completed, cut them out.
· Then attach a piece of string to the bird body and the colored cone canopy.
· Add as many birds to the edge of the canopy until the composition is satisfying.
· The stabile will appear almost as a merry-go-round of birds.
· If the towel roll appears dull, decorate it with crayon or cut paper. (See Figure 9–14C)

A wonderful place to display the stabiles would be as a centerpiece in the school cafeteria. What a great way to say Spring has Sprung!

TEACHERS' SUPPLEMENT: Another way to use this lesson would be to make the shape into a mobile. Use the cone canopy with the birds attached to it as a hanging. Just tie a string from the point of the cone and the mobile is ready to attach to a light fixture for display. (See Figure 9–14D)

Figure 9–14B

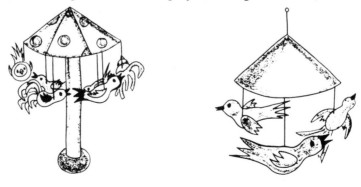

Figure 9–14C   Figure 9–14D

Our Bird Friends

Craypas

This is a wonderful way to introduce bird drawing to your class. However, although a sketch of something can be shown to the children, it should not be copied by them. Show what is to be shown and then erase or remove the sketch immediately.

Figure 9–15A

Basic Materials: 18 by 24 inch colored construction paper, craypas.

Procedure:

- Here is an unusual way to use the blackboard when aiding the children with a sketch. Use a small sponge and water for the drawing tool. The sketch remains just long enough for a visual picture of it, and as the water dries the picture disappears. Try the idea!
- A bird can be made with a large oval body and a small oval for a head.
- If the bird is walking on the ground, show his legs in walking position, his tail up and his beak and eyes down.
- Add a wing on the side closest to the drawer, and a suggestion of a wing sticking up on the other side. (See Figure 9–15A)

Figure 9–15B

- A flying bird is shown with an oval for a body, a smaller oval attached for a head.
- The tail is straight in line with the body.
- Add one wing spread out above the body, and another wing outspread below the body.
- The eye and beak are in line with the body, but the legs are not visible, they are tucked under the bird. (See Figure 9–15B)
- The front view of a bird is drawn with a large oval for a body, and a smaller oval for a head.
- His legs are drawn on each side of the body below the little wings.
- The eyes are placed on each side of the head, and the beak in the lower middle portion of the head. (See Figure 9–15C)

Figure 9–15C

- Birds in a nest are drawn with an oval body, smaller oval head and beak and eyes upward. (See Figure 9–15D)
- When the demonstration is ended, give the children paper and craypas.
- Suggest that they draw a picture of birds in any manner or fashion they desire, stress large drawings. The birds can be imaginary or familiar birds like robins, sparrows, wrens, blue jays, juncos, cardinals. Many various types could be shown in one picture.
- Next suggest that a suitable background be drawn for the birds in the picture. Trees, bird houses, bird baths, fences, telephone wires, city, country or town scenes are ideas that can be utilized. (See Figure 9–15E)

Figure 9–15D

Figure 9–15E

- Suggest that the craypas be used heavily so a nice oil paint effect will be created.

The completed pictures are large and vivid in color. A good place to display them might be on the walls in the main hall of the school. Entitle the exhibit: *Our Bird Friends* or *We Draw Birds*.

Paper Bag Birds

Bag Construction

Here is another interesting way to utilize the paper bag. Since it is spring, a bird project is always desirable. Suggest that your class make Paper Bag Birds.

Basic Materials: 2 paper bags, newspaper, strings, assorted colored paper, scissors, paper cement, felt tip markers.

Procedure:

- Crumple newspaper lightly into a ball and place it in one of the bags.
- Tie it closed, this is the head of the bird.
- Again crumple newspaper, but this time make the ball larger for the body.
- Put the newspaper ball in the second bag and now tie this to the head shaped bag. (See Figure 9–16A)
- Cut wings, tail, beak, eyes and legs out of colored paper and cement them to the body of the bird.
- Add felt tip marks to accentuate feathers and other areas of the body.

When the birds are completed, attach string to the body and hang them from light fixtures in the school corridor. Everyone will enjoy the spring aura that the birds will create. (See Figure 9–16B)

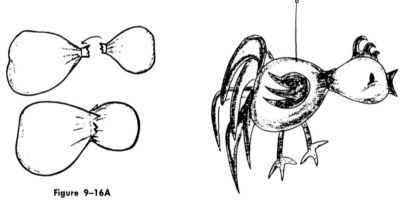

Figure 9–16A

Figure 9–16B

Cylinder Birds

Paper Construction

It is always nice to see the birds returning in the spring. Add this idea to the spring display in your class.

Basic Materials: 12 by 18 inch paper (any color), stapler, scissors, scraps of assorted colored paper, paper cement, felt tip marker.

Procedure:

- Staple the 12 by 18 inch paper into a cylinder shape which will become the body of a bird.
- Cut colored paper shapes into wings, beak, eyes, feet, tail, crest for the bird and attach them to the cylinder with paper cement.
- Cut chips of paper for breast feathers, and curl the tail and crest for the bird with very impressive plumage.
- Add felt tip marker to portions of the body for more prominence. (See Figure 9–17)

Place the birds in a different kind of display. Take brown paper strips and attach them like branches at all different levels on a huge bulletin board. Then carefully tack the birds to the board from the inside of the cylinder. The exhibit will look like a giant aviary. Entitle the display: *Personal Aviary— (Your class' Name!)*

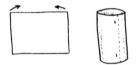

Figure 9–17

The Birds Are Back

Pastels

Spring means the return of many of our fine feathered friends. Why not utilize the bird arrivals in an art project?

Basic Materials: 12 by 18 inch light blue construction paper, pastels.

Procedure:

- In 2 areas of the blue paper trace your 2 outstretched hands lightly with pastels.
- The hand sets will become wings of 2 birds.
- Now between the bird wings, draw a body and head for the bird, and then start to color the entire bird with colors that are typical of birds in your vicinity.

Figure 9–18

- Color the birds carefully and be sure to keep your fingers away from areas that are already finished.
- Pastels are great to use but they become messy if we are not careful.
- Next draw a suitable background for your picture. (See Figure 9–18)

Spray the pictures with hair spray and mount them on a dark piece of paper. Tack the pictures to a bulletin board in the classroom and label it: *The Birds Are Back!*

The Circus and everything involved with it is one of the most exciting experiences during the spring season. Following are some ideas which will utilize the subject during art lessons.

Circus Animals

Crayon—Paper

The animals in a circus are ofttimes the main attraction. Everyone loves the elephants, zebras, seals, monkeys, lions and tigers. In the art lesson suggested here, ask the children to draw their favorite circus animal, which will be placed in a paper cage.

Basic Materials: 12 by 18 inch manila paper, crayons, strips of red paper 1 by 18 inches and 1 by 12 inches, paste, 2 red squares of paper, scissors.

Procedure:

- Draw a large circus animal on the manila paper with heavy crayon.
- When the animal is completed, paste the red 12 inch strips vertically on the paper for the bars on the cage.
- Then paste the 18 inch strips horizontally, one at the top and one at the bottom of the cage.
- Cut out 2 red wheels and add them to the cage.
- When the cage is completely cemented on the animal picture, decorate the wheels and top of the red cage with yellow scroll designs. This will make the circus cage very authentic looking. (See Figure 9–19)

A good way to display the pictures would be to use them in a circus parade on a huge bulletin board. They are nice just this way but the display can be made more elaborate if the class draws circus people, side shows, other animals which can be cut out and tacked among the red cages for a huge circus parade.

Figure 9–19

Moveable Clown Faces

Cut Paper and Crayon

This clown idea is gay and impressive. It is a wonderful lesson to use as a prelude to circus fanfare during the month of May.

Basic Materials: 9 by 12 inch white paper, 12 by 18 inch pastel colored paper, scissors, brad clips, crayons.

Procedure:

- On the 9 by 12 inch white paper sketch with crayons a large oval for the face of a clown.
- Now add with heavy crayon the eyes, large nose, mouth, hair, ears and funny little hat. (See Figure 9–20A)
- Lay the head aside and start to make the collar.

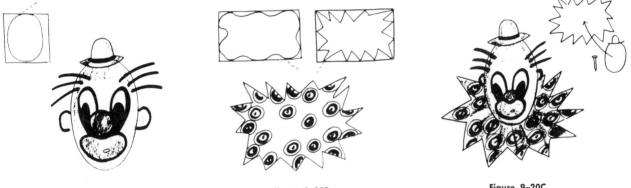

Figure 9–20A   Figure 9–20B   Figure 9–20C

- The edge of the paper can be cut away in wavy, pointed, or scalloped shapes. (See Figure 9–20B)
- Then with crayon decorate the collar, with lines repeating the cutout shape or with stripes, polka dots, stars, flowers—any decoration at all.
- When the collar is completed, take the clown head and place it on the collar.
- Add a brad fastener through the nose of the clown and through the collar.
- Flip the ends of the brad open and the clown is attached to the collar. The finished product is a gay moveable clown head. (See Figure 9–20C)

The most desirable spot to display the clown heads might be in a tricky way. Arrange them in fan shape on a bulletin board. In this arrangement they will appear like spectators. Under the clowns, print a small sign on a cut paper circus flag saying: *The Clowns Are Watching You!*

Fabric Clowns

Mixed Media

Send an S-O-S signal to class mothers for any pieces of scrap fabric they may have left over from their latest dress pattern for this novel art lesson. A fabric clown art project will be an interesting experience for all.

Basic Materials: Scraps of gayly printed fabric about 12 by 18 inches in size, crayons, scissors, felt-tip markers, paper cement, 18 by 24 inch manila paper, scraps of colored paper.

Procedure:

- Suggest that a suit be made from the donated fabric for a circus clown's picture.
- First turn the fabric to the wrong side and with a black crayon make a large X shape which fills the piece of cloth.
- Then draw an inflated outline around the X making it a large X shape. (See Figure 9–21A)

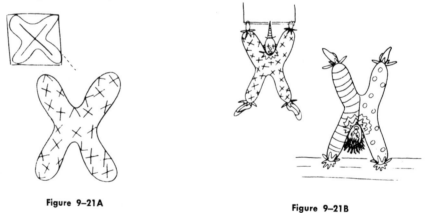

Figure 9–21A   Figure 9–21B

- Now cut this out for the clown body. Paste it anywhere on the manila paper.
- Next make the clown performing some form of action.
- He can be planned with his head drawn or made of cut paper pasted at the bottom of the X and the 2 extensions of the X can be his arms and body doing a cartwheel.
- He can be made with his head at the top of the X and his arms could be outstretched holding the bar of a swing; or he could be in the same position with his feet on a horse, a tight rope walk or a platform. (See Figure 9–21B) These are only suggestions, the children will devise many different creative ways to display the clown.

- When the position of the clown has been decided, add a face, feet, hands, hat, collar with crayon or cut paper.
- Now draw an environment for the clown. Suggestions might be a huge audience behind him, a scene of the three rings of the circus with each one highlighting a performer, or a circus parade.
- Color important portions of the picture darker than others, and then outline the picture drawn with felt tip markers for a dramatic effect.

The pictures will be best displayed taped to the walls in the corridor of the school. Label the exhibit: *The Clowns Are Coming!* or *Clowns for the Day!*

Three Dimensional Clown Face

Mixed Media

Circus time is fun time for everyone. An art lesson using the circus theme is always a success. Here is an idea which uses the clown face in a unique way.

Basic Materials: 12 by 18 inch manila paper, crayons, scissors.

Figure 9–22A

Procedure:

- Fold the manila paper in half the short way.
- Draw a clown face on one side of the paper using the fold as the tip of the clown nose. (See Figure 9–22A)
- Now cut the face shape, but be sure that the fold at the nose tip stays intact. (The clown face won't stand if the fold is not substantial.)
- Next decorate both sides of the clown face with heavy crayon.
- With cut paper paste additional decoration on the clown, like a hat, collar or buttons. (See Figure 9–22B)

When all the clowns are completed, set them on the window sills in the classroom. They will make a great clown exhibit for all to enjoy. Have a little contest to decide upon the best name for these clowns. Award the winner a circus balloon.

Figure 9–22B

Clown Bank

Mixed Media

This personal clown bank art project is one which is not only pleasing to the eye, but one which can be utilized in a very special way by thrifty children.

Basic Materials: two 6 inch paper plates, assorted cups of tempera paint, brushes, paper cement, scraps of colored paper, scissors, yarn.

Procedure:

- First glue the 2 paper plates together. This is the base for a clown head.
- Carefully cut a slit in the top of the clown head for coins.
- Now paint a clown face on the paper plate.
- When it is complete, set it aside to dry.
- Then cut out a paper hat, collar, and ears for the clown and attach them with paper cement.
- Yarn hair is an attractive addition also.
- Fasten a yarn holder on the back of the clown head so it can be hung on a chair, a door, or bed post. It will be difficult to keep these great clowns in school for more than a day. Just encourage the children to get the project home safely!

Zany May Flowers

Tissue Paper

Large, brilliantly colored flowers are especially welcome during the month of May. This art project will make outstanding spring displays.

Basic Materials: 24 by 36 inch colored construction paper, scissors, assorted colored tissue, paper cement, a bottle of metallic sparklers, scraps of green construction paper.

Procedure:

- Cut a huge flower shape from the large colored paper. Any shape will do as long as it is big. (See Figure 9–23A)
- When the shape is complete begin to crumple and cement pieces of the tissue to the flower shape.
- The tissue pieces can be arranged in many ways—around the edge to form a border, completely covering the shape, or in spots of design in areas of the flower. (See Figure 9–23B)

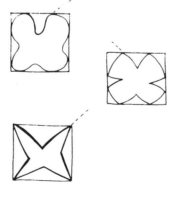

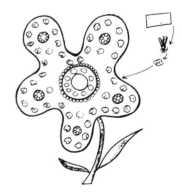

Figure 9–23A

Figure 9–23B

- Next add cut green leaves and a stem to the flower. (The next step is optional, but the children love it.)
- Lay the flower on newspaper.
- Spread paper cement in areas of the flower and sprinkle metallic sparklers in the cement.
- Each time it is done, lift the flower and shake it lightly to rid it of the excess sparklers.
- When there are enough sparklers on the flower, put it aside and pour the remaining sparklers which have collected on the newspaper into the container in preparation for the next flower.

Tape the completed zany flowers helter-skelter on the walls of the auditorium or all-purpose room. The flowers are so gay and bright that they will add to the appearance of the room during the month of May.

Loyalty Day and Memorial Day are both important as Patriotic Days. Here are some suggestions you might want to try for those occasions.

Patriotic Hat

Paper Fold

This wonderful patriotic hat will fit every head, and can be decorated with all sorts of materials.

Basic Materials: 18 by 24 inch sheet of manila paper or a sheet of newspaper, red-white-blue paint in small cups, brushes, red-white-blue crepe paper, scissors, crayons, scraps of red-white-blue paper, paper cement.

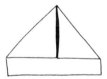

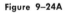

Figure 9–24A

Procedure:

- Fold the paper in half the short way.
- Find the middle point in the top folded edge of the paper. Make a small crease at this point.
- Next fold the right edge of the paper into the middle point.
- Then fold the left edge of the paper into the middle point. Your shape now looks like a pyramid. (See Figure 9–24A)
- Now fold the front bottom flap over the hat as far as it will go.
- Turn the hat over and repeat the fold with the remaining flap.
- Paste the two flap edges together. (See Figure 9–24B)
- Now the hat can be decorated in any number of ways. It can be painted red, white and blue, it can be decorated with cut paper stars and stripes, it can be decorated with patriotic symbols in crayon.
- Streamers of crepe paper can be added to one side, or at the top. The children may decide to use combinations of materials to decorate the hat. (See Figure 9–24C)

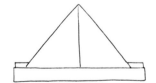

Figure 9–24B

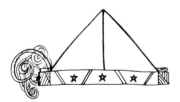

Figure 9–24C

On Loyalty or Memorial Day the children will enjoy wearing the creation in the town or school parade. Suggest they criss-cross crepe paper streamers across their chests to add a final touch to their costume.

Patriotic Holder Decorations

Paper

Three dimensional art projects that can be used by the children make wonderful incentives for a lesson. Use the old fold trick—"cat stairs" to produce all sorts of holder decorations.

Basic Materials: strips of paper 3 by 18 inches long in red, white and blue, paper cement, stapler.

Bonus Materials: white paper napkins, 12 by 18 inch white paper, scraps of red, white and blue paper, scissors, paste, crayons.

Procedure:

- Paste 2 colored strips together in perpendicular shape.
- Now fold one strip over the other until the strips are used up. (See Figure 9–25A)
- If longer strips are needed, new strips can be attached with paste to the ends of the first strips.
- When the desired length is reached, glue the strip ends together, bend the cat-stair around into a circle and staple it. (See Figure 9–25B)

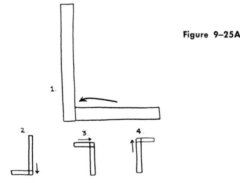

Figure 9–25A

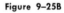

Figure 9–25B

- The shapes can be used for all types of decoration. You can make large circle rings to fit a vase, flower pots, jars.
- Small cat-stair rings can be used to make napkin holders for a Patriotic Party, or as decorations for candle holders.

If you are using them as napkin holders, why not have the class make a place mat and decorated napkin to go with it? Use red, white and blue cut paper and crayons to decorate a white napkin and a 12 by 18 inch white paper mat. When the work is completed, you have a wonderful Patriotic Luncheon set. Use the set the week prior to Memorial Day in the cafeteria or classroom. Have extra sets made during free time to take home for family use over the Memorial Day Weekend.

Red, White and Blue Pop Art

Cut Paper

A Patriotic holiday should be welcomed by a good red, white and blue picture. Here is an idea which breaks away from the conventional stars and stripes, and yet remains patriotic in color and spirit.

Basic Materials: 1 by 1 inch paper squares in red, white and blue; 12 by 18 inch gray paper, paste, blue felt tip marker.

Procedure:

- Distribute the gray paper and a handful of the red, white and blue squares,
- Now suggest that the children move the colored squares around on the background paper until the squares form an interesting composition.
- Do not cluster or clump the squares, scatter them, overlap some, allow areas of paper to show for added interest.
- When an arrangement is pleasing, piece by piece pick up the squares, apply paste and return them to their original position. (See Figure 9–26A)
- When the pieces have all been fastened securely, take the felt tip pen and design an all-over pattern on top of the composition to pull it all together. (See Figure 9–26B)

Figure 9–26A

Figure 9–26B

When the pictures are finished, mount them side by side on one large bulletin board. The effect will be one huge patriotic design. Entitle the display: *A Design Can Be Patriotic, Too!* or *Red, White and Blue Pictures.*

Three Dimensional Stars

Paper Fold

Large 3-D stars are special Memorial Day decorations. Stars can be used in innumerable ways for patriotic designs. Here are the basic instructions for a star, and one way they may be used in an art project.

Figure 9–27A

Figure 9–27B

Basic Materials: Squares of paper—12 by 12 inches, 9 by 9 inches, 6 by 6 inches in red, white and blue construction paper; scissors, 12 by 18 inch white paper, paste, crayons.

Procedure:

- Fold a square corner to corner to form a triangle.
- Now follow the illustration carefully for the star fold. (See Figure 9–27A)
- The slanted cut end when opened is the star.
- Refold the creases so the star has high and low alternate folds. (See Figure 9–27B)
- Cut several stars, and paste them to the white paper background.
- Add stripes and smaller stars with crayon in red, white and blue.

Display the 3-D star pictures in a straight line down the school corridor during May. The exhibit will spark everyone with patriotism.

SPECIAL NOTE: A White on White Picture can be made by just pasting a multitude of various sized white 3–D stars on white paper. This creates a most dramatic effect. Use the idea for another lesson.

DRAWING IDEAS FOR THE MONTH OF MAY

1. Draw a portrait of Mother.
2. Draw the many things Mother does for you.
3. Make a Mother's Day card.
4. Draw "you" first thing in the morning.
5. Draw a picture of the prettiest garden you ever saw.
6. Draw the Memorial Day parade.
7. Draw the funniest thing in a circus.
8. Design a soldier's uniform for yourself.
9. Draw the thing that makes you swell with patriotism.
10. Decorate a folder for May in red, white and blue.
11. Draw the letters in May three different ways.
12. Draw a May Pole Dance in monochromatic color.

10

![decorative banner]

June

June—the end of the school year! A time for reflection and tying up the loose ends. A happy time loaded with summer expectations for the children. This month commemorates two important days. Father's Day and Flag Day. During the month we slip from spring into summer. Use the following ideas to the best advantage during the closing weeks of school.

June Garden Fold

Mixed Media

This June garden is quite unique. Have each child in your class plant one during an art period. The flowers will be thankful!

Basic Materials: 6 by 24 inch manila paper, scissors, assorted scraps of colored construction paper, paper cement, crayons.

Procedure:

- Fold the paper the short way 3 times, there will be 8 3-inch rectangles.
- Now refold the paper in an accordian fold so your paper has ups and downs. (See Figure 10–1, Steps A, B, C, D)
- Decorate the up folds that face you with various types of flowers in cut paper and crayon designs.

209

Figure 10–1A

Figure 10–1B

Figure 10–1C

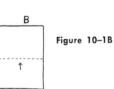

Figure 10–1D

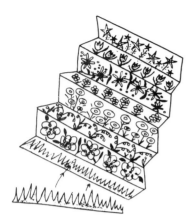

- Use a different type of flower and color combination in each panel for an interesting composition.
- At the bottom of the first panel paste a line of cut paper grass to complete the June Garden. (See Figure 10–1E)

This art project makes a different kind of runner display for a table or desk. Let the librarian borrow them for the reading tables in the library, they will bring summer indoors.

Figure 10–1E

Illustrate the Alphabet

Crayon

Figure 10–2A

This lesson is a wonderful one to utilize on a busy day. It takes a minimum of materials and the results are extremely creative.

Basic Materials: 18 by 24 inch manila paper, crayons.

Procedure:

Figure 10–2B

- Fold the paper 4 times, creasing the paper well after each fold.
- Open the paper, there will be 16 rectangles.
- Now have the children put a letter of the alphabet in the upper corner of each rectangle. (See Figure 10–2, Steps A, B, C, D, E)
- When the last rectangle is used, turn to the other side and begin lettering on that side until all the alphabet has been printed.
- Now suggest that the children become illustrators, and draw a picture representing the letters in the alphabet. However, stress the importance of unusual ideas for each letter. For instance an aardvark, abacus or albatross could be used for "A" instead of the usual apple; and bagpipe, boomerang, brontosaurus could be used for "B," instead of the usual boy or ball.

Figure 10–2C

Figure 10–2D

When the alphabet is completely illustrated it can be cut along the fold, assembled in a colored paper folder and stapled to make a personal alphabet book. These can be shared with the kindergarten classes or young brothers and sisters at home.

Figure 10–2E

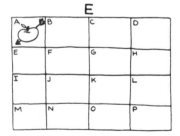

June in Design

Paint

Paint can be applied to paper in a variety of ways. Have the children try paint applied with string for a new art experience.

Basic Materials: 12 by 18 inch gray or black construction paper, sheets from old telephone directories, scissors, paste, pieces of string about 12 inches in length, bottles of red, yellow, blue paint, brushes.

Procedure:

- Cut the large letters J-U-N-E out of the telephone directory pages.
- Make 2 or 3 sets, and each time a set is cut change the shape and style of the letters.
- Next experiment placing the letters on the gray or black paper.
- Place them vertically, horizontally, in interesting arrangements.
- Use as few or as many sets of June as needed. (See Figure 10–3A)
- When the composition is pleasing, lift the letters one by one, apply paste and return them to the original position.
- Then take a piece of string and drop one end into a paint jar.
- Pull the string out between the jar and a paint brush to remove the excess paint.
- Now trail the wet string around the entire letter design.
- Repeat the application of paint with string in other colors on the composition. Notice the exciting effects that occur when wet paint of one color meets wet paint of another color. (See Figure 10–3B)

Tack the completed pictures side by side on a class bulletin board. Cut huge bright letters from construction paper for the word—JUNE. Tack them over the designs for a dramatic touch.

Figure 10–3A

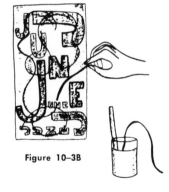

Figure 10–3B

Things I See During June

Chalk—Crayon

So many wonderful things are seen during the month of June. Why not have the children record some of these things in a very different way?

Figure 10–4A

Figure 10–4B

Basic Materials: colored chalk, ad sections of the newspaper cut 9 by 12 inches, black crayons.

Procedure:

- Make blocks of 3 different colors using the side of the chalk all over the newspaper.
- The color blocks are interesting if they are in different shapes and sizes. (See Figure 10–4A)
- Blow away the excess chalk powder, and sketch a preconceived design right over the chalk composition with heavy black crayon.
- Scenes that are prevalent during June make good designs—boating, fishing, swimming, hiking are some of the topics that can be drawn. (See Figure 10–4B)

Mount the pictures on black paper and place them on the wall near the office of the school. Entitle the display: *Things I See During June.*

June Seascape

Paint

Sailing begins its rise during the month of June. Whether the children live near the water or not, they will enjoy this vicarious art experience.

Basic Materials: 12 by 18 inch light blue paper, 9 by 12 inch manila paper, crayons, scissors, dark blue paint, white paint, paste, easel brushes, small pieces of sponge, newspaper.

Figure 10–5A

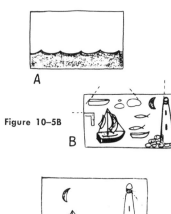

A

Figure 10–5B

B

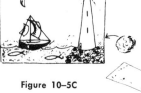

Figure 10–5C

Procedure:

- Cover the work area with newspaper.
- With an easel brush paint the light blue paper with dark blue paint for a water scene.
- Put the picture aside to dry.
- Now sketch and crayon heavily pictures on manila paper that can be used in a seascape. Boats, fish, docks, lighthouse, piers, bulkheads, buoys, are all things that can be drawn. (See Figure 10–5A, B)
- Cut the shapes drawn and paste them to the dried sea scene.
- Add highlights to the scene with crayon wherever needed.
- Now take the sponge, dip it in white paint and pat on newspaper to remove the excess paint.
- Then carefully dab the sponge in the various areas of the water to simulate foam and sea spray. (See Figure 10–5C)

Mount the pictures on a sheet of black paper and display them in the hall corridor. They will make a refreshing sight for all to enjoy. Label the exhibit: *Seascapes Near and Far.*

NOTE: Sponge was used to paint a portion of the picture in this project. Why not paint a complete picture using a sponge as your brush at another time?

Stand-Up Travel Folder

Colored Pencils

Most children are eagerly anticipating a coming vacation or trip during the closing days of school. Let them record their thoughts in an art lesson, and add interest to their coming experience at the same time.

Basic Materials: 12 by 24 inch white construction paper, colored pencils, scissors.

Bonus Materials: crayons, felt tip markers, paint, brushes.

Procedure:

- Fold the paper the long way 3 times. There will be 8 sections when the paper is opened.
- Now refold the paper in an accordian fold with high and low folds. (See Figure 10–6, Steps A, B, C, D)
- Cut the folds in 2 places on 2 of the folds. (See Figure 10–6E), and bend the cut sections back to give added 3 dimensional depth to the fold.
- On the first panel fold, place the area title of the vacation experience.
- Then in each panel thereafter draw descriptive sketches illustrating encounters that may occur in the vacation spot. (See Figure 10–6F)
- Add felt tip marker or crayon to highlight areas if need be.

Use these wonderful folders at the last exhibit in the display case before the summer holiday. Entitle the exhibit: *Where I Hope to Be—Soon!*

The patriotic ideas which have been offered in this book are interchangeable. Here are a few added ideas with a patriotic theme for Flag Day.

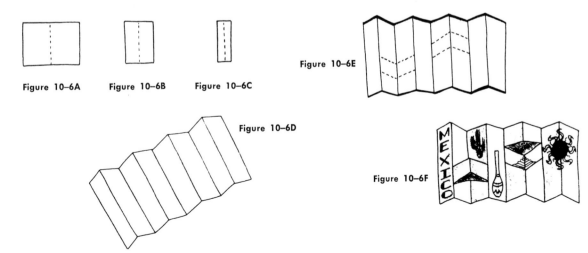

Figure 10–6A   Figure 10–6B   Figure 10–6C

Figure 10–6E

Figure 10–6D

Figure 10–6F

Personal Flag Replica

Tissue

On Flag Day it would be nice to have individual replicas of our flag. In an art lesson preceding this special day, suggest that the children create the American Flag with tissue.

Basic Materials: 9 by 12 inch manila paper, red-white-blue tissue paper, paste.

Procedure:

- Very simply sketch the outlines of the American Flag on the manila paper with pencil. Be sure that the field of stars is in the left hand corner.
- Next tear the pieces of tissue (the color needed for an area), crumple them and paste them to the flag outline on the manila paper.
- Fit the pieces tightly together so none of the background paper will show.
- Use white tissue for the stars, medium blue tissue for the field, red and white tissue for the stripes.
- Continue to tear, crumple and paste the tissue until the entire flag has been filled with color. (See Figure 10–7)
- The flag is beautiful just this way, however, it can be pasted to a black paper mount, and a yellow cut paper holder and stand can be added.

Cover an entire bulletin board with the completed tissue flags for a special patriotic gesture. Another impressive way to display them would be to use the individual flags mounted like blocks to form the word FLAG across the bulletin board.

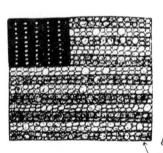

Figure 10–7

Three Dimensional Parade

Crayon

This idea for developing a parade scene is quite unusual and refreshing. Try the project with your class.

Basic Materials: 12 by 18 inch manila paper, crayons, scissors, scraps of manila paper.

Procedure:

- Fold the manila paper in half the short way.
- Open the paper and draw a parade scene for Flag Day on the upper top half of the manila paper. (See Figure 10–8A)

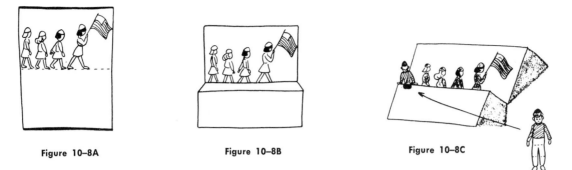

Figure 10–8A   Figure 10–8B   Figure 10–8C

- When the parade has been drawn, fold the untouched lower half of the paper in half again and bend the fold up. (See Figure 10–8B)
- Now on scraps of paper draw and color heavily little figures of boys and girls. (Make the figures in proportion with the parade people.)
- Next cut them out; fold the figures at the buttocks and knees and place them on the front fold in a sitting position. They appear as an audience watching a parade. (See Figure 10–8C)

A good way to display the project would be first during a show and tell about art time. Then, when the children have had an opportunity to show and discuss their pictures, tack them to the chalk sill all around the room for one long continuous parade scene.

Transparent Stars

Fused Crayon

Utilize old red, white and blue crayon stubs for a special Flag Day lesson.

Basic Materials: scraps of red, white, blue crayons, 2 pieces of 9 by 12 inch waxed paper, 12 by 18 inch blue paper, electric iron, scissors, pad of newspaper.

Procedure:

- Scrape the red, white and blue crayons on one of the pieces of waxed paper. Many shavings of color are needed.
- Now place a second piece of waxed paper over this.
- Use a warm iron to press the waxed paper and crayon sandwich together. (See Figure 10–9A)
- The heat will fuse or laminate the waxed paper into a transparent sheet.
- Take the blue construction paper and cut a large star shape in the center of it. (See Figure 10–9B)

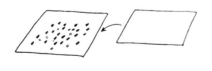

Figure 10–9A   Figure 10–9B

- Then lay the crayon transparency on the blue paper so it fills in the cut star shape.
- Tape the transparency to the blue paper with scotch tape—this is the back.

For display purposes, tape the stars into portions of your windows in the classroom. The results will be great blocks of transparent stars. A wonderful way to commemorate Flag Day!

Father's Day is almost nondescript. We seem to pass over it lightly, and yet, it should be an important time, shouldn't it? The following ideas may help to make this a special day for Dad.

Dad's Necktie

Crayon

Most fathers are vain about their neckwear. As an art lesson and gift for him, design a tie that you think he might enjoy, and use it also as a Father's Day Card.

Basic Materials: 6 by 12 inch manila paper, crayons, scissors.

Procedure:

- Fold the manila paper in half the long way, then lightly draw a tie shape on the paper with crayon using the fold as one side of the tie. (See Figure 10–10)

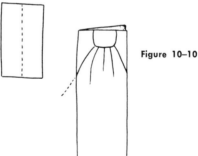

Figure 10–10

- Now cut the tie shape card, and decorate it heavily with crayon on both sides.
- Use Dad's favorite colors.
- When the tie is completed, think up a good verse for father and carefully print it inside the card. Dad will surely enjoy the effort that was put into his project.

Dad's Car Bag

Plastic Bag Decoration

This idea is inexpensive and most effective for a Father's Day gift. The children in your class will enjoy making the project during an art lesson.

Basic Materials: box of 11 by 14 inch plastic bags, colored felt tip markers, scissors.

Procedure:

- Cut a small hole near the top of one side of the plastic bag.
- Make it large enough to fit one of the knobs on the dashboard of Dad's car.
- Now decorate the front of the bag with felt tip markers.
- Draw scenes or designs that will appeal to Dad. It might be an idea showing his hobby—fishing, golfing, tennis, gardening, or it might be designs using his favorite pipe, car, or book as motifs. (See Figure 10–11)

Figure 10–11

Complete the art work on the bag and carefully wrap it with paper that Mom donated. Present this great gift to Dad on his Day.

Letter Holder

Mixed Media

Dad can always use a desk accessory. During an art lesson have the students design a "Letter Holder" for father.

Basic Materials: 4 by 4 inch square of cardboard, crayons, felt tip marker, thumb tack, wooden clothespin, paint brushes.

Procedure:

- Choose bright, vivid colors.
- Decorate the square of cardboard with a crayoned geometric design.
- Outline the design with felt tip marker.
- Put a large thumbtack up through the middle of the cardboard base, and attach the painted clothespin head to the thumbtack. (See Figure 10–12) The project is ready to be wrapped and taken home.

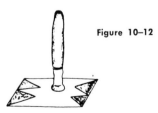

Figure 10–12

Dad's Paperweight

Polymer Medium

A paperweight is always a welcomed gift. Here is an idea that is different and produces a very professional looking gift.

Basic Materials: old magazines with shiny surfaced paper, polymer medium, brush, water, a nicely shaped stone with a flat surface.

Procedure:

- Thumb through a magazine and find a picture which is pleasing and fits the flat stone surface.
- Next coat the stone with a thin layer of polymer. Also coat the picture and immediately place it on the stone face side down.
- Press the picture as flat as possible on the stone surface. (See Figure 10–13)
- Now place the stone aside overnight to let it set.
- The next day place the stone in a container of water until the paper from the picture soaks off. The results will be a duplicate on stone of the magazine picture—a most pleasant surprise.

Figure 10–13

Wrap the stone in tissue and present it to Dad on his day. Be ready to answer the endless questions pertaining to how you managed to place the picture on the stone.

NOTE: Be sure when using the polymer that the brush remains in water when not being used. Also, clean the brush in water when work with it is completed.

Giant Butterflys

Crayon

The familiar fold and cut idea can turn out an almost endless supply of giant paper butterflys for a June display. The children will enjoy them so much they will want to create more than one.

Basic Materials: 18 by 24 inch manila paper, scissors, crayons.

Procedure:

- An outline representing half a butterfly's body is drawn on a folded sheet of manila paper. (See Figure 10–14A)

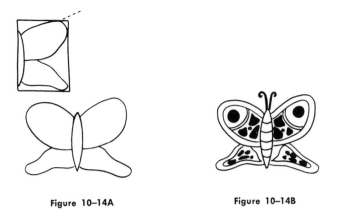

Figure 10–14A

Figure 10–14B

- The paper is then cut along the outline and opened flat for the complete butterfly.
- Now color the butterfly shape with heavy crayon implementing designs wherever needed.
- Add 2 black paper antennae, and the project is completed. (See Figure 10–14B)

Tape the butterfly shapes everywhere—on the wall, windows, ceiling, even on the side of a table or desk. When applying the tape to the surface of the display area, bend the butterfly in positions that will make the shape 3 dimensional and very realistic.

Styrofoam Menagerie

Styrofoam Carving

Styrofoam, a comparatively new material, is used abundantly in the packing field. It is such an inexpensive item that it is readily discarded, and therefore available just for the asking. Collect enough discarded styrofoam for a class and try this great idea for an art lesson. June is zoo time—make a private menagerie.

Basic Materials: styrofoam, any of the following cutting tools—saw-toothed knife, dull kitchen knife, nail file, scissors—pipe cleaners, cups of assorted tempera paint, brushes.

Bonus Materials: small blocks of wood or heavy cardboard, Elmer's glue.

Procedure:

- Give each child a piece of styrofoam, a cutting tool and some pipe cleaners.
- Suggest that they create an animal of any type using the styrofoam pieces and the pipe cleaners to attach the parts together. (See Figure 10–15)
- Keep the animal simple.
- When the animal is assembled, paint it with tempera paint, and if you have the bonus materials mount the animal to a base of wood or cardboard.

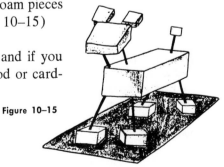

Figure 10–15

Display the menagerie in the display case, with a little sign and entitle the display *Krazy Kreations* or *Kreative Menagerie*.

Illustrating a Funny

Crayons

There are some art ideas which seem to work more advantageously if they are done at the end of the school term. A rapport between teacher and class has been developed over the school year, and the response to certain ideas may be more relaxed, and therefore free and more creative. Try this idea during June.

Basic Materials: 18 by 24 inch manila paper, crayons, felt tip markers.

Procedure:

- Suggest that the children imagine that they are authorized by a famous magazine to illustrate a Funny Saying.
- Next distribute the paper and crayons.
- Then write a number of sayings on the chalkboard, so the pupils can choose the one they would like to illustrate. Some of the ideas might be:

    A dog has a bark,
    Can it cover a tree?

    An elephant has a trunk,
    Can it be opened with a key?

    Monkeys have tails, do they tell
    a good story?

    The window has a pane,
    does it hurt?

    We saw a boat sail,
    was it sold?

- When the children reach a decision about the saying they plan to illustrate, suggest that they proceed with the idea.
- Crayon important areas heavily and other areas lightly.
- Highlight the main ideas with felt tip marker.
- Under the illustration print the idea that was used for the picture. (See Figure 10–16)

The results will be quite humorous—display the pictures in the hall for all to enjoy.

A dog has a bark
Can it cover a tree?

Figure 10–16

Magic Circle Plant

Mixed Media

There are not too many types of plants that can have a variety of different blossoms on them at one time—but—an artist can change all that. Have your class create with art materials this very special plant for a June lesson.

Basic Materials: 12 by 18 inch blue paper, cut paper circles in all sizes and colors, crayons, assorted paper and fabric scraps, scissors, paste.

Procedure:

- Paste 3, 5, 7, or 9 circles on the blue paper.
- Do not clump them together or have them all on one level—scatter them so there are spots of paper showing in areas.
- Now use the crayons, assorted paper and fabrics to decorate each flower in a different manner.
- Next give the plant a stem and some leaves with one of the materials available.
- Complete the plant by adding a cut fabric container at the bottom of the picture.

A nice way to display these magic plants would be to cut them with an outline of the blue paper all around. They would look most attractive as a display above the chalkboard. (See Figure 10–17)

Wax Resist

Water Colors

A fine line drawing will appeal to the children. Most boys and girls like little details, and this lesson will lend freedom to this desire for "little" shapes.

Basic Materials: 12 by 18 inch waxed paper, 12 by 18 inch white paper, pencil, box of water colors, brush, cup of water, newspaper.

Figure 10–17

Procedure:

- Cover the working area with newspaper.
- Now place the waxed paper over the white paper and fasten it with a paper clip.

- Then draw a picture with pencil, pressing the wax lines down into the white paper.
- The sketch could be a plane, or a car model that the boys might plan to build during the summer months; or it could be designs of clothing that the girls might be planning to make for their dolls.
- When the picture is completed, remove the waxed paper and brush a wash of water color over the white paper.
- What a pleasant surprise to see the lines of the picture appear. They are fine lines and almost create the appearance of etched lines. (See Figure 10–18, Steps A, B, C)

Mount the pictures on black paper and display them on a bulletin board in your room. Entitle the exhibit: *Summer Hours Spent in Good Use!* or *Summer Fun!*

Figure 10–18A

Figure 10–18B

Figure 10–18C

Cardboard Painting

Tempera Paint

This is a wonderful way to use the small quantities of leftover paint you may have at the end of the school year.

Basic Materials: tempera paint, liquid laundry starch, pieces of cardboard about 4 by 2 inches in size, scissors, 12 by 18 inch manila paper.

Procedure:

- Notch the pieces of cardboard with the scissors.
- Now cover the manila paper with a thin layer of liquid starch.
- Spoon small puddles of tempera paint on different parts of the paper.
- Then with the notched edge of the cardboard spread and mix the colors. (See Figure 10–19)

The results will be vivid abstract paintings that will look most handsome taped to the walls of the cafeteria during June.

Figure 10–19

Fused Color

Crayon

June—school is just about over. There are all sorts of odds and ends in the art supply corner. Here is a wonderful way to use all those crayon stubs.

Basic Materials: crayon scraps, any shiny surfaced paper like shelf paper, fingerpaint paper, magazine pages; an electric iron, scissors, newspaper padding.

Procedure:

- Scrape the crayons on the shiny paper with scissors. (See Figure 10–20A)
- Place a second piece of paper on top of the sheet with the shaved crayon pieces.
- Use a warm iron to press the paper sandwich.
- Then remove the top paper, there are 2 sheets of colored waxy surfaced paper to use.
- On one, draw a picture of birds, butterflies, flowers, fish with a piece of black crayon.
- The other sheet can be used to scratch into the waxy surface with scissors and make a line design.

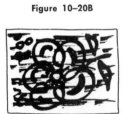

Figure 10–20A

Both pictures are a special bonus from old crayon stubs. Fold one of the pictures in half and use it to store some of the papers that accumulate during June. (See Figure 10–20B)

Figure 10–20B

Three Dimensional Fish

Paper

June is the time for fishing and water fun. This 3 dimensional fish is easy to make and most handsome when completed.

Basic Materials: 12 by 18 inch colored construction paper, crayons, scissors, string, cardboard.

Procedure:

- Draw the largest fish possible on the colored paper.
- Two curved lines make a wonderful fish. (See Figure 10–21A)
- Cut the fish.

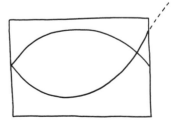

Figure 10–21A

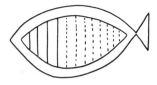

Figure 10–21B

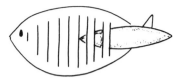

Figure 10–21C

- Now leave a margin of about ¾ of an inch and draw a smaller fish outline in the larger fish.
- Then draw straight lines from the top of the outline to the bottom. (See Figure 10–21B)
- Next cut these lines into slits.
- Take a piece of cardboard the length of the small fish shape, and cut it with a smooth curve at top and bottom. (See Figure 10–21C)
- Then weave it into the slots of the fish.
- When it has been woven through, bend it so it pushes the slots of the fish out on each side and makes the fish 3 dimensional.
- Decorate the fish with crayon and tie a string at the top.

It makes a wonderful moving shape to hang from a light fixture for the closing month of school.

A New You for Summer

Crayon

Everyone at one time or another has been curious about how they might look with a different color hair, or a new hair styling. Here is a fun art lesson for both girls and boys to try. It will help to determine your appearance with a varied hair coloring and style.

Basic Materials: 12 by 18 inch oaktag, scissors, crayons.

Procedure:

- Draw an oval toward the center of the oaktag which is approximately the size of a face.
- Cut the oval, but leave the frame intact.
- Now create a hair styling with light crayon.
- When it is pleasing, color it heavily with crayon, the color of your choice.
- Fill in the remaining area of oaktag with the side of a crayon. (See Figure 10–22)

Figure 10–22

Spend a portion of an afternoon just to let the children trade their "New You Look" with each other. Make sure mirrors are available when trying the homemade stylings. It is interesting to note the transformation that takes place with the paper styling. Suggest that the children each write a story about the "look" that they like the best and why.

Summer

Paint

Have you ever considered how a seasonal word could be decorated? Everyone has a definite idea about how this could be accomplished. Suggest that your students decorate the word *Summer* during the closing days of school.

Basic Materials: white paper 12 by 18 inches, cups of assorted tempera paint, brushes, pencil, scrap paper.

Procedure:

- Make a trial sketch on scrap paper to develop the idea.
- Start by printing *Summer* across the middle of the paper and proceed to decorate the area around it with appropriate decoration.
- Summer might mean flowers, swimming, fishing, boating, camping, outdoors. Incorporate one or all of the ideas the way you think they should be used.
- When the trial sketch is completed, transfer the idea to the white paper and paint it with tempera paint. (See Figure 10–23)

Figure 10–23

Cut around the designed area of the white paper and paste it to the cover of an 18 by 24 inch construction paper folder. Use the folder for summer sketching projects.

Use the idea for each season—autumn, winter, spring, summer. They are all excellent subjects to use.

Spray Painting

Tempera Paint

Just before school closing, have a desk cleanup day. The many forgotten treasures will create a unique picture as a parting June art lesson.

Basic Materials: spray window cleaning bottles or spray guns, 12 by 18 inch manila paper, tempera paint diluted with water, miscellaneous objects from a desk like: scissors, old pencils, erasers, clips, rulers.

Procedure:

- Fill the spray containers with the diluted paint.
- Cover the work areas with newspaper and place the manila paper on this.

- Now arrange the found objects on the manila paper. (See Figure 10–24A)
- When the arrangement is pleasing, hold the spray container a short distance from the object-composition and start to spray the paint.
- Use more than one color spray if desired. (See Figure 10–24B)
- Now allow the paintings to dry, and remove the objects.

Figure 10–24A

Mount the pictures on black paper and tack them side by side on a bulletin board. Entitle it: *Found Objects* or *Recent Discoveries.*

Figure 10–24B

Circle Art

Crayon

So many wonderful shapes that we see during this season are made basically with a circle. Why not see how clever your class can be about identifying a variety of circle shapes.

Basic Materials: 12 by 18 inch manila paper, compass, crayons.

Procedure:

- Draw a variety of different circle shapes with the compass on the manila paper.
- When at least 5 to 7 circles are completed, start to identify each circle with an object or person associated with spring. The round face of a clown, flower, the sun, baseball, fruit, shells. (See Figure 10–25)
- Crayon each circle picture gayly.

Figure 10–25

It will take a little thought, but the students should come up with great picture ideas.

Cut out the finished circles and paste them on 12 by 18 inch colored paper that has been folded into a booklet shape. The booklets will be excellent for holding school work during the month of June.

Giant Insects

Crayon

This is an excellent lesson for dramatizing June. Utilize the fold, draw and cut idea for making huge insects. Correlate the art lesson with science and you will have blown-up replicas of the real thing.

Basic Materials: 18 by 24 inch manila paper, crayons, scissors, felt tip markers.

Procedure:

- Fold the manila paper in half the long way.
- Draw half an insect on the paper using the fold as the center of the insect's body.
- Cut the insect drawing, and open it flat for the complete insect body. (See Figure 10–26)

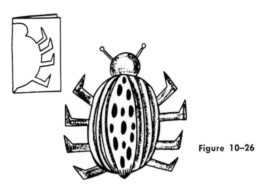

Figure 10–26

- Next start to color the shape heavily with crayon, adding insect markings —spots, stripes, wing webbing, dabs of color until the insect is completely colored.
- Then outline each section with felt tip marker.
- Now add 2 thin black cut paper shapes for antennae.
- Fold the original crease and each leg inward so the insect appears alive.

Attach paper springs to the under portion of the insect and tape the projects helter-skelter at different levels of the wall. For fun tape a couple to the ceiling in realistic stance. It will appear that your class is swarming with insects.

Imaginary Insects

Paint Blobs

A child's imagination is a wonderful thing. Here is a great way to discover the individual's personal world of fantasy in this June art lesson.

Basic Materials: 12 by 18 inch manila paper, black paint, brush, crayons.

Procedure:

- Fold the manila paper in half the long way.
- Reopen it.

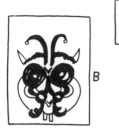

- Put a blob of black paint on one side of the paper.
- Close the fold, and rub the paper with your hand until the paint inside spreads and becomes dry.
- Now ask the children to look at the dried black blob and decide how they can make it into an imaginary insect by using added crayon sketching.
- Nothing more need be said. The blobs will become fantastic insects. (See Figure 10–27)

Mount the insects side by side on a large bulletin board, for one of the last bulletin board displays of the year.

Figure 10–27

EXTRA SUGGESTIONS FOR DRAWING

1. Draw a flag for outer space.
2. Draw "you" in a parade.
3. Draw your backyard in the summer.
4. Draw a house being built.
5. Draw a pair of large socks. Decorate them for Dad.
6. Draw how you keep cool.
7. Draw your "Dream Vacation."
8. Draw what you like doing best during summer.
9. Draw how you plan to treat Dad during Father's Day.
10. Draw your favorite teacher.
11. Show what you like to wear during the summer.
12. Draw how you think you will feel the last day of school.

11

July

July . . . summer. Most schools are closed, children are away at camp or on vacation. The main holidays during summer months are negligible. However, July 4th is one of our important National holidays, and should be recognized with an art lesson if you are working with groups of children.

The ideas in the last two chapters are geared to the maintenance of a good craft program for summer camps, scout activities, after school activities, organized summer programs, trips, and the use by enlightened parents who would like to initiate their children to good craft projects in the home.

Fourth of July Rocket

Mixed Media

A rocket would make a wonderful art lesson to commemorate July 4th. Try these simple directions.

Basic Materials: cardboard towel roll, red-white-blue tempera paint, brushes, 6 inch circle of red paper, scraps of red-white-blue crepe paper, paper cement, scissors.

Procedure:

- Paint the cardboard roll in any patriotic theme desired using the red, white and blue color scheme.

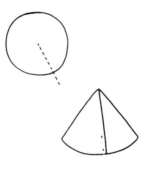

Figure 11–1A

- Set it aside to dry.
- Next cut a slit to the center of the circle and bend it around to make a wide cone. (See Figure 11–1A)
- Staple it together.
- Attach the cone to the cardboard tube with rubber cement.
- Complete the rocket by cutting long streamers of crepe paper and attaching them to the bottom of the rocket with rubber cement. (See Figure 11–1B)

Many patriotic holiday ideas have been listed previously in the book. Refer to them for other ideas pertaining to the patriotic theme for July 4th.

Figure 11–1B

Weaving

Mesh Bags and Yarn

Orange mesh bags are always easily obtainable. Use them along with donated yarn for an inexpensive craft project.

Basic Materials: pieces of orange mesh bags approximately 9 by 12 inches, 9 by 12 inch manila paper, pencils, felt tip marker, yarn, scissors, large-eyed needle or bobby pin.

Procedure:

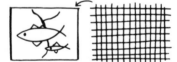

- On scrap paper draw a design dealing with the sea. Fish, boats, anchors, or shells are all good subjects to use for a design.
- Place the sketch under the mesh and with felt tip marker retrace the design on the mesh. (See Figure 11–2A)
- Now thread the needle or bobby pin with yarn and start to weave, over and under the mesh fibers.
- Continue the weaving process filling in areas solid with yarn until the design is finished. (See Figure 11–2B)

This project makes an impressive wall hanging or pillow cover when completed.

Figure 11–2A

O'jos de Dios

Yarn Cross

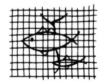

O'jos de Dios or God's Eye are constructions that come to us from a group of Mexican Indians. They are colorful woven designs which make beautiful hanging ornaments.

Figure 11–2B

Basic Materials: wood shapes like: twigs, tooth picks, pop sticks, thin dowels, assorted colored yarn, scissors.

Procedure:

- Tie 2 pieces of wood that are even in length together in cross fashion. This is the loom.
- Now tie the yarn in the center and begin the weaving by wrapping the yarn around one part of the cross and then spanning the yarn to the next part of the cross (See Figure 11–3A)
- Continue this procedure changing the color scheme and yarn thickness from time to time for interest.
- When the cross is completed, cut and tie the end of the yarn to the cross.
- Add beads or wool pom-poms at the wood points for added decoration. (See Figure 11–3B)

The yarn cross can be as small or as large as you care to make it. The individual crosses are wonderful decorations to hang from light fixtures or windows. However, the Indians customarily use a large cross which is made by making 5 God's Eyes the same size and attaching them to 2 large dowels which have been fastened together in cross fashions. (See Figure 11–3C) This ornament is used as a wall hanging.

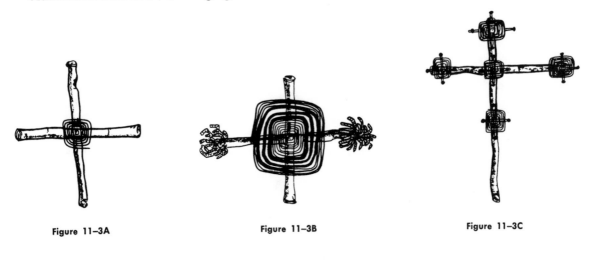

Figure 11–3A   Figure 11–3B   Figure 11–3C

Treasure Box

Fabric Collage

Everyone enjoys a box of their very own. It is an invaluable storage place in which to house precious items. This box literally costs nothing to make; it involves materials which can be found at home.

Basic Materials: shoe box or comparable box, glue, miscellaneous scraps of fabric, scissors.

Procedure:

- Cut the fabric scraps into medium-sized squares and rectangles.
- Attach them in helter-skelter patterns on the box with glue.
- Try to keep similar fabric designs apart.
- Mix solid and patterned fabrics for a more interesting arrangement.
- Be sure to glue the edges of each piece carefully, so it stays flat.

The completed box resembles a patchwork design—a different type of box decoration. (See Figure 11–4)

Figure 11–4

Insect Box Puppet

Hand Puppet

I have suggested previously that there are any number of different puppets to create. Here is a good Insect Puppet that can be made during the summer.

Basic Materials: 2 small cereal boxes, cups of assorted tempera paint, brushes, assorted scraps of colored paper, scissors, an old sock, paper cement, masking tape.

Procedure:

Figure 11–5A

- Tape the ends of the two square cereal boxes together. (See Figure 11–5A)
- Paint the puppet to resemble an imaginary insect of some sort.
- Use unusual colors and add additional decorations with cut colored paper.
- Next cut the toes off an old sock and cement it to the outside of the insect head for the body of the puppet. (See Figure 11–5B)

The children will enjoy giving a puppet show outdoors for their peers. A yard show or camp show are always excellent times to display the puppet creations.

Personalized Stationery

Inner Tube Prints

A wonderful summer activity is to make your very own stationery. This suggestion utilizes discarded inner tubes in an interesting way.

Figure 11–5B

Basic Materials: discarded inner rubber tubes, scrap sketching paper, 9 by 12 inch white paper, cardboard, tempera paint with soap flakes added for thickness, brush, scissors, spoon, glue.

Procedure:

- Sketch initials, or a design exemplifying a particular interest on the scrap paper.
- Cut this out and use it for a pattern to trace the same design on a piece of inner tube. (See Figure 11–6A)
- Now cut the rubber shape with scissors and glue it to the cardboard. This becomes the printing plate.
- Next brush tempera paint on the rubber plate.
- While the paint is still wet, cover the plate with a piece of white paper cut the size of stationery and rub it with a spoon to transfer the picture to the paper. (See Figure 11–6B)
- When the print has been pulled, lay the picture aside to dry.
- Then cut out the shape and transfer it to other paper or use the paper print the way it is for your stationery . . . custom made.

Figure 11–6A

Figure 11–6B

Bottle Folk

Papier Mâché

Here is a wonderful papier mâché project which uses a bottle for a base.

Basic Materials: bottles of various sizes and shapes, newspapers, paper towels, masking tape, wool, wallpaper paste, tempera paint, buttons, beads, glue, shellac.

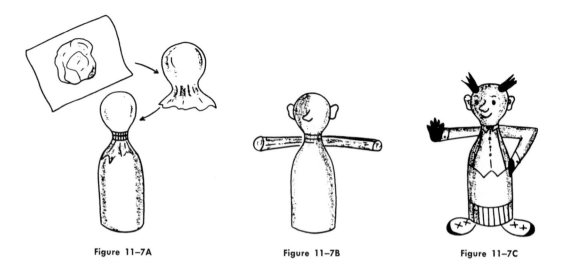

Figure 11–7A   Figure 11–7B   Figure 11–7C

Procedure:

- To form a head and neck, wad a sheet of newspaper about the size of a fist, and wrap it in paper towel; twist the ends of the towel at the bottom, secure it with tape and insert it in the bottle opening. (See Figure 11–7A)
- For nose and ears, wad smaller bits of newspaper and secure to the head with tape.
- Make arms by rolling the newspaper into long thin rolls and fastening it to the bottle with tape. (See Figure 11–7B)
- Papier mâché is made by tearing strips of newspaper about 1 inch wide and 3 inches long. School paste diluted with water can be used instead of wallpaper paste.
- Use the paste freely and apply the strips to the head and work down.
- Use black and white newspaper print for the first layer, comics for the second, and black and white print again for the third. (This helps you to see the areas you have covered.) Allow the project to dry overnight.
- Now decorate the Bottle Folk! Glue wool on the head for hair. Buttons and beads for eyes.
- Paint facial features and clothing.
- When dry, shellac the bottles for preservation. (See Figure 11–7C)

Dry Print Photograms

Developing Technique

Here is a wonderful summer project that can be done by children of all ages. It is especially desirable when working with natural materials like field weeds, flowers, ferns and grasses.

Basic Materials: a package of developing paper which is known commercially as Helios or Ozalid paper, a bottle of 28% ammonia water, a large mouthed gallon jar with tight cover, a collection of natural materials, scrap paper.

Procedure:

- First put a few drops of ammonia water into a large mouthed jar with a good cover.
- Set it aside.
- Then work in a semi-dark room or working area. (A shady wooded area would be fine!)
- Experiment first with the placement of the natural materials that are to be printed.
- When an arrangement is satisfactory, place it on the yellow side of the developing paper. (See Figure 11–8A)
- Cover the arrangement with a piece of scrap paper and carefully carry the paper sandwich to a sunny area.
- Take away the scrap paper and expose the arrangement to the sun until the yellow paper turns to white (about 1 minute).
- Put aside the natural materials and quickly place the developing paper in the ammonia-treated jar. (Roll the paper to place it in the jar if the mouth is too small.)
- Replace the cover of the jar and allow the paper to remain in the jar 1 or 2 minutes.
- Remove the print when the picture silhouette appears. (See Figure 11–8B)

Figure 11–8A

Mount the print on black paper, and label the specimens. A nature scrapbook of photograms makes a wonderful project for science study at camp.

Figure 11–8B

Sand Sculpture

Plaster Relief

Casting in sand is one of the most exciting and creative art activities that can be done. The work takes little preparation, and is most rewarding in the final analysis.

Basic Materials: plaster of Paris, discarded ½ gallon milk cartons, strong flat cardboard box, dampened sand.

Procedure:

- First fill the cardboard box ¼ full with wet sand. Then with your fingers as a tool or with a stick, sculpt a design or picture in the sand. (See Figure 11–9A)

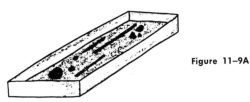

Figure 11–9A

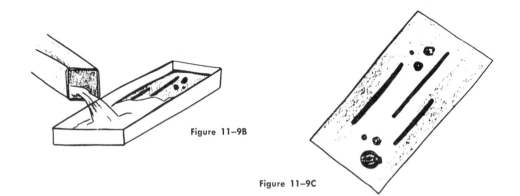

Figure 11–9B

Figure 11–9C

- Add pebbles, shells, beads, glass or other miscellaneous materials to the sculpture to create interest.
- Now prepare the plaster. The plaster must be carefully mixed.
- Fill the milk carton ¼ full with lukewarm water.
- Slowly sprinkle the plaster into it, using your hand as a mixing tool.
- Rub the plaster between your fingers during the stirring process. Be sure that the dry plaster at the bottom of the container is absorbed into the mixing process.
- When the plaster is creamy and fluid, pour it over the wet sand sculpture. (See Figure 11–9B)
- Place a hairpin or paper clip in the plaster mold for future hanging.
- Then allow the plaster to set about an hour, or until it is dry.
- Now remove the plaster cast carefully from the sand.
- The cast relief will pick up a sand texture which is interesting and enhances the project. However, most of it can be removed by brushing it off with a stiff brush if a smoother finish is desired. This must be done carefully because the plaster relief is quite brittle.
- Added interest may be added to the plaster relief with tempera paint if desired. (See Figure 11–9C)
  NOTE: Plaster dries rapidly. Wet plaster cannot be added to dry plaster. Therefore, if extra plaster is needed, the area to be filled in must first be dampened with a wet sponge before the new plaster is poured on it. Vinegar slows the hardening process of plaster. The addition of salt speeds the process of hardening plaster.

Mock Ceramic Jewelry

Plaster of Paris Blobs

Pins made with Plaster of Paris are coveted items when they are handmade. Experiment with plaster of Paris in this new and creative way.

Basic Materials: plaster of Paris, aluminum foil, discarded ½ gallon milk containers, water, flat backed pins, Duco cement, water color paints, brush, colorless nail polish.

Procedure:

- Mix the plaster and water to the consistency of whipped cream in the milk container.
- Next slowly pour the blobs of mixture on a sheet of aluminum foil in small cookie shapes. (See Figure 11–10A)
- When the shapes are dry, carefully remove them from the foil and paint them with water colors.
- Coat them several times with colorless nail polish to produce a shiny strong finish. (See Figure 11–10B)
- Next attach a flat backed pin on the back of the plaster shape with Duco cement to complete the project.

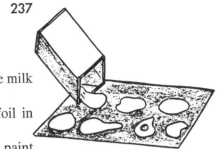

Figure 11–10A

When displaying the pins for a craft show, fasten the pin to a square of oak-tag to give it a professional look.

Plaster Sculpting

Plaster of Paris and Balloons

Figure 11–10B

Plaster of Paris is a most valuable craft media. There is a wide variety of projects and techniques that can be creatively utilized. Here is one that is lots of fun to try!

Basic Materials: plaster of Paris, collection of balloons in assorted small sizes, discarded milk cartons, water, felt tip markers, sandpaper.

Procedure:

- Mix the plaster and water in the milk container until it is the consistency of whipped cream.
- Then slowly pour it into a small balloon, and fasten the balloon top. (See Figure 11–11A)
- Set the shape aside and allow the plaster to harden.
- Next remove the balloon and carefully sandpaper the rough areas of the shape.
- When the shape is smooth and satisfactory, decorate it with felt tip marker. Any little animal, bird or fish would make a good subject. (See Figure 11–11B)

Figure 11–11A

Make several little balloon sculptures. They make ideal gifts to take home from camp.

Figure 11–11B

Facial Tissue Beads

Modeling

Wonderful jewelry can be made by using this method.

Basic Materials: paper tissues, Elmer's glue, water, toothpicks, discarded milk containers, tempera paint, shellac, brushes.

Procedure:

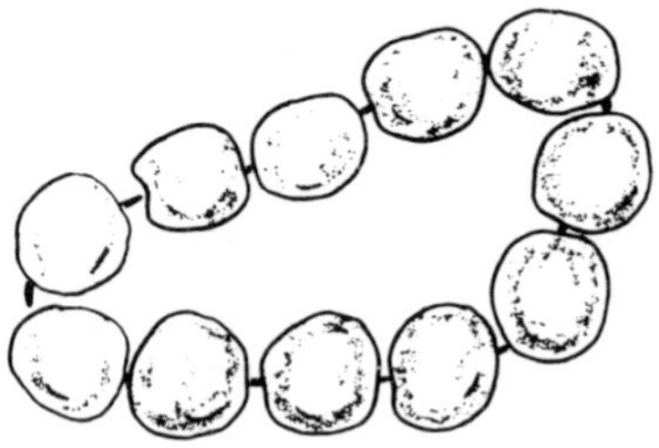

Figure 11–12

- Shred about 20 facial tissues in the milk container.
- Add a mixture of ½ water and ½ Elmer's glue to the shredded tissue and mix it to a pulpy consistency.
- If the mixture appears too fluid, add more tissues.
- Let the mixture soak about 5 minutes, and begin to shape the pulp into beads using a toothpick to make each hole.
- Allow the shapes to dry overnight.
- Now decorate the beads with paint, and when they are dry, shellac them.
- String the beads into desired necklace lengths. (See Figure 11–12)

The beads are a most impressive project. Make several necklaces with different shaped beads and different colors.

SUGGESTIONS FOR SUMMER DRAWING

1. Sketch scenes in your city or town like: churches and synogogues, stores, library, railroad or bus stations.
2. Sketch trips to: the beach, the zoo, a parade, amusement park, a park, a fishing trip, a car ride, a train ride, a carnival.
3. Sketch your family—eating, watching television, on a picnic, in the back yard, at a drive-in.
4. Sketch clothing for people of different eras—early man, the Egyptians, the Greeks, Martians.
5. Sketch a news event that you may hear on radio or see on T.V.
6. Draw feeling pictures like: how you feel when you are tired, sad, happy, bored, grateful, lonely.
7. Draw pictures of groups of birds, fish, animals.
8. Draw pictures showing different terrains like: deserts, valleys, mountains, an oasis.
9. Draw textures like hair, stone, brick, fuzz, cotton, sand, velvet.
10. Draw the things you might like to do when you grow up.

12

August

August—a wonderful time of the year. Vacation is still upon us. Children are beginning to anticipate the new school year . . . the renewal of old acquaintances and the making of new friends. They are in search of projects to do and exhibit to their peers during the first month of school.

This is an excellent time to reflect on areas of the craft suggestions which could be utilized to complete a successful and fruitful summer. A craft project is one which is enjoyed during the preparation of it, and remains a cherished visual memory for years. Enjoy working with the following suggestions!

Wax Sculpting

Wax as a Media

Ever since man discovered that forms could be made from mud and clay, sculpting has played an important part in our civilization.

Many forms of sculpting have been utilized over the years. Here is one that is most desirable and yet is not utilized to any great degree.

Basic Materials: old candle stubs, large metal coffee cans, discarded milk cartons, dull knife or nail file for carving.

Procedure:

- Cut and discard the wicks from the old candle stubs.

- Then put the candle pieces in the can and carefully melt the wax over a low heat.
- If colored wax is desired, drop a few old crayons in the mixture to obtain the correct color effect.
- When the wax has melted, pour the contents of the can into the empty milk carton.
- Let the wax harden overnight.
- If a hollow appears in the center of the wax shape, add more liquid wax to fill it.
- Now peel the paper carton from the wax form, and the shape is ready to sculpt.
- First draw a picture of the form to be sculpted or start with a preconceived idea and work freely.
- Shave the wax with the tool in developing the shape.
- Keep the sculpted piece simple.
- Work slowly and while modeling turn the shape from time to time so all sides are considered as a part of the whole shape.
- If a portion breaks, heat it slightly with a match flame and return it to its original position.
- When the project is completed, mount it on a block of wood or corrugated cardboard by just heating the bottom long enough for the wax to melt and adhere to the mount. (See Figure 12–1)

Figure 12–1

Soap is also a good medium to use for sculpting. Use large square bars of white or colored soap for various effects. Soap sculpting is a bit more difficult than wax sculpting, so become proficient with wax sculpting before attempting soap sculpture.

Mosaic Collage

Mixed Media

Any number of materials can be used for making a mosaic, or a collage. Several types have already been outlined earlier in the book. Try a mosaic-collage using unusual tesserae for the composition.

Basic Materials: tesserae which could be: dried beans, peas, cereals, shells, pebbles, pasta, beach glass; Elmer's glue, plywood or wood panel, shellac, brush.

Procedure:

- Choose a suitable subject or theme for the composition of the mosaic-collage.

- Sketch the idea first on scrap paper and then transfer the sketch to the piece of wood when the idea is satisfactory.
- Next glue the tesserae piece by piece directly to the base.
- Continue to add pieces until the areas of the sketch are completely filled.
- A variety of tesserae can be used on one composition to create interest. (See Figure 12–2)
- If fragile materials like cereal or seeds are used for the project, shellac the entire composition for durability.
- Attach wire to the back of the wood base for hanging.

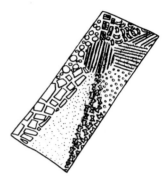

Figure 12–2

Tin Foil Sculptures

Aluminum Tray Construction

A simple craft project can be produced with discarded aluminum food trays.

Basic Materials: aluminum food trays, scissors, scrap paper, pencils.

Procedure:

- Experiment first by planning a pattern the size of the bottom of the tray for an animal on scrap paper.
- Cut the pattern, and test the construction by bending and folding it into positions for standing. (See Figure 12–3A)
- If changes need to be made, recut the pattern.
- When the pattern is satisfactory, trace it on the bottom of the aluminum tray and carefully cut it out with scissors. The foil edges are sharp so precautions must be taken when cutting the shape.
- Next fold and bend the foil to make it a 3-dimensional form. (See Figure 12–3B)

Don't stop with one animal, make several.

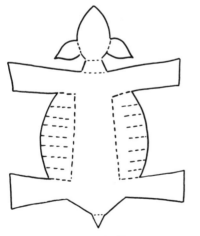

Figure 12–3A

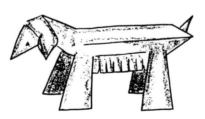

Figure 12–3B

Snowfall Paper Weight

Mixed Media

Here is a wonderful idea that can be utilized by all age groups. When completed, it will bring hours of delight to those who watch its movement.

Basic Materials: small nicely-shaped jars with screw top lids, moth flakes, Duco cement, small plastic or ceramic figurine, water.

Procedure:

- Glue the figurine in the lid of the jar.
- Put it aside to dry thoroughly.
- Next put 2 teaspoons of moth flakes into the jar.
- Add water to the jar almost to the rim. (See Figure 12–4A)
- Put glue around the rim of the jar and the lid.
- Carefully screw the lid to the jar and allow it to stay in the upside down position until the glue dries thoroughly. (See Figure 12–4B)
- Now paint and decorate the lid with spray paint for added decoration.

The Snowfall Paper Weight is complete.

Figure 12–4A   Figure 12–4B

Sawdust Painting

Sawdust as Media

Painting is always fun—no matter what you use for paint. Try using sawdust for a different way of painting.

Basic Materials: sawdust, rubber cement, cups of assorted tempera paint, brushes, 12 by 18 inch manila paper.

Procedure:

- Draw a picture of a simple idea . . . a boat, fish, animal or bird.
- When it is completed, decide upon areas that you desire to add sawdust texture.
- Cover these areas with a thin layer of rubber cement, and immediately sprinkle sawdust on the wet cement. (See Figure 12–5A)
- Do small areas at a time, and continue to add the sawdust until the picture is pleasing.
- Now fill in areas not covered with sawdust with tempera paint.
- When the sawdust and glue are thoroughly dried, these textured areas can also have color applied to them. (See Figure 12–5B)

Mount the picture on a piece of contrasting construction paper to complete this unusual project.

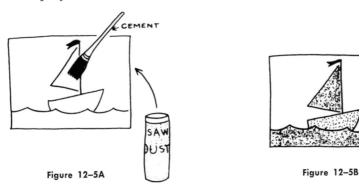

Figure 12–5A   Figure 12–5B

Yarn Jewelry

Yarn as Media

Children love to make things that they can wear. Here are a few ideas you may want to develop with an art group.

Basic Materials: pipe cleaners, scissors, cardboard strips, staples, assorted yarn.

Procedure:

- A ring can be made by bending a piece of pipe cleaner to fit the size of a finger, then twist it closed.

- Next take yarn and wrap it tightly around the ring shape, changing the color scheme whenever desired. (See Figure 12–6A)
- End the ring by tying the yarn to the base.
- A bracelet can be made by bending a cardboard strip into a circle shape and fastening it securely with a stapler. (See Figure 12–6B)
- Next wrap the yarn around and around the shape until the circle is completely covered.
- Now cut the yarn and glue the end to the inside of the bracelet.
- The bracelet and the ring can be further decorated with scraps of felt cut into designs and glued to the yarn shape. Other possibilities might be the addition of a fancy button, bead or stone. (See Figure 12–6C)

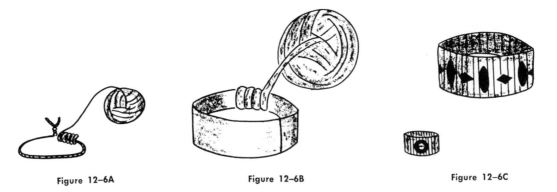

Figure 12–6A   Figure 12–6B   Figure 12–6C

Six Layer Paper Trays

Papier Mâché

Here is a wonderful papier mâché technique which you will enjoy.

Basic Materials: newspaper, paste, assorted cups of tempera paint, brushes.

Procedure:

- Give each child six equal-sized pieces of newspaper.
- Have them cover each piece of newspaper consecutively with paste, and cover with a new piece of paper, building sandwiched layers of paste and paper. (See Figure 12–7A)

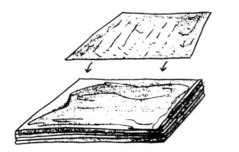

Figure 12–7A

- Do this until the top sheet is the only remaining piece of paper; this one is not pasted on top.
- Now quickly draw a light pencil shape; either a leaf, abstract form, square or circle.
- Carefully cut out the shape.
- The paper is now very flexible, and the sides can be gently shaped up to form an interesting dish.
- Set the piece aside to dry.
- The scraps of papier mâché can be cut into small shapes like fish, birds, flowers and animals that can be used for pins. These too, must be set aside to dry.
- When the projects are dried, they are strong and hard.
- Paint, decorate and shellac them for durability and preservation.

The containers can be used readily for holding nuts, cookies, and candy. However, they cannot be immersed in water. A damp sponge will wipe out any soiled areas. (See Figure 12–7B)

The small shaped pieces can be attached to pin backs and make wonderful pin ornaments.

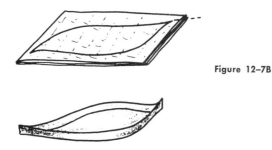

Figure 12–7B

Light Bulb People

Bulb Based Constructions

It always seems as if we are accomplishing great things when a discarded or used article can be salvaged and used in an art lesson. The commonly used electric bulb becomes very uncommon when it can be used in this way.

Basic Materials: discarded light bulbs, Plasticine, vinegar, assorted tempera paint, brushes.

Bonus Materials: yarn, assorted cut paper, paper cement.

Procedure:

- Dip the old light bulb in vinegar; this will permit the paint to adhere to it.
- While it is drying, make a base for the bulb with Plasticine.
- Next place the bulb in its Plasticine base and paint it with tempera paint.
- A complete face with features and hair can be painted on the bulb, or yarn and cut paper can be used for decoration. (See Figure 12–8)

Make a family of people or animals; the completed project will be different and a sure treasure.

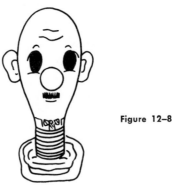

Figure 12–8

Fancy Bottles

Enamel Paint

This project makes an excellent craft lesson. Little is needed and all age groups can be involved.

Basic Materials: bottles, pail, water, enamel paints.

Procedure:

- Each child should furnish his own nicely shaped bottle.
- Next, fill an old pail ¾ full of water.
- Gently pour different colored enamel paints on the water.
- The enamel will float on the top.
- Carefully dip the bottle in the pail.
- Swish it around so that it has a coating of the enamel all over it.
- Turn the bottle upside down to dry.
- Replenish the enamel paint whenever necessary.

The completed project is a long lasting memento of a different craft experience. (See Figure 12–9)

THINGS TO DRAW DURING AUGUST

1. Concentrate on people. Sketch them whenever you are able to do so. Make rough quick sketches while you are on a bus, walking, shopping. Redo them when you have free time.
2. Find a large mirror and make sketches of yourself. It takes practice, and is lots of fun. Take the best sketch and make a pastel portrait of yourself.
3. Design costumes for people who will live in the 21st century.

Figure 12–9

Index